Céline

PHILIPPE BONNEFIS

Céline

THE RECALL OF THE BIRDS

Foreword by JEAN-FRANÇOIS LYOTARD

Translated by PAUL WEIDMANN

University of Minnesota Press
Minneapolis
London

The University of Minnesota gratefully acknowledges funding provided by the French Ministry of Culture for the translation of this book.

Originally published as *Céline: Le Rappel des oiseaux.* Copyright Presses Universitaires de Lille, 1992

Published by the University of Minnesota Press
111 Third Avenue South, Suite 290, Minneapolis, MN 55401-2520
Printed in the United States of America on acid-free paper

Library of Congress Cataloging-in-Publication Data

Bonnefis, Philippe.
    [Céline. English]
    Céline : the recall of the birds / Philippe Bonnefis ; foreword by
Jean-François Lyotard ; translated by Paul Weidmann.
        p.   cm.
    Includes bibliographical references.
    ISBN 0-8166-2646-4 (hardcover). — ISBN 0-8166-2647-2 (pbk.)
    1. Céline, Louis-Ferdinand, 1894–1961 — Criticism and
interpretation.   I. Weidmann, Paul.   II. Title.
PQ2607.E834Z55913   1996
823'.912—dc20   96-20552
                                                           CIP

I always had an object in composing all these pieces:
different occasions provided it to me.
Therefore the titles correspond to the ideas I had;
let me be excused from accounting for them.

COUPERIN

CONTENTS

FOREWORD

Jean-François Lyotard

Why do we write about literature? Is it in order to shed light,[1] or to bring ourselves closer to the enigma concealed within the work, at all costs, and without ever uncovering it? "My books," declares Bonnefis, "are written against clarity. They are lampshades, visors. I shall not add to the ranks of the shedders of light; they are numerous enough without me, and rather active as well, blinding us daily on television screens, on the radio, and in the newspapers. Shedding full light on the event, as they say. You get the picture! This is exactly the picture on which I would like to shed a little darkness!"[2]

Bonnefis calls upon Roland Barthes and Pascal Quignard, learning from the latter that literature is "a way of being within language while remaining in silence." And from Barthes, he takes this deceptively timid conjecture: "It is very possible that society currently needs a slightly more difficult zone of thought or communication."[3]

There is something of the prophet in Bonnefis, one of those whom biblical exegesis called lesser prophets. "Persevere," he tells us, "in wanting transparency; continue to obey the rules of *correctness*,[4] to fabricate theories, to cause the proliferation of comparativism; in this way, literature and the reading of it, those masterpieces in peril, will disappear completely, and with them the truth, so difficult to communicate, that they possess. They posit in *fact* that no object is identifiable as such.

The name that the object bears, of place or person, and even the common noun, admittedly designates it; but this name refers to something beside itself, something that remains anonymous under this name, as the 'fatal sign' of something undefinable, 'the thing,' tied to the object and yet apart from it. This is why Blanchot can write to his Japanese translator that the name 'is a mask that transforms everything into a mask and that nothing unmasks.' "[5]

Bonnefis's favorite objects, be their names Céline, Baudelaire, Maupassant, Flaubert, Vallès, Laforgue, Zola, or Cendrars, do not adhere to their designated identities; quite the contrary. The art of writing is practiced in the gap, both immense and exiguous, that separates the name from the thing: it is a separation lodged "within proximity itself."[6] The writer is one who "enters into a loss of identity,"[7] one who discovers himself or herself to be "absolutely foreign" to his or her own name. At the expense of interminable twists and turns practiced in the language, the writer tinkers with the arrangements of phrases, inventing an idiom in the hope of making himself or herself understood by the other thing, and of making the thing understood.

Literature, without a doubt, is communication, a treasure of the community, because it is a work of and in language. Yet in the general exchange, it occupies an exceptional place: it suffers, so to speak, from a slightly suspicious condition because it seeks to make contact with an assumed addressee. Does this addressee speak, in fact? Its language is unknown. It is nowhere else but in the community, and even in the private life, of each of its members, again very near, inevitable, but as a stranger, an immigrant who stands in silence or asking unintelligibly for a response on the threshold, on the *step,* as if waiting for someone to recognize his muteness.

The writer makes himself or herself both the accomplice and the hostage of this illicit presence. And if we decide to ignore this clandestine one, which is what takes place in ordinary interlocution — and which, perhaps, is what ordinary interlocution requires — if we question the name alone, without the thing, in view of obtaining a definition of the object that concerns us (as is the case with the textual commentary, for example), in that case, the language of the mute filters through us; it expresses itself in our place and from our position as subject, and we no longer know what we are saying, because it is the other who whispers it to us without our hearing it. It is a discourse ventriloquized by a phantom; formerly, this was called ideology, and passed for limpidity.

It is very common, and undoubtedly quite necessary to everyday exchange, as well as to theoretical construction, to forget the mute *thing*. But if, on the contrary, we were to try to recognize it, its silence plunges us into an agonizing dilemma: to make the stranger talk, as they say at the police station, is to impose our language upon him; and to let the stranger speak his own language, supposing that he has one, is not to let him express himself, as no one will understand the message. The gap between the identity and the thing, where the writer plays out his work, must be negotiated. The work is this negotiation.

Although Freudian analysis does not take as its object the literary thing, there is an analogy to be made between certain rules imposed upon clinical practice and the experience, in writing (and in reading), of an incessant negotiation required of the language in order for it to reach the unknown idiom. The rule of "free association," from which it is expected that the unconscious will be given the opportunity to have its say, leads one to think of the wandering maneuvers and the groping — the "work," as Freud would have said — to which writing submits itself in order to approach and seduce the strange mute. Here and there, the cobbling together of an idiom uses similar detours. Moreover, the notion of anamnesis outlined by Freud indicated a mode of "presence" of the thing that was foreign to the mind and that required of it neither victory nor abdication; as with literary writing, the question was how to avoid both the recollection of a real scene to be localized in the history of the subject and the inexplicable repetition of the trouble in the form of a symptom. The search for a psychosocial origin, the diagnosis of a syndrome: what literary critic has not fallen into these traps?

Literature demands that the distance of the thing not be reduced or *retracted*, however close it may be. On the contrary, literature wants to say it *as such*, and thus to sustain the insane hearing of it. But then the same problem arises: In which language is the alterity of the other, its surplus [*à-côté*], to be written? In its own, or in mine, which is that of all of us? In the second case, there is no work, but only an ordinary message, a "paper,"[8] a piece of cultural merchandise to be consumed. As to the first supposition, either the language of the other remains unknown, as we have already stated, and the work that will write it will be a scrawl (Balzac's *Chef d'œuvre inconnu*) or a blank page (Mallarmé); or we are able to translate the other's language into our own, and the other ceases to be "absolutely foreign." Why, then, this work of reading and writing, if it were only a question of translating? Unless translation also already demands this work of giving voice to that which is first mute, and unless translation is a form of literary writing.

There is no brute appropriation or disappropriation in writing or in reading (or in translation). It is a word-for-word negotiation, at all costs. Everyday language is beseeched, commanded, to allow a mutant language, perhaps a monster, to generate in its womb, and without compensation; a language that would give the unknown idiom of the other thing its due. Is this what, in the old days, was called style? At any rate, here we are, writers and critics, on the other side of the world from the theoretical or rhetorical promise, absorbed in a practical task of cobbling together, between language and thing, a chimera of words, hilarious and futureless. Do you wish to stay *clean*?[9] "I find that none of those babblers is 'INSIDE THE THING,'" writes Céline to Paulhan. "They are frantically beating off OUTSIDE."[10] The cleanness or the ownership of the name is found outside the thing, and is ignorant of bargaining with the thing. But how does one write without compromising oneself in the altercation in which the language-mother and the thing come to blows?

So be it. But how does one know, in all the confusion, that the thing has been given its due? "Where, then, is the balance?" asks Bonnefis. "And who will tell me when it's enough and that I now have every reason to consider myself satisfied?"[11] No one hits the mark exactly; no one, writer or critic, can ever express satisfaction. And no thinker can settle the difference. "From the *not-enough* to the *still-more*: this is the movement that takes over my reading."[12] The idiom invented will always lack something. The thing moves away as one approaches it. One has to supplement, add, fill in the cracks. Writing, haunted by its infirmity, is constantly tempted to remedy by inflation. A precarious exercise, which Claude Simon summed up in his response to the idiotic question, What does the act of writing mean for you? "To try to begin a sentence, to keep going, and to end it." To *finish* it . . .

Bonnefis says that the literary or critical text is a kind of fetish. It never forms a complete totality or an identifiable unit. One must continually add complements: "I don't know what, shattering glass, a nail, a citation, a note, a page . . ."[13] The work is a fetish, the critical work as well: insecure objects, suspected of inconstancy and even of nonexistence, more or less cobbled together; they bear the mark of a lack that they are not meant to fill, but rather to manifest. They are melancholy works, in which can be perceived the persistent and silent complaint of the stranger.

As a rule, reading and writing "postpone the moment of reunion," devoting themselves to "the perpetual deferment of satisfaction" through a thousand "delay tactics."[14] At this cost, however, writing traces a path toward the unknown; advancing close to it like a crab, writing gives itself a lead on what the thing says and makes clumsy advances toward it. Writing casts out little threads of diversion around its "object," violating the correct strategy of adjustment and appropriation that discourse implies.

In the war that the critic wages against lucidity of vision in order to perceive the thing that is "present" in the work he or she is commenting on, he or she rejects the lens of precision, aided by a bizarre "trick lens," which Bonnefis names a "polemoscope": a lens so blurry that, while aiming at the center of your target, you land "wide of the mark."[15] The mark? In truth, no one knows. Yet it is certain that this sort of "parallax error" has engendered the anamorphoses or the paramorphoses that the great visual works, in all periods, have inflicted upon common perception. This is equally true in literature: the work, and criticism as well, can only hope to make understood that which the thing silences by shaking up the apparent order of vocabulary and syntax, and by making this order "work" against itself.

But, common sense demands, what good are these stratagems, these childish ruses, these calculations based on an absence? Obviously, they have no utility, and the pleasure that they may give is always altered by contradiction. Is this not perverse? Yes, without a doubt, argues Bonnefis; but there is an obligation to the work. The fact of inaccuracy, the fact that a surplus is hidden in the identifying name, is felt as a disquieting strangeness, and understood "as a perverse *you must*. Like the imperative of an unending debt. Yes, a demand, I insist upon it: a terrible demand. From the pen of Karl Abraham, psychoanalysis invokes here an 'imprisonment by naming' [*contrainte par nom*]."[16] (A century ago, the unpaid creditor was still authorized by law to exercise the penalty of "civil imprisonment" [*contrainte par corps*] upon the debtor in default, as a last result.) We are indebted to a silence that is quite close by. A voice inside us complains of being abandoned, like the voices of the dead. "Interior intimo meo," wrote Augustine of Hippo. However, the saint, and Christendom after him, believed that this voice inside our ears was that of the living God, that it spoke love, and that one had only to love it to hear it.

Undoubtedly, it is not mere chance that the corpus of authors to which Bonnefis has become attached, from Baudelaire to Cendrars and Céline, belongs to the moment in occidental civilization (a moment that is a constant component of this civilization, and not only of an epoch) during which the voice ceases to say anything comprehensible or pleasant and loses its divine authority. To simplify, let us say that the feeling of abandonment that results from this silence finds its acme in the "crisis" to which Nietzsche, Mallarmé, and Valéry all eventually sign their names, and which shakes the arts, the sciences, politics, and ethics at the turn of the century.

The "wisest" of minds console themselves for this mourning by substituting some sort of "replacement value" for the deceased father. Ersatz is too paltry to fool the desperation of orphans. The most positive among them argue that we have lost nothing, but rather gained liberty, since God was nothing but a scarecrow created by despots and not by priests, and that we can easily do without his so-called commandments. But why was it necessary to invent this decoy [*leurre*] and believe in it, if everything was going along fine without it?

Writers and artists, before any doctrine, use their practice as a guide; if there were no strangeness in the familiarity of names and objects, from where would the obligation to create [*faire œuvre*] come? Does nothing nameable remain today to designate the thing to which the work refers? Bataille would have said that the constraint to write, for not being authorized, is all the more sovereign. That which remains when there is nothing else left: literature is that remainder, that resistance. Vain, defeated in advance by the elusive thing, and by the stiffness of language.

Céline knows in advance that his matter is not resolved. He knows that he is lost, that he has lost. He doesn't look for the idiom apart from ordinary language, through a gesture of distinction, neoclassical, neo-elegiac, neodeclamatory, as many around him are doing at the time. He remains in the most common facet of language, that of the down-and-out; he takes it against the grain through popular parlance, drives it in and smashes it up with idiomatic turns of phrase, onomatopoeias, interjections, and parataxes. "The beautiful thought he is secretly nursing, his writer's dream, his hope *to flee into language.*"[17] Without fleeing the language, without putting it at a distance, rummaging through its belly for the idiom that is already there, that makes it stammer, rage, moan, laugh, avoid conclusion. The surplus of the thing is there somewhere, in the language-mother's uterus, never where one thinks it to be, less and more there than there, "beyond"-there [*outre-là*].

Bonnefis has written some subtle pages on the entry of this neologism in the Célinian text and the career he makes of it. "There are indeed two *outres* in French: the *outre* that comes from *ultra,* which in Latin means 'beyond'..., and which Céline sometimes writes, archaically, '*oultre*'; and the *outre* that comes from *uter,* which in Latin means 'belly.'"[18] Let us add to this fetish the other Latin *uter,* the interrogative pronoun that asks (is it pure chance?) "which of the two..."; which of the two meanings is the correct one, for example. If we are to believe the critic, such is the confusion that Céline takes as his obligation, the disorder to which he is indebted, as if the flimsy beyond-there, this beyond lodged in the bulbous stomach, imposed upon his writing the direction to take in order to inquire after the other thing. This is how you *must* make it understood, this thing, and make yourself understood by it: in the din that its saraband makes at the heart of the language-womb, bursting it.

The first part of the study is entitled "Bridges" [*Ponts*]. The purpose of these Célinian works of art is not to step over obstacles: they explode, cave in, and sink. "A bridge is an essentially unstable structure."[19] The ramp of the bridge at Courbevoie, a suburb of Paris, is the place from which Louis-Ferdinand Destouches, his legal name, first saw the light of day, a day marked in advance by the crawling and the bent, and doomed to come to a sudden stop. For bridges lead nowhere, a ramp gives access only to end. "The bridge of Kiel, end of the German odyssey (Céline seeks refuge in Denmark); the bridge of Bezons (another suburb), end of the medical career (of Doctor Destouches, obstetrician); London Bridge, end of the English adventure (Céline's); the bridge of Beresina, end of History."[20]

Bonnefis goes from bridge to bridge across the Célinian continent, as if he were writing a literary *thème*: here is an object-name, let us deploy it, and make of it the first word of a luminous hermeneutic... But no, it was a stratagem. The reader has scarcely settled into this passage when Bonnefis causes it to explode, in the same way that the writing of its author mines the language and uses it to explode itself. The passage is destroyed, the impasse remains.

Bonnefis takes up his quest for the Célinian secret by way of the "Steps" [*Pas*] and the "Passages." Terrific writing, writing of terror, which explodes the enormous bypass that is language, all the bridges of syntax and semantics that are supposed to straddle the void, from sentence to sentence, and constitute the coherent discourse by means of which reality is sustained. Mined and ignited by the idiom of beyond, the vast prison of language explodes in disastrous bursts. Its din resonates in the Célinian phrase, in scansions of *Boum, Radaboum, Taraboum, Broum,* and *Broomb, Blam, Bang,* and *Bzim,* not to mention the lines of *Vrrroum*— with which Bonnefis makes a methodical and cynical inventory on the text of *Normance.*[21]

The poetics of argot, a language beyond language, which Hugo already had attributed to *Les Misérables,* that misery of language, swells again to bursting, and exhausts itself in the onomatopoeia of enormous percussions. And yet a rare music filters through the din. The eardrum of the writer, shattered, remains capable of nuancing the excessive vibrations. How does one write the racket of the end of a world? Which is also the end of a subject. By giving rhythm to the prose, by hammering it to the meter of the fragments, by tempering it, sprinkling it with the fine fallout from the explosion; "[to] go like dust in the wind" [*passer poudre*],[22] writes Bonnefis, and "to stuff us back in the oven,"[23] the pulverized machinations in the maternal sack, the "metro" of the *mêtêr.*[24] For "there is no outside and... everything is inside, beings and things in the same bag."[25] The so-called birth is an "appalling slip,"[26] a passage to death. By burning the bridges behind oneself, the fulminating retreat of writing with the womb gives true life to the stillborn thing.

The bridge was not a simple motif of reading. In the catastrophe of the "Steps" and the "Passages" that give their titles to the second and third parts of his study, Bonnefis reveals the very pace of Céline's prose, his manner of trying to pay his debt to the thing. He detects a sort of music or dance that wells up in the heart of the writing of disaster. The mother limped a little, of course; moreover, the limp outlines a dance step. She sold lace; in the enormous din, her son hears a sonorous texture without warp or weft, a fragile piece of embroidery in the process of fraying.

Céline had a fondness for light opera; he wrote ballets; he was in love with the English language, which he said was all accents, and whose sonorous dance enchanted him. "For three months (in London), I didn't blink . . . I was jolly comfortable with it."[27] As if a return to the uterine hell was enough to transform the racket into a celestial melody. Grace in terror? Perhaps it is thus that the thing is felt, in hysteria or otherwise. Céline has called the acme of joyful devastation "*jouissance.*" The exercise in reading in which Bonnefis indulges is admirable, as I will leave the reader to judge. The onus is on him or her to go off in search of his or her other, across the continent of Bonnefis, beside his name.

A few more words on the privilege accorded by the commentator to auditive sensibility. This privilege is clearly claimed. Comparing his author to the "founding fathers of French realism," the Flauberts, Maupassants, and Zolas, who all suffered from ophthalmia, Bonnefis asserts: "All I know is that, from Céline onward, the question is no longer the same: having become, from a question of eye that it was up to him, a question of ear. The image of the body is radically altered. And, along with it, literature's own representation of the world."[28]

The mother's limp, the limping that is essential to real prose, the idiom that hobbles along for better or worse from its good leg to its bad one (Céline goes so far as to fantasize his mother with a wooden leg), translates to a sonorous tempo. Céline's hypochondria invented a head wound and a trephination that supposedly so disturbs the system of the inner ear that the writer claimed he suffered from Ménière's vertigo. With Littré, Bonnefis invents an etymology that leads from *clopiner* to *clocher*, from misstepping to misunderstanding. "The lame, limping, vanish into the deep landscape of hearing."[29]

If it is true that writing or reading requires one to lend an ear to the idiom of the thing, then the question of literature is also asked under the regime of hearing; in that case, the better ear to lend must be the bad one, since what the thing "says" is cacophonic. It is still necessary to make dissonance audible as dissonance, and to accommodate the idiom to the common order of the language.

Hence the infinite negotiations, the skirmishes, the collisions and uncouplings from which the art of writing earns its living. What results is a music of timbres and rhythms: "Rather than airs (the melodies that link sounds), he likes notes."[30] Notes: this is still too much to say of a music by a "lunatic" [*timbré*].[31] The piece by Rameau that gives Bonnefis's book its aegis, "The Recall of the Birds," perhaps still maintains inordinately the dissonances under the harmonic rule of their "resolution." Rather, one imagines diabolically unresolved pieces, insoluble, such as those by Thomas Mann's Leverkühn in *Doktor Faustus*. Or else, one should hear, mistake,[32] in Rameau, a work by Varèse or Messiaen, in which the rough recording of the music exceeds itself, becomes outraged, to the point of giving voice to the wailing of sirens or the cries of birds.

To sum up, perhaps there is still too much goodness and grace in the song, however discordant, that Bonnefis tries to hear in Céline's prose. However, it is true that when it comes to questions of idiom, there is no classicism. Shakespeare, Dante, and the suave Racine are no less crazy about misunderstandings [*mésentente*] than Céline or Beckett. It is this madness that makes classicism, whatever the season. And I wait calmly for Bonnefis to lend his bad ear [*sa male oreille*][33] and his polemophone to the discord, the twisting and tortures that shape the prose of a Montaigne or the verse of a Céline — to speak only of the francophone domain.

"What?" the astonished kindly souls say. "You have nothing to say about the abject anti-Semitism that merited Céline's prison and exile?" "We simply had to get back to that. — Did we really?"[34] And why not? Is not the trilogy of anti-Semitic pamphlets — *Bagatelles pour un mas-*

sacre, L'École des cadavres, and *Les Beaux draps*—published between 1938 and 1941, an integral part of his oeuvre? One could quibble on that point. The pamphlets are without precedent and remain without a follow-up; their existence is denied in the correspondence of 1947, and most important, they were not "writings," negotiated, as were the other works. These texts were vomited, or rather excreted, "acted" as one says of an "acting out."[35] Céline later qualified them as "beasts." "That isn't saying much, given the nature of the crime." True. But they are beasts as regards writing. To vomit, to banish, to will to extermination was at least to admit that a name remained *outside* of the hysterical negotiation between the language and the thing, which Céline's prose practices. "The Jews are the fathers of our civilization. Sooner or later, one always denies one's father," says Céline by way of an excuse in a letter to Milton Hindus from 1947. His anti-Semitism was perhaps a dreadful slip; at least it reveals the extent to which the frenzied debarment of the father, common to many writers of the murdered God, and here underlying the desire to return to the language-womb back to the end of his night, was sometimes unbearable.

I do not mean to continue after Bonnefis has stopped. He will forgive me the overtime, as they say in soccer: pure inflation on my part, provoked by the fetish object, his *Céline,* which he gives to me to read. It is understood: for some time, there has not been a critical work that has given me such a sense of the subtle veneration that we owe, and that the philosopher especially owes, to literature. It is not romantic, nor even novelistic, except to the depth of discourse of the intellectual leaders, to judge that with the writing of a Céline, with his reading-writing by a Bonnefis, is revealed the most critical *fact* of language: its inappropriateness to itself, its excess, and its flaw regarding what it "means/wants to say" [*veut dire*]. On this inappreciable gap, literature casts and recasts its lot. Literary Studies must fully consecrate itself to affirming this intimate estrangement, work after work, without the hope of mastering it by means of some "theory." A bit of darkness cast over the lucid calculations of profitability, including the "cultural" profession, by which the world itself is henceforth confirmed. In this way, literature and literary theory resist, without a strategy.

Resistance by elision: language is brought to its state of weightlessness. Bonnefis, after Céline, lightens the weight of significations, referents of usage, and meanings; he returns the writer's prose to its volatile essence. Literary matter affects the corporal soul of the reader with vanishing strokes of odors or timbres. Every vibration fades and drifts away.

Translated by Kristine Butler

TRANSLATOR'S NOTE

As often as possible, we have cited Céline's work in the Bibliothèque de la Pléiade edition, prepared by Henri Godard and published by Gallimard.

Voyage au bout de la nuit and *Mort à crédit*: tome I
D'un château l'autre, Nord and *Rigodon*: tome II
Casse-Pipe, Guignol's band I and *Guignol's band II*: tome III

It is to this edition we are referring whenever, in the notes, the page number is preceded by a tome number.

⤶

For the works that are not available in the Pléiade, however, we have made use of the N.R.F. or the Folio text, published by Gallimard.

L'Église (N.R.F., 1952)
Normance (N.R.F., 1954)
Entretiens avec le Professeur Y (N.R.F., 1955)
Féerie pour une autre fois ("Folio," 1977)
Maudits soupirs pour une autre fois, ed. Henri Godard (N.R.F., 1985)
Lettres à la N.R.F. (1931–1961), ed. Pascal Fouché (N.R.F., 1991)

⤶

The "pamphlets" have been cited in the original editions.

> *Bagatelles pour un massacre* (Denoël, 1937)
> *L'École des cadavres* (Denoël, 1938)
> *Les Beaux draps* (Nouvelles Éditions Françaises, 1941)

↩

The related texts (medical thesis, various letters, interviews, etc.) have been consulted in, and occasionally cited from, the *Cahiers Céline* published by the N.R.F. (Gallimard).

> No. 1, *Céline et l'actualité littéraire (1932–1957)*, 1976
> No. 2, *Céline et l'actualité littéraire (1957–1961)*, 1976
> No. 3, *Semmelweis et autres écrits médicaux*, 1977
> No. 4, *Lettres et premiers écrits d'Afrique (1916–1917)*, 1978
> No. 5, *Lettres à des amies*, 1979
> No. 6, *Lettres à Albert Paraz (1947–1957)*, 1980
> No. 7, *Céline et l'actualité (1933–1961)*, 1986
> No. 8, *Progrès* suivi de *Œuvres pour la scène et l'écran*, 1988

All the translations of Céline's work are mine.

A WARNING

Touit-Touit, piouït! piouït! *tuii . . . tui! . . .* Pïouït!¹

Or else this:

Taa! . . . too! o! o! o! oo! . . . the call of the Swans.²

Repeated to you. Or rehearsing. As they say in the countryside, noon is rehearsing.

> "Can't you hear? . . . Taa!!! . . . too! . . . too! . . . too! . . . too . . . too . . . Taa! . . .
> Taa! . . . how the winter wind carries it?" . . . I sing it to him so he can hear
> better . . . lah! fa! soh! lah si do! lah! Do! so he can hear the whole call! . . .
> Do sharp! soh sharp! . . . of course! . . . fa sharp minor! It's the tone! The
> charm of the Swans! . . . the call, friend! the call! . . .³

‿〜

Of all the titles collected in the first of the four great harpsichord suites composed by Jean-Philippe Rameau, *The Recall of the Birds* is undoubtedly the most mysterious. What does recall — what does *rappel* mean? An imitation, an acclamation, a call to order, or a cry of alarm? If it is a call to arms, who then is sounding it? Is it the birds recalling, calling each other? Or is it the bird-catcher practicing his chirruping, his warbling? The "purring of pigeons,"⁴ the caterwauling of crows, the saw rasps of the crested tit . . . ? Call or birdcall? Who is calling whom, and why?

All questions without an answer. You can play the piece over and over: far from being appeased, your disquiet, each time, only increases. Not only does the performance of the piece not solve any of the difficulties presented by the title, but it adds the discomfort of listening to them.

This music, indeed, jostles you; sharp and sour, it taps on your fingers and demands an explanation. Rages, tantrums, a flurry of wings; capercaillies, gannets, shrikes, linnets, pipits, peewees ... all the birds together, the whole species; "the most divided" of the animal species. So says Giono, who knows everything about birds, about their names, their babble, their plumage, and that it's colored glass on which God is walking.[5]

God ... or Satan. Lucifer, the Prince of Darkness ... *The Recall of the Birds* is a disheveled piece; it contains more chaos than, in spite of their titles, *The Whirlwinds* or *The Limping Woman*; more breaks, more discordances than *The Cyclops*, where the keyboard technique, with its hammering of the two hands, alternating like drumsticks, nonetheless fragments the score in a terrifying manner.

⌒

Such, or such, no matter what, this is indeed the music that will have chased me throughout the following pages. Less an accompaniment than a sort of theme song; a *jingle*: ringing, clinking. A bell. Yes, a warning.

1

BRIDGES

Sidestepping or what? The fact is that on the verge of entering Céline's work, it's Flaubert's work that comes to my mind. And more precisely, within this work, *Bouvard et Pécuchet*. Shortly after the moment when the two inseparable ones decide that their vocation is history.

> "Would you like us to try and write a history?"
> "I'd like nothing better! But which one?"
> "Indeed, which one?"

We know that their choice soon settles on the life of the Duc d'Angoulême. Having completed their archival research, they draw up an outline, and, in doing so, are struck by a strange coincidence. "One must note," they observe, "the importance of bridges. First, he exposes himself uselessly on the bridge of l'Inn; he carries the Pont Saint-Esprit and the Lauriol bridge; at Lyons, the two bridges prove fatal to him, and his fortunes end before the Sèvres bridge."[1]

Basically, I have nothing else to say about Louis-Ferdinand Céline. I only wish to note, as far as his work is concerned, the significance of bridges.

From the very start, bridges attract him. And he makes no bones about it. "I cross bridges at the drop of a hat..."[2] He likes bridges, the way others like trees, flowers, or God knows what. But bridges also like him, spanning the breaks, throwing as it were gangways between the blocs, the separate pieces of a life. To the point of giving it, of finally giving it the coherence, the rigor of a geometric abstraction. A life that would resemble, according to Rimbaud's expression, a "bizarre drawing of bridges."[3] From the Pont de Neuilly, close to which he comes into the world (a child found under the arch of a bridge), to the famous bridge over the Kiel canal, at the Danish frontier, in *Rigadoon*. A forest of beams, buttresses as high as the first story of the Eiffel Tower; and the whole thing being bombed: "Should've seen the bridge lift up and the tracks and our platforms . . . and *broum!* . . . everything fall back down! . . . better said everything waves . . . a true roller coaster . . ."[4]

The Kiel bridge marks the end of the German odyssey. For that matter, all of Céline's endings take place at the foot of a bridge: the end of a medical career at the bridge of Bezons; the end of the English adventure at London Bridge; the end of *Conversations with Professor Y* at the Pont des Arts . . . The bridge is a punctuation mark. A period. Let us add that the whole Célinian autobiography is punctuated in this manner. In Céline bridges always place periods and commas in the general discourse of History. Consider his preface to Albert Serouille's book, *Bezons throughout the Ages*:

BEZONS, in the dictionary? Two lines and sullen . . . What a villainy! What filth! But the whole of French History runs through Bezons! Precisely! Specifically over the bridge of Bezons. Are the years of France abundant, prosperous, happy? The Bezons Fair is going full swing! Hunting at Maisons-Lafitte, the troops parading toward Carrières, we have roaring processions, joy, revels, on both shores all goes well!

Are the years baneful? Are woes raining on France? . . . The vanguards of the disaster are camping at Bezons . . . The bridge blows up! . . . It's the great sign! . . . Go see it . . . They hardly fix it . . .

What Bezons needs is almost a removable bridge . . . Ten times throughout History it blows up, blows up again, now in boats, now in oak, now in stone, it always disappears! . . . each time! . . . and the steel then! . . . The bridge of Bezons won't hold . . . Truth of ages . . . I was there on that parapet in June '40! What a *badaboum!* Saltpeter! Smokes! Dust of History! . . . What an outcome! Twenty centuries in the water! . . . The water of Bezons![5]

It blows up, the bridge of Bezons. But, if it blows up, it blows up the way all bridges blow up, and they are bridges precisely because of the way they blow up. There is indeed no doubt that the explosion of the bridge (an explosion that lasts, like a single held note, a single infinitely broken-up note) constitutes the womb that serves to produce the motif itself. Here is the motif of the bridge, better named the "archbridge" in the prologue of *Guignol's band*:

> The dancing there was even worse than on that other one, a hundred thousand times like on the Avigne!... in the forge of God's Thunder!... And *broum* and *tzimm!* and Saint Mary! and dead and dead! in the Satchel of the Hurricanes!... Here!... Here!... No importance! The world right there flipped over, old umbrella all deadbeat soft!... It sailed into the cyclones!... Too bad for it!... *Wrroub!*... And *Bing!*... *Braoum!*... I saw it pass over the Grand Hotel! At quite a clip! I saw it sailing... swinging all up there... madcap in the clouds!... The brolly and the archbridge![6]

"Archbridge" gives us everything. In one word, all the arches, all the *archi,* all the *arkhe;* the arch per se, which is the vaulted part of a viaduct; Noah's ark, the sepulchral ark; the two triumphal arches of life and death... All the arches, all the archaisms. Chaos.

— But, above it, the bridge?

— Only on top of it. Extra. Among others. But chaos first and foremost. No question of bridges without chaos. Bridges and chaos hold together. Order and disorder, established one upon the other; drawing their strength from the relation that unites them so close to each other... And then one still wonders about the instability of works of art (as they say). This instability is built in. A bridge is essentially an unstable structure. If a bridge wasn't tottering, if it didn't wobble on its arches, if it wasn't shaken, racked with spasms, well, it's simple: in Céline's eyes, it wouldn't be a bridge; I mean a real one, what is called, in his language, a bridge.

Real successes would not have more value than Bichelonne's successes. Bichelonne, in charge of trains under Laval's government, and "let them arrive anyway!... in spite of everything and everyone! Herculean task!... all the networks, switches, schedules, diversions, in his head!... down to the minute, to the second!...with what blew up every night, aqueducts, ballasts, stations, you can picture the fun! and I reblam you!... patch you up here!...divert there! restart!...and it reblows immediately! and then again elsewhere! the fifis didn't let him sleep!"[7] Always beavering away, galloping back and forth, reestablishing connections. Mercury himself.

—Minus the wings!

—Minus the wings, that's a fact. Céline's Olympus, ever since *Thunderbolts and Arrows,* is only peopled with cripples. A lame Hermes, therefore. Yes, the man of the bridges, the man of the ways limped. And "no 'distinguished limp' for him...a true gimp."[8] A work-related injury, basically.

For it must be restated: war or no war, the Célinian bridge is never too steady. It always looks, on the contrary, as if it's leaning, but leaning...Enough to make you fear that, in the end, it will surrender to the call of the chasm; that after so much flirting with the abyss it will embrace it with open arms. And the necessary consequences be damned. Even should we perish when we cross bridges or simply read the story of the crossing. But these are the distinctive difficulties of Céline's text, the ones that this text encounters on its way, the ones to which it exposes its reader.

One must do this justice to the forewarned reader. Céline himself would have been careful to warn him. Even if the warning comes a little late, and if, to make any use of it, we will have to wait for *Conversations with Professor Y.* To wait, in other words, for Céline to share with us the story of his Pascalian illumination. The story that invokes the author of the *Pensées,* that places itself, at least, under the authority of Pascal's name. A name rustling with memories of *Exodus,* of Passover (in French *Pâques,* from which the adjective *pascal* derives), the Hebrew word that signifies "passage of the Lord." *Passage*...we have seen Céline worse inspired. No doubt that he thought he had found in Pascal a brother; that he had found in this solitary man—as open as him to the anxieties and the terrible pleasure of the passage—his partner in debauchery.

"Blaise Pascal!...you remember Blaise Pascal."
"Yes!...Yes!..."

"The revelation he had on the Pont de Neuilly?...his bolting horses?... his spilled carriage?...a wheel torn off?...how he damn well nearly took a bath?" [...]

"The *Pensées* one?"

"Exactly! exactly, Colonel! the one who could no longer see anything but a gulf! always a gulf!...from that day on!...from the fright!...the gulf on his right!..."

"Yes, on his right!" [...]

"And then in the air, Colonel! in the air after, *Infinite spaces frighten me!* by Pascal too, Colonel! a hell of a thought of Pascal's!...do you remember?"

"Yes! yes! yes!"

"It transformed his life, that terrible bridge accident!...from top to bottom! freed the genius! his genius!..."

"Ah?"

"Yes, Colonel!...me! look at me, Colonel! I'm a Pascal type of guy. [...] I too have felt!...exactly!...or very nearly...the same fright as Pascal!... the feeling of the gulf!...but me, it's not at the Pont de Neuilly...no! It happened to me at the metro...in front of the stairs of the metro...of the North-South!...the revelation of my genius, I owe it to the 'Pigalle' station!..."[9]

Not Neuilly...And yet Neuilly. Between the Pont de Neuilly, near where he was born, and the "Pigalle" station, we will have noted more than one connection. Besides which Pascal, if needed, would make the link. Pascal, seized with fright at the Pont de Neuilly, and, by this very fright, with the feeling of the gulf that Céline then attributes to him, Pascal who connects the maternal arch of all fecundity to the obscure womb of the metro. Pascal who, to every tunnel, thus connects every bridge, inasmuch as, all of them, bridge of Bezons and bridge of Kiel, bridges of Orléans or Paris, bridges here, bridges elsewhere, they do nothing but echo, and as it were, redeploy in space the traumas of the first bridge.

Even were they only imaginary...The moment has not yet come to settle this. There is a time for everything. And it's already enough that the bridges have been plugged into the tunnels for us. What more could we ask for, having thus gained the assurance that, when we plunged into the night of the metro, far from leaving the bridges, we on the contrary entered more profoundly, progressed in the knowledge of our object? Having been given to understand, if we hadn't understood it yet, that the function of Céline's bridges is less to cross gulfs than to raise the gulfs, so to speak, up to their level.

So that Céline's bridges, with the abyss, are immediately on an equal footing. That is, if they do not yield the heights to it . . . A single bridge on the horizon, you would think the world was upside down. And isn't the bridge now sagging, the bridge wedding the abyss? As for the abyss, don't seek it down below anymore; it's opening up above your heads. It's from its yawning mouth that these sticks of mines and the whole excremental fauna are falling, the cloud of *aroplanes* [*aravions*] that whine, buzz, whir around the bridges like a swarm of dirty flies. "*Poum! Pou! Pou! Poum!*":[10] from bridge to bridge (from book to book), the same drummer. So as to hammer the cliché into our brains and to force us to wholly penetrate ourselves with this truth, that Hell is no longer under the earth but in the skies.

Pascal's words: *Infinite spaces frighten me!*

Céline could not quote more appropriate ones. To the point that, upon these fine words, there was nothing left for him but to dive in headfirst. To put his words into action. To proceed, that is to say, with the engulfing of the bridges. And it's the magical gesture of the metro-writing:

"Friend Pascal, in a 'deux chevaux,' I'd like to see him try it, from the Printemps to the rue Taitbout! . . . It's not a gulf he'd be afraid of! . . . twenty abysses! the Surface isn't safe anymore! . . . the truth! . . . there! . . . so? . . . me I don't hesitate! . . . it's my genius! that's my genius! no two ways about it! . . . I cart everybody off in the metro, excuse me! . . . and I charge along with: I take everybody! . . . willy-nilly! . . . with me! . . . the emotional metro, mine! without all the inconveniences, the congestions! in a dream! . . . never a single stop anywhere! [. . .] all the passengers locked up, chained, bolted in! . . . all in my emotional train! . . . no whining! . . . I can't tolerate whining! no question of their escaping! . . . no! no! [. . .] all in my emotional metro! . . . houses, people, bricks, biddies, little bakers, bicycles, automobiles, shop girls, cops with them! piled in, 'ground emotional'! . . . in my emotional metro! I don't leave the Surface anything! . . . everything in my magical transport! [. . .] I don't leave the Surface anything! I don't leave it anything! neither the Morris columns, nor the harassing young ladies, nor stub puffers under the bridges! No! I take everything along!"

"The bridges too?"

"The bridges too!"[11]

The metro carts off the bridges. The metro, to tell the truth, is only taking back its own. The difference between a train on its viaduct and a metro in its tunnel? Nil. The difference is nil. On either side, press, congestion. The same circulation, and as it were the same *transit*. Same cramming and crushing. On the surface, you are pounded; underground, "ground emotional."

— But the grind is finer.

— Finer, says who? bombs pulp pretty fine; they pulverize. And besides, such quibbles are out of date. Powder for powder...

Should one wish, at all cost, to distinguish between bridge and metro (since we must renounce the distinctions provided by our senses: they are of no help to us here), one could be tempted to point out how much relief, in the lexical landscape of French, the word *pont* (bridge) has, putting into perspective as it does all the *arches* of this language — were this not neglecting the obvious fact that Céline's ghost train connects every *metro* to it. However, could it be that in French there are not as many *metros* as there are *arches*?

We were flitting, a little earlier, from *arch* to *archi* and from *archi* to *arkhe*. Let us now skip from *metro* to *metro*. From the *metro* in metronome (which sends us back to *metron*, measure) to the *metro* in metropolis (which sends us back to *mêtêr*, mother). And, if we pushed all the way to the *metro* in metrotomy, we could even get as far as *mêtra*, womb.[12] And thus as deeply. The same trip, basically; and the same crossing of the same archaisms.

All the peculiarities, all the singular thoughts that feed Céline's interest in bridges reappear, as such, with the engulfer of the metro. His phobias, his obsessions, and even his aesthetic preoccupations. Because bridges give rise, for Céline, to a problem of art. Let us follow Sosthène, he is a good guide; an artist, in his own way, he is the man to introduce us to it. Sosthène on London Bridge. He is going to cross the Thames. And, just above the river, in the very middle of the bridge, he finds nothing better to do than to sing a song. Yes, Monsieur sings. *La Petite Dame du Métro*, "The Little Lady of the Metro," a song by Mayol.

> He comes up, old Sosthène. He plays the tease, the rascal...
> *Are you the little lady?*
> *Same as that other, then?*

He sings all falsetto...
   All close to me in the metro...
He jigs, he works himself up... The gusts of wind catch him... carry him
off. He goes whamming into the parapet...[13]

And nearly goes overboard. But "he doesn't give a damn, he's gig-
gling too much." Happy as a lark... And the best thing is that it's the
bridge that puts him in this state, that capsizes his soul. Even though
it's just a bridge. For a bridge, with Céline, remains a bridge. Over there,
besides, on the other bank, "right next to Cannon Dock," the zeppelins
remain as threatening as ever. *Boum! Boum!... Boum!* The hullabaloo
is de rigueur.

As I've said, the explosion is essential to the constitution of the motif.
And I am not retracting anything I've said. Yet if the explosion is a necessary condition, it is nonetheless manifestly not a sufficient condition.
The cacophony, it's clear, requires the addition of a touch of melody; a
little musical phrase, something that will flatter the ear a bit... Clear, consequently, that Céline's bridges are the products of din and of harmony.

And *brang!* and *proum!* go the bridges, and *prrag!* and *pataclac!* But
the Célinian being is so made that, even under the worst bombings, he
starts hearing tunes. Sumptuous tunes, but which he alone hears. No
matter how much he asks around him, asks Lili, "she hears the sirens...
that's all." And Felipe, who listens, but who doesn't hear any music either,
"just the showers of mines" and, he too, "plenty of sirens."[14]

It would be far too sad if the din of the strafing were to render us, too,
insensible to the little music of the bridges. Oh! frail, barely perceptible
(I will grant it), a distant music, but how refreshing for whoever knows
how to catch even two or three notes of it. The memories, then, that
come back, the echoes! How they sing, Céline's bridges! How they dance,
all of a sudden! We dance on the abyss. We dance all in a circle.[15]

Try resisting, for instance, the charms of this nautical evocation:

> It's there on the bridge that we came to listen to the accordion, the one
> from the barges, while they wait in front of the gate for the night to end
> so they can pass the river. The ones especially that come down from Bel-
> gium are musical; they wear color everywhere, green and yellow, and to
> dry linen all over the strings and then raspberry slips that the wind swells
> by leaping into them gust after gust.[16]

A little wind in some color, a little accordion tune, "the echo carrying itself away...the notes...the bridge."[17] There is no bridge but the one in Avignon. Whether in Bezons, whether in London, Pest, or Paris ("dive from the bridge of Pest?"),[18] Céline's bridges all say the same quest for an impossible rigadoon. Oh! certainly, they shake, and shake us, but, after the surprise, how much hope they leave us with. The hope, perhaps, that a dance step might eventually pull us from this tight spot, from this danger spot?

If this is indeed the hope, the mad hope with which bridges lull us (with which they wave us and shake us), we will have to pay all the more attention, when we are carted off in Céline's metro, to the exigency of a meter or a measure that, there as much as anywhere, never fails to impose itself, and just as implausibly.

> For a little nothing...you blow it all: ballast! vaults!...a breath! a cedilla!...go tumbling! a thousand miles per! your story capsizes! derails! your train plows! it's a total squashing, truly vile! shameful! you and your six hundred thousand readers!...cursed disaster! for a breath!...on a breath!...into jelly![19]

A mistake in scanning, "a little off-beat hitch patatrac":[20] disaster. But it is only a disaster so quickly because the metro-writing retains, in relation to the disaster, the greatest, the closest proximity. The entire secret of the new music lies therein, in this art Céline has, that in any case he claims as his very own, the art of flirting with catastrophe.

∽

Who has never, as a child, danced to the tune of the broken bridge? Of the Magdeburg bridge, *die ist zerbrochen*; of the London bridge, *London Bridge is broken down.*

The little girls and little boys take each other's hands and form a line. In a line they pass and pass again under the arch formed by the upraised arms of the first two. And, as each one trembles fearfully that the arms will fall, that the arch will collapse on him, imprisoning him, they all take up the song together:

> London bridge is broken
> down,
>   Broken down, broken
> down,

London bridge is broken
down,
   My fair lady.

Build it up with wood and
clay,
   Wood and clay, wood and
clay,
Build it up with wood and
clay,
   My fair lady.

Wood and clay will wash
away,
   Wash away, wash away,
Wood and clay will wash
away,
   My fair lady.

Build it up with bricks and
mortar,
   Bricks and mortar, bricks
and mortar,
Build it up with bricks and
mortar,
   My fair lady.

Bricks and mortar will not
stay,
   Will not stay, will not stay,
Bricks and mortar will not
stay,
   My fair lady.

Build it up with iron and steel,
   Iron and steel, iron and
steel,
Build it up with iron and steel,
   My fair lady.

Iron and steel will bend and
bow,
   Bend and bow, bend and
bow,

Iron and steel will bend and
bow,
    My fair lady.

Build it up with silver and
gold,
    Silver and gold, silver and
gold,
Build it up with silver and
gold,
    My fair lady.

Silver and gold will be stolen
away,
    Stolen away, stolen away,
Silver and gold will be stolen
away,
    My fair lady.

Set a man to watch all night,
    Watch all night, watch all
night,
Set a man to watch all night,
    My fair lady.

Suppose the man should fall
asleep,
    Fall asleep, fall asleep,
Suppose the man should fall
asleep,
    My fair lady.

Give him a pipe to smoke all
night,
    Smoke all night, smoke all
night,
Give him a pipe to smoke all
night,
    My fair lady.

Now in boats, now in oak, now in stone, "and the steel then!" as the
preface to Albert Serouille's book hammered out; the celebration of the
bridge of Bezons in which Céline, not without a little malice, rewrites

History to the tune of "London Bridge." A tune that could seem written especially for him, this dance or nursery rhyme — this lullaby[21] — that associates the mysterious image of a bridge that must constantly be re-built, to the image of children who, no matter how lightheartedly they sing it, nonetheless surrender to the delights of very ancient fears. For how could we doubt that fear isn't a little bit part of the game? All the more delicious for being vague, and, so to speak, without object.

But, if they don't know its object, others, in their place, understand it, who remember; who have learned, at their own expense, that rivers hardly like to be crossed. And that they often receive the most discrete structure, the least little bridgelet, as an insult. Of course, they obviously have ended up by consenting. But at what price! The Hooghly Bridge, in Calcutta, rests on a bed of skulls; *on a layer of children's heads,* the chronicles say. The bridge of Halle hides in its foundations the skeleton of a child. And even London Bridge itself, so the rumor goes, was at the time of its construction ritually sprinkled with the blood of the innocent.

Once again, it is only a rumor. But how this rumor grows, how it is able to impose itself, when, reflected by the vaults, its echo is suddenly amplified! Then, yes, we are willing to believe; and we would even like nothing better than to give credit to the wildest of tales. To the legend, for instance, assigned by Breton tradition to the bridge of Rosporden, legend that claims that if one only removed, pried free a few stones, at a certain place, one would assuredly find the remains of the young boy the first builders installed there and walled in alive, a candle in one hand, a piece of bread in the other. Having, essentially, light and food for his immobile journey, while the local residents, from shore to shore, went about their business in all safety.

And tranquil they certainly could be. But then neither more nor less than we ourselves are every time we set foot on a bridge. What would we have to fear? The dear angels have paid; "cute brats of the fog,"[22] they watch over our steps. Their light troop floats over the river, forming frag-ile rings, as the little girls and boys of Wapping used to form in the lost streets of the London docks, with their "sweating passages of distress."[23] A whole farandole, to the lively strains of which the narrator of *Guignol's band,* who has been stamping his feet, wearing out his soles for so many and so many pages, finally surrenders in desperation.

So that we soon find ourselves wondering if it isn't of them, quite simply, of their dizzying and gentle swirling that Céline is still thinking when, at the end of the journey, in *Rigadoon,* worried about the footbridge that must carry them to safety, to the other side of the Kiel canal, he sends forward as his scouts, he dispatches the little cretins who, on their own initiative, ever since Berlin, had placed themselves under his protection:

> Let them cross the bridge . . . it'd already be proof that it's possible, that the iron can maybe pass, that the tracks hold . . . the roadway and the enormous beams had for a moment distended themselves, bent, in a way that the worst was to be feared . . . no! . . . our droolers arrive, they rejoin us, they seem to have had fun . . . happy as can be! . . .[24]

And happy, obviously, because they are naturally gay. Happy also because nothing delights children as much as crossing and recrossing bridges. Which is why they describe them in their rounds, recite them in their songs. Bridges are their domain, the true stage of their games. A great theater that speaks to them of life and speaks to them of death. In the right words, and especially the appropriate tone. Such a music! Music of the Passage, how else to call it? That used to be well known, but that has, alas, since been forgotten.

Hence the fact that Céline, in his books, keeps striving to rediscover the lost music. Singing scales any old how, "Re! . . . fa! . . . sol sharp! . . . mi! . . . Shit!" (*Death on the Installment Plan*); "Sol sharp! . . . sol! la sharp! . . . si!" (*Rigadoon*).[25]

To tell the truth, he's trying out notes all the time, "do! do! do! fa mi re do si!" "Mi! do! do! sol!" "fa! . . . la! . . . si! . . . do! do!"[26]

— Ah! yes, dodo. To go sleep, to go lie under the bridge of the great rest, of the long slumber . . .

And he's also humming tunes to himself all the time. All the time . . . Long before the chorus of *Journey,* the enigmatic *Song of the Swiss Guards.* As far back as the thesis he defends in 1924 — Céline having always considered that this thesis, which was meant to sanction the end of his medical studies, in fact inaugurated his literary career. A retrospective illusion? Yet, when examined, how pregnant it seems to be with the work to come! Through its climate, first, which is so immediately Célinian. A first book that, in one bound, transports us to the "melodious country," to a dream Hungary, where "music surges effortlessly into the open,"[27] Semmelweis's native country; Semmelweis, the doctor whose eulogy Céline (his name may not yet be Céline, but Céline he nonetheless already is, and to the hilt) is about to undertake. Wishing to salute in Semmelweis the man of science who brought to light the infectious process of the puerperal fever, but who, no matter how much of a man of science he may have been, kept a mind innocent enough, a soul fresh enough to force us to hear, in the classic question, so frightening to grown-ups, of how children are made, the question that, in truth, should frighten them even more, and that bears, on the contrary, on the reasons why, having made them, they immediately destine them to death. Because after all, at that age (who doesn't see it?), the two questions go hand in hand, even if, through a sort of slip, and a very understandable slip in the mouths of our little ones, one often takes the form of the other.

This slip, the appalling slip that birth is: such is the object of Céline's thesis.

And the object, consequently, of the first of his books, if it must be repeated. In one fell swoop, swoop of the wing or swoop of the bow (it's one and the same, after all), Céline goes to the heart of the matter. He has barely begun, and the great imaginary scene of his work is already in place. Set, so to speak, at the frontispiece; established, what is more, on facts confirmed by History.

The facts, here they are. We are in Vienna. In the maternity ward of the Hospital of Vienna, where the ward of Doctor Klin (*recte,* Klein) and the ward of Doctor Bartch both face and oppose each other. Two workrooms, two methods. Whereas Bartch uses midwives, Klin only uses students. The result: his department is a slaughterhouse. The statistics evince, for Klin, a considerable failure rate. All the more considerable inasmuch as Céline, to better damn the enemy, stretches the numbers; inasmuch as he even pumps them up beyond all reason, inasmuch as he is not afraid to accuse Klin of losses whose total, expressed in percentages, would make us dizzy. Not far from 100 percent; 96 percent, if precision were to still have any meaning here and if these weren't doctors' accounts.

As if death, on its side, kept detailed accounts! Charon's ferry, in Céline's work, is called *La Publique, The Democrat.* The only truly public transportation. Jam-packed around the clock, a permanent rush hour. The holocaust, round-trip.

Arithmetic ends where death begins. Céline, in his mathematics, can afford to be inaccurate. Doesn't he know for a fact that in Professor Klin's obstetrics ward there is no life left for anyone? Ever since Death, the bitch, desecrated "the vagina tabernacle"...[28] Having wrapped up his investigation, Semmelweis rapidly reaches the conclusion that if expectant mothers run fewer risks when they are handled by midwives, it's because, unlike students, midwives are forbidden to perform autopsies. "It is the fingers of the students, soiled during recent dissections, that carry the fatal cadaverous particles into the genital organs of the pregnant women and especially at the level of the cervix."[29]

Woman is in labor, and she is giving birth to death. There is decidedly something rotten in motherhood, something lame. And, of course, she limps, Ferdinand's mommy: not a reader of Céline who doesn't know it. There have even been a great many disputes over this maternal disgrace, and over Céline's exaggerations where it is concerned. But things, in these arguments, haven't always been kept straight; the part of allegory, in the all-too-vivid picture the work paints of this limp, hasn't always been made clear. If Clémence, on her woolen leg, waddles like a duck, it's a sign that motherhood, in its principle, rests on shaky grounds; that motherhood, finally, is but a fool's bargain.

Céline to Albert Paraz: "Women give life and take it back."[30] It would be difficult to bring back to a more prosaic level the exemplary destiny of Philippe Ignace Semmelweis; difficult to denounce more crudely the scandal against which he leads his quixotic combat, which is nonetheless the scandal all of Céline's revolt feeds on: the scandal that makes him, one day, pick up a pen, write his first book, set the cornerstone of his work. And at the same time helps him find (not the least remarkable fact), helps him immediately find its addressee. Céline having dedicated his thesis to Doctor Brindeau: to the professor who taught him obstetrics, no doubt; were it not, moreover, to the distinguished music lover the honorable practitioner could become when the mood was on him — "an orchestra fanatic."[31]

A double address: medicine and music. All of Céline is in this coincidence. The work, there, takes its chances. With a single roll of the dice, a single stroke, a single envoi. Addressing itself to music, over medicine; and, ultimately, trusting the ear to judge everything, the smooth running of things or, on the contrary, their lameness. Let Semmelweis, for instance, fail to impose his ideas, and it's in the ear, his ear, that the failure will ring; the pathetic failure that is the failure of his life, but that is also the failure of all of medicine, or at least of this science of the passage medicine is when medicine, as is here the case, is reduced to obstetrics . . . To his friend Markusovsky, who has come to talk with him in professor Klin's maternity ward, he admits that "the sickening sound of the bell that precedes the priest bringing the viaticum has forever entered the peace of my soul."[32]

Klinn! . . . Klinn! Klinn! Klinn! . . . His ears are ringing. And this little bell of obsession soon cuts him off from the world of reason. Madness, alas, takes hold of his mind. Semmelweis raves, Semmelweis goes trippingly on the path of life. How far is the student, the spruce streamjumper Céline showed us at the beginning, crossing "the Danube bridge every Sunday."[33] The time of the fall has come for him. "At a few days' interval he first breaks his arm, then his left leg in one of the tortuous, inaccessible staircases so common in his neighborhood."[34]

One can still see, in the present-day capital of Hungary, the house that Semmelweis was born in. Now a museum devoted to his memory, it is a fine residence in the neoclassical style, located in the Tabán neighborhood; formerly the neighborhood of the ferrymen, those whose made their living transporting merchants and their merchandises between Buda and Pest . . . I do not know if Céline ever visited this house. But everything seems to suggest that he never did. The beautiful epitaph, superbly symbolic, he wouldn't otherwise have failed to compose: *Born in a world of ferrymen, he botched his passage.*

You always believe you have crossed the passes, have passed the bridges. But after this one, there is that one; and after that one . . . "the towboat whistled; its call passed the bridge, another arch, another, the lock, another bridge, far, even further . . ."[35]

You always believe you have crossed the bridges . . . Céline doesn't believe anything. He knows. He who came into this world on the hither side of the bridges. And who, since then, and forever, remains on the other shore. Forever the man across. Won't he have told us, have dinned it into us often enough: "I didn't start too good . . . I was born, I'll repeat it, at Courbevoie, Seine . . . I'll repeat it for the thousandth time [. . .] you can never repeat things enough for the hardheads! . . . Courbevoie, Seine, Rampe du Pont . . ."[36]

And again, and always, "Rampe du Pont, 11, Courbevoie":[37] the only noise in the work. Let those who can hear . . . But who is talking about hearing? The word for the passage is a word that won't pass. At the birth registry, the lady pretends she can't hear you.

—A little hard of hearing, maybe?

—No! It's the word itself, and it's the thing; it's the bridge that is drilling her ears. *Pont, pont, pont, pont* . . . The great tune of the bridges (Ludwig van and Beebeecee).[38] How many decibels? Céline, at the Kiel bridge: "no ear can resist, no head, mine you can imagine!"[39] Pétain, under the great bridge of Sigmaringen: "he had become so senile he didn't even hear the bombs or the sirens anymore."[40] Deaf in the vicinity of the bridges, and of all of them as they are; deaf as the pontiff, who is keeper of the bridges, is deaf; deaf as the ferryman is deaf.

For deaf the ferryman is, as Ulysses in the straits of the Sirens. See *From Castle to Castle* . . . At the end of the hundred or so pages that serve as an introduction to the story itself, yet seem but a labyrinth solely conceived to make us despair of ever finding its exit, Céline, in one of those magic tricks he always has up his sleeve, suddenly retires from the front of the stage—where he nonetheless was, till then, living it up with such style and making such a row—and lets Charon take his place to rescue the reader from the impasse into which he, Céline, had a little too carelessly misled him: in such a way, it might be worth pointing out in passing, in such a manner that with the Boatman of the Styx it is death, and death alone, that ushers us into the heart of the matter.

From the window of one of his patients, a cancerous old woman who is stubbornly refusing to pass on and, her final coquetry, is lingering at the doorstep, Céline sees, thinks he sees, a curious craft pull up to the dock. It's a sort of *bateau-mouche,* similar, come to think of it, to one of those old barges that used to provide the service along the river, back in the distant days of his youth. *La Publique,* one can read on its badge, "number: 114."[41] For while it is night, a pitch-black night, the eyesight is nonetheless in no way diminished. Céline, staring, can even follow on the landing stage the long line of passengers. Each one pays his place, he can see that too; and each one, one after the other, is repaid with a great oar blow to the head.

—Well, the dead have to be re-killed. You always die twice. Once, to leave the world of the living; the second time, to enter the realm of the dead. The trauma of the passage isn't doubled for any other reason . . .

—Except that of all this, nothing, of course, is explained. Not a word of commentary. As if the unusual sight didn't require any. One can at best deduce, from the observer's unruffleable calm, his satisfaction at noting how everything here is unfolding according to an immemorial script. It isn't death, that troublemaker, death and all its trimmings, that could still surprise him. The surprise comes from another quarter; and only then does the fairy tale begin. Céline suddenly recognizes in the attendant a temporary ticket-taker whose services Charon has availed himself of for the occasion, the silhouette of his friend Le Vigan. An uncertain silhouette, of course, but as befits the silhouette of a movie star who has vanished from the screen and who only barely exists in the memory of the public, where he survives, it must be said, thanks to a phenomenon more akin to retinal persistence than to the resurrectionist faculties of memory; a "man from nowhere,"[42] with that faraway look that never leaves him, so vague since he's no longer in vogue. The same Le Vigan we will see Céline drag after him like his shadow throughout the German trilogy; and in *North*, especially, where Le Vigan, now only La Vigue (the diminutive as the ultimate stage of shrinking), is portrayed as a fading, taciturn, and haggard character. One of those beings who, by reaching their minimal weight, as Frédéric Vitoux so felicitously puts it,[43] have reached perfection. Who no longer have to force themselves to enter into a state of absence, nor even to be silent to overcome the natural gravity of speeches. When Le Vigan finally deigns to emerge from the silent roles he prefers, it is only to whisper, if not to intersperse his inaudible murmur with a frequent "*Hush!! Hush!!*"[44] addressed not so much to his interlocutor as to himself. As if, not satisfied with evolving in a world of silence, he still had to protect himself from the sound of his own voice. To break with the complicity of the mouth and the ear on which every speaker bases the power of seduction he exerts over others . . . Yet another proof that deafness indeed affects all passages; proof that it is the affection of the passage.

It was simply up to Céline to complete the allegory. And complete it he does, with all his con man's skill, he who could sweet-talk us into buying the Brooklyn Bridge, his illusionist's talent, which grows more prodigal as the years go by, and which gives his last books a hint of the enchanting charm of fairy tales . . . Near the ship of the deceased appears Le Vigan, as we have noted; but a Le Vigan wearing a sombrero, boots, and spurs: a fantasy gaucho. Disguised, it seems. But neither more nor less, in fact, than any of the others. Than Sosthène in his Chinese robe, Titus in full regalia. Céline's novels are peopled with costume parades, with mid-Lent carnivals; fake this, fake that: the so-called. Not too serious, all these fine folk! But that's the world. Life is a theater whose actors, whose extras, no matter under what aspect they appear, catch you by surprise. A happy being is the Célinian being, for whom the real is a permanent surprise. The wise man, so goes the old saw, has gotten over everything. But Céline has gotten over nothing. He's only just getting there. Eternal Huron who greets the event with a *No! you're kidding,* with an *Impossible!* . . . And whose exclamations are a delight to us. Céline exults, and the discovery of the incredible nature of reality implies, for him, adherence. It's a question of tact. While you mustn't give the cold shoulder to Providence's favors, you musn't surrender to its advances on the spot either, you have to play hard to get. Céline's methodical disbelief is but a delaying tactic. The answer is postponed but in no way ambiguous; its terms, on the contrary, unequivocally manifest the intention he has always had of submitting, in the end, to the obvious: that there is nothing sensible to be said about the world. With only one reservation, the afterthought that if the science of the world is an insane science, it is also, after all, a gay science. Of gaiety as the supreme elegance. Céline would have been worthy of a place in the pantheon of postmodern fame, between this painter and that musician, amid the wits, sparkling and light, spirits of fire and of the air, celebrated by Clément Rosset.[45]

But, for all that, and were he to put even more gaiety into it than usual, Céline knows what he knows. He knows that, released on bail after a hard-labor sentence for collaboration, Le Vigan went to seek refuge in Argentina. Thus is solved the mystery of the sombrero.

— But not of Argentina. We are in Paris.

— In Paris, fine! In other words, wherever you please. Anywhere... Always remember that Céline's gaze on his contemporaries is the gaze of a ghost. Of a Huron (I have just shown it) and of a ghost. Because Céline is the ghost of the bridge. Because Céline haunts the passage, forgotten by the previous century, which ended without him, disdained by the current one, which didn't wait for him to start. The ghost, however, knows nothing of the divisions by which we partition space, serialize time. He confuses the here and the there; confuses the present and the past... One eye on the present, the other on the past. Never both eyes in the same direction. A cross-eyed gaze. And it's this strabismus of Céline's ghostly gaze that explains that at this point, and thus at the moment the story is finally about to open — beneath the gaucho with the imposing headgear, slowly appears the silhouette of a Le Vigan wrapped in an enormous turban. A memory of bygone times. It was a winter day in Sigmaringen. Céline, that day, had gotten into an argument with his partner in misfortune.

> Let's see! let's see!... down there?... on the dock?... La Vigue?... well, he was in a gaucho outfit... Le Vigan ticket-taker... that I recall! that I remember exactly! and that's all!... fever no fever! exactitude! [...] that I've lied? excuse me! [...] that La Vigue wasn't a gaucho!... no sombrero!... that he was wearing an enormous turban! well, of course I know it! shit! the enormous turban!... I tore it off him in the fight!... and in the snow!... actually, why were we fighting?... it was a bandage, his turban!... a bandage for his ear infection!...[46]

Come on! We are nearly out of the woods. The genie of the passage is about to officiate. With this bandage for his ear infection, he is now dressed in his insignias, equipped with his attributes.

The bridge and the cloth-eared, *le pont et le sourdingue.* Between the *ding! ding! ding!* of the bell tintinnabulating in Semmelweis's ear, in Professor Klin's maternity ward, and the *dingue* of the *dinguerie,* the barminess Céline so likes to simulate, when he comes to us weaving (he who, however, never drinks anything but water) and raving like an old drunk bum who has spent his last night under the bridges.

↜

Few pictorial references in Céline's remarks on his work, interviews, statements to the press, radio or television programs. The standard recollections or citations for such occasions: *The Raft of the Medusa, The Breakfast on the Lawn, The Church of Auvers*... Kind words, however, for Seurat: "he put *trois points,* three dots everywhere; he thought it aired his painting out, made it flutter. He was right, that man."[47] And how right we ourselves would be to smile, if the irony of the remark didn't conceal an artistic connection quite seriously claimed, and even often reaffirmed, as Henri Godard has pointed out.[48] In this Baudelairean quest for an imaginary double, no doubt that Seurat occupies a prize position. But why this fixation? Where exactly, in truth, does Céline's approbation go? The question is worth asking. Is it to the inventor of pointillism, or to the painter of the *Bridge of Courbevoie*? To a praxis, or to the mysterious necessity that apparently subordinates it to the depiction of a site to which, more than half a century later, Céline still remains as attached as ever? As if some part of himself had remained there, had never crossed the bridge: eternal ferryman of that part of himself that couldn't cross the bridge and to which, from the other shore, he is madly waving his arms...

Letter to Albert Paraz, October 4, 1947: "I was born in Courbevoie, 12, Rampe du Pont." In *Faerie for Another Time*, it's 11 ("Rampe du Pont, 11, Courbevoie"). 11 or 12... The difference, for the time being, has no meaning; the stereotypical nature of the utterance is far more important to us. Céline gives you the place of his birth just as someone else would rattle off their name and occupation. Just as mechanically. Born in, etc. And, fifty years later, still born. Never failing to. Never getting over it, literally. Born, that's all he ever is.

We have thus found that his birth is his station in life. But we don't yet know if it's a bearable one, nor, in the end, what this way he has of being truly is. Though we may soon find out.

I was born in Courbevoie, 12, Rampe du Pont, in 1894, the Seine was frozen, my mother was coughing up blood, like you, from poverty, it must be said, she lived seventy-four years. She was a lace maker. She died blind. We've always been damned hard workers in my family. And damned idiots. Arletty, my buddy, is also my homey; she was born in Courbevoie, a little further down, Rampe du Pont. When you get out you'll go see the barracks, they are famous for their Restoration military architecture, Vigny was garrisoned there.

Henry IV nearly got drowned, Rampe du Pont, at the old ford, going to visit some whore. More exactly passage de l'Ancre, a little dead end behind the ramp, ah we know a few things about the suburbs! My heart is still there.[49]

A frozen river, a consumptive mother (as was indeed feared), and this king who barely escapes drowning: so many predicaments, all of a sudden! And just when the reader was discovering that nowhere else does Céline feel more at ease. Never so sure of being at home, on his own ground, than in the middle of the worst quandaries. Should difficulties appear, various obstructions, passage difficulties, how he immediately jumps on the opportunity! Bedlam on the bridge:

In love, I can say, with passage difficulties, visions in the straits, those oh so rare instants when nature lets you observe it in action, so subtle, how it hesitates and makes up its mind ... at the moment of life, if I dare say ... all our theater and our belles-lettres are on coition and around ... fastidious repetitions! ... the orgasm is mostly uninteresting, all the hype of the giants of the pen and the cinema, the millions for advertising have only ever displayed but two or three little spasms of the rump ... sperm does its work far too much on the quiet, far too intimately, it all escapes us ... childbirth, now there's something worth seeing! ... spying on! ... down to the minute![50]

Born we know where. And, as a result, following the *circulus vitiosus* traced by *la courbe voie,* the curved path of his destiny, ending up as an obstetrician. Obstetrician or doctor of the dead: another one of the circle's properties is to make the starting point meet the point of arrival. Which explains why between the wail and the rattle, between the first cry and the last sigh, Céline soon no longer knows where to listen. "I keep watch over [...] hiccups" (Copenhagen Hospital, cancer ward).[51]

Wails all fascinate me ... just think, years at Tarnier! ... Brindeau, Lantuéjoul ... the first cries ... the first cry! ... all thick and full of phlegm ... my business! ... the tiny little mugs, beet red, bluish, already strangulated! ... did I ever help beings to be born! ... How they come! ... you're putting me back into memories here! "Push, my good lady! Push! ..." I've heard quite a few cries... I'm an ear man... but the childbirth duo mommy the little brat, there's a chord to remember... the mommy just done screaming, the kid takes it up...[52]

Thus turns the wheel, from death to life, from life to death. But whether it turns one way or turns the other, Céline is there. Where needed. Where it's happening. Where the *event* is taking place: the event of the passage, the only one that counts (the rest, compared to it, is just literature, *tcetera, tcetera*..., as he says); the only one that Céline cares to record, and that he struggles to reproduce, sentence after sentence. For the sentence itself is a passage. Or at least, in order to write, he must convince himself it is. And, let us not doubt it, he certainly does see the sentence pass, and hears it. Except that once past, he loses all interest in its fate. He is waiting for the next one. The next train, the whole train of words already taking shape in his head. The Rapid... If Céline despises "*la phrase filée,*" "the smooth sentence," he loves, on the contrary, and loves above all else, *la phrase qui file,* the sentence spinning out of control.

The poetry of the railroad, indeed, with its *Blue Train,* its *Star of the North,* its *Orient-Express,* with its posters on which modern art, in the 1930s, attempts the first depictions of speed, invents in a hurry its esthetics, is to a certain extent where Céline, pell-mell, goes fishing for his images. The metaphor of the railway takes the place, for him, of an *ars poetica.* It is even, in truth, his guarantee. Not only does it comfort him in his conception of his own style, but it furthermore convinces him that this style is imperative, that it is the most adequate, the one best related to his eternal interests, to the curiosity that the doctor in him (still so childlike, in this respect, *puer æternus*) has never lost for the things of life, for everything dealing with the mysteries of gestations and parturitions, the little secrets of birth. And thus does he cart the question of childbirth off in his train (train of words, train of sentences, pleasure train, scenic railway and roller coaster, the great haulage of the fantasies), just as he carted the bridges off in his metro.

Between the Sigmaringen railway station, for instance, and a maternity ward, the similarities are misleading. All these women *expecting.* Expecting the following one, expecting the next one. The latest born, the last train: they aren't too sure anymore. Everything is getting muddled in their heads, bewitched. The maneuvers of the machines have bewitched them, "the farandole of the shunting,"[53] all the traffic of the convoys ... Might they, like Céline, harbor the suspicion that "life on earth must have begun in a railway station?"[54] One could hardly explain, otherwise, their presence in this place, and the reasons, too, for their strange migrations. Because, on top of it, they are traveling. If not next to the tracks, you can see them in the cars. The train, their universe. At the least stop it's a stampede. Women and children first!

> our two carriages have barely stopped, already we're invaded! ... we don't exist anymore! swamped under brats and old biddies! ... a wave, the way they spill, pass over us, squash us! crush ... they're coming through every hole [...] the train rattles ... but not too much ... where can it go now? we'll see! [...] immediately they start squawking! and then there's singing! and all together! how many are they? ... forty? fifty? ... in three parts, all together, and in tune! and cheerful! ... the children are from Königs-berg ... the pregnant women from Danzig ... I still have their tunes in my head ... *tigelig!* ... *ding!* ... *digeligeling!* a song about bells ... for Christmas, no doubt ...[55]

Please notice: it's as if the passage, all of a sudden, was coming clear. There is music, we hear songs. And it's true that after singing Christ-mas so much, it would be a shame if in the end it didn't come; and if didn't come, along with Christmas, feast of the Nativity, everything that should come, and would assuredly come if the *ding!* ... *digeligeling!* that they all take up at the chorus didn't reawaken the echo of the little bell forever tinkling in the head of poor Semmelweis — if the memory of his martyrdom didn't toll the knell of all our hopes.

Besides, this train, a train bearing children, this heavy female entrusted with the cartage of the species — this train is returning from a funeral. A delegation from the Vichy government, then enclaved in Sigmarin-gen, had wanted to pay a final homage to one of its servants, deceased way up there, to the northeast of Berlin, from the consequences of a surgical operation. "Twelve hundred kilometers ... all of Germany."[56] Two days to go up, as many to return. An infernal journey, then, whose sole prospect is a return to the Sigmaringen pocket, that bag of tricks, that little swelling on the path of the invasions, that hysterical pregnancy of History. Without a future, therefore. The tracks, beyond, are cut off. Last stop. Everybody off. Even the text itself comes to an end. End of the line, end of the novel. The machine has stopped, banked its fires. Soon all that is left in the train, all that is left in the book is Céline; Céline and a German woman, blonde, with pale skin, bluish like motionless milk: a German woman from Memel, about to give birth. And thus are, inevitable, the last words of the story: "I've got Memel!...my Memel!... [...] mustn't get there after the birth! a woman nearly 'at term' who's been knocked around awful, terrible, you could say!"[57]

Could one dream a more perfect image of motherhood than the one that transpires through the name Memel? A name, as Claude Simon comments,

> that makes you think of *Mamelle,* Mammary with in its aspect I don't know what (the two white "e"s perhaps) of frigid a black city crowned with snow near a frozen livid sea inhabited by the Slavonic women with linen hair with heavy breasts (the two "l"s of *mamelle* suggesting the vision of the *jumeLLes,* the twin forms swinging)...[58]

But, oh women of Memel, who offer us the basket of your breasts, why do you remind us of those figures, those half-figures in their stone sheaths, that used to be placed in gardens, at the corner of an alley, between two lawns? Is it because these figures were called *terms*? Is it because of this word and all it suggests, to our ears, of hopes satisfied, of promises accomplished?

Alas! though she's nearing term, this one hasn't reached it; nearly at term, only. *Nearly.* But for this little word at the end of the line everything would end, the journey and the book, and, who knows? the work itself perhaps... As if, ultimately, *something* refused to end or spilled over the end. A little *something* that will cause the novel to end prematurely. For that is how it always ends. This structure of the premature is what gives all of Céline's ends, end of this or of that, end of a chapter and end of a work, end of a sentence, their so eminently suspensive dimension.

↵

We will note, in this connection, the complete absence in Céline's texts of the most expected of all Célinian motifs. An obsession with childbirth inhabits the work, and yet the work does not allow itself the slightest evocation of it. Of the promised marvels of that "childbirth duo mommy the little brat," not a peep. Perhaps the work itself can't hear them, aside from a rare few aural visitations. And hardly angelic ones, for that matter. Closer, assuredly, to the visions tormenting Flaubert's holy hermit than to Mary's Annunciation. Neither celestial concert, nor music of labor. What the condemned man had taken a little while ago for a baby's wailing is in fact the shouting of the abortionist, the woman in the cell next to his, the prisoner of the "28" who is screaming "I'd say like twenty-five newborn babies!"[59] Nursery cries: a crèche all by herself.

— Because the assassin always returns to the scene of the crime?

— Because there is something, in the obstetrician, akin to the tyrant of Syracuse... Because the obstetrician bends toward the bellies of women like Denys in the Latomies, attentive to the moans, the calls, the imprecations "that stir your innards," "the tragedy of matter, the depths of the world imploring you."[60] Because auscultation is his great passion and all resonant objects equally seem to invite him to explore the "musician hollow nothingness"[61] they take shape in; "the hole of the hole of the depths of the Butte,"[62] in *Normance*; this Montmartre, mount of the martyrs, we see offering the resonance chamber of its entrails, tunnels, cavities, "crypt beneath crypt [...] vaults that are three...four thousand years old!"[63] to the gong strokes with which the war, above, hammers the sky of Paris. Bombs, "catacombs directly."[64] So that later, knocked for six as they've just been, wandering amid the quasi-Pompeian ruins of the city of Hamburg, they will all find nothing better to do, the little cretins, the cat Bébert, Lili, and her whole court, than to penetrate, in turn, into the enormous swell of dirt rising before them, whim of the elements unleashed, a bell of clay: "giant bell in fragile clay...bell... basically a blister."[65]

Good example of the "hysterical twist"[66] Céline's reflections rather naturally take where acoustics are concerned. From the bell to the blister — from the sound, "basically," to the womb of the sound: this is the trail that must be followed in every case; the trail that must not be lost, for any reason whatsoever, until "the entrance of the cave." Then, he explains to Robert de Saint-Jean, in 1933, "'Ho...Ho...' I go 'Ho' and it answers me."[67]

The Echo. The hollow of the Echo. Only, once you are there, beware: "the hollow of the Echo is sacred."[68] For instance, the "hollowed-out trunk" of the cathedral tree on which, "with sixteen sticks," the Pahouins

of Cameroon beat out their tam-tam, "Bikobimbo 1916":[69] Céline, modest trading-station guard that he was for a time, would never have been
imprudent enough to go near it. "I who was a hundred meters away, my
hut, I never went to see."[70]

A wise move. You don't joke with these things. The prologue of *Death
on the Installment Plan,* in this respect, is still as relevant as ever. One
look, and "it's over! it's enough! you're damned forever!"[71] The ear is
the gate of Hell. The ear, at least, that they call inner. Not the one, open,
that blossoms under the refreshing shower of the waves, under the rain
of sounds, but the black box, Michel Serres's "tempestuous box"[72] in
which Bachelard, already, had located the "sense of night," "and of the
most sensitive of nights: the underground night, enclosed night, night
of the deep, night of death."[73]

Let us add with Céline the left ear, we won't be adding much. The
left, as Michaux observes in *Passages,* partakes of "the vegetative, the secret, the reverse." On the left, consequently, everything in our body that
leads a life apart, that enjoys an existence so seemingly superfluous it
always manifests itself in an underhanded way, our organs, our entrails;
on the left, the stomach that Cendrars's fantastic medicine assimilates
to a "cosmic eardrum";[74] and, on the left, and with all the more reason,
the ear I was speaking of, plunging its roots into the thickness of the
infinitely deep biological night that our flesh wraps with a silky and
shivering sheath, with the bronze shimmers one sees in tar, and where,
somewhere, in the mysterious zone of the otolites, all along the semi-
circular canals, roll the unceasing rumblings of the great nocturnal and
bloody disturbance that haunts, for Céline, the depths of the world. His
bad ear, all obstructed with fossil noises, with "underground echoes,"[75]
"a great selection of memories of breaths."[76] Céline's plugged ear, his
deaf ear; his ear, rather, that turns a deaf ear, that only has ears for the
shadow mouth, the Dodonna oracle, for the storm brewing in the Sibyl's
flanks: his left ear. Ear that will have nothing to do with his right ear,
nothing to do with this latter's skill, which is, however, immense: "a cat
going by, the least mouse . . . I hear everything."[77] The keen ear, sensitive,
but sensitive . . .

Sensitive in proportion to how little the other one is, that should
have been obvious. The sense of hearing, functioning according to the

optical principle of the blind spot, develops here from a point of essential deafness; or, more precisely, originary deafness. By which we should
understand that it is first, of course, but also that it goes back to the
source. A fantasy of the origins, this belief in the existence of a deaf
spot. Which is to say, at the same time, how determinant it is. And it
indeed determines, for Céline, nothing less than his great aesthetic op-
tions; the idea, especially, that literature should be a praxis of listening,
an art of "stethoscopic fine-tuning."[78] A mad idea, as mad as any idea in
this realm, but an idée fixe, the hobbyhorse he rocks, bells in hand, before his bemused interlocutors. Who are asking themselves if they should
believe their ears, should seize the key he is handing them with so much
insistence. Until the moment when they are forced to admit that not
only does this key not open anything, but it only serves him to padlock
the system. A work can establish itself in duration only as long as it
rests on the unawareness of its own source. Should the writer, under
the pretext of explaining and justifying himself to the reader, actually
be muddying the waters, it isn't so much in order to retreat into the
bastion of his collected works as to seal off his own access to it. And
this is how (explanations coming on top of explanations) the question
of the deaf spot soon finds itself at the center of the most dizzying of
interpretative deliriums . . .

It being restated, however, that the question is an inaugural one. Inscribed as it were on the tympanum of the work; and thus inscribed at
its place, which is nonetheless the most improper place one could imagine. Not at all a treatise on acoustics, some novel reflection that might
provoke controversy, shake such and such of our certitudes in the matter of otology, but a work discussing the science of obstetrics. The thesis on Semmelweis.

Céline has just dealt with Semmelweis's birth, "at Budapest on the
Danube, in the profile of the Saint-Étienne church, in the heart of the
summer, precisely July 18, 1818."[79] But, having established this date, which,
with its repetition of the number 18, looks like a standstill of History,
Céline pauses momentarily. He skips a few lines, leaves two or three
blank lines, and, instead of continuing in the chronological order cus-
tomary for biographies — this order, Céline reverses it. As if 1818 couldn't
begin anything. The date, no more than the mention of the place of

birth, doesn't begin anything whatsoever. One must go back in time and further in space.

> In the profile of the Saint-Étienne church?... near the Danube... let us look for a house. It no longer exists. Nothing... Let us look further. In the world... In time. Something to guide us toward the truth... Let us look! Over there maybe in the frantic round drawing away... 1818... 1817... 1816... 1812... Let us go back in Time... In space now... Budapest... Bratislava... Vienna... 1812... 1807... 1806... 1805...: "On December 2, at four o'clock in the morning, the action began in a fog that was soon dispelled..." AUSTERLITZ...[80]

It's no longer a chronology, it's a countdown. Ebb of time, it pulls back in two movements, two series of dates; then, at the joint of the two series, the pivotal date of 1812, just as the eighteenth century is becoming the nineteenth and History is groaning on its hinges. Turning point of centuries, charnel house of History: the trenches of 1914, and, in 1812, the crossing of the Beresina. "Eblé's sappers!...,"[81] "Eblé's pontoneers,"[82] all gone like ghosts, vanished in the ice. The two bridges cracking, collapsing under the feet of the Great Army in distress. For three interminable days. More than a third of the men swallowed up. An indescribable crush... The work has barely begun and Céline's imagination is already haunting the bridges of the Beresina. Around which lurked the letter to Albert Paraz of October 1947. We haven't forgotten the frozen Seine, his mother coughing up blood, nor the good King Henry caught in the old ford. We might especially recall the slip that causes Céline to take one number for another, to drop the 11 of the Rampe du Pont for the 12 of 1812 — to drop the Rampe du Pont for the bridges of the Beresina and so relocate himself in History. In the negative utopia, at least, that serves him as History. A History entirely made of disasters, of course, but of muffled disasters, nearly muted. In which even the worst catastrophes are but petty change, a day-to-day, small-time Apocalypse.

To the rhythm of the convoys that Céline, long after, can still hear starting up at a "certain station where are loaded every evening the coffins of London." *Waterloo on the Bridge,* "over the Bridge,"[83] how was it?... Henri Godard, on this subject, quotes an unpublished letter by Céline, a request for information sent, in September 1934, to his English translator, John Marks, and which shows him quite preoccupied, all of a sudden, with this "railway station of the dead."[84] *Cemetery Station,* located "at the foot of the Waterloo Bridge," as Gordon Biddle tells us;[85] immediately past the bridge, at the exit of which an undertaker, the London Necropolis Company, has provided, ever since 1850, for the daily transportation of the cadavers to their final resting place, "a distant cemetery," at Brookwood, to the southwest of the capital ... Basically, whether it's the Thames you're talking about, whether it's the Danube, the Loire at Orléans, the Seine at Courbevoie, you're always crossing the river on the bridges of the Beresina. In the end: the bridge. "The song of Roland started France; I can see France ending Rampe du Pont."[86]

What can we add to this prophecy, if not that by preferring the half-frozen white waters of a Russian river to the red waters of the History of Rome; that by rejoining, in his thoughts, "the four hundred thousand hallucinated emberesinated to the plume,"[87] Céline was also identifying his literary start with the slow numbness of the end of a reign ... If not that, by choosing to enter life over the same bridges that once saw the Great Army reach its spectral existence, he was himself entering it the way one enters the other world: "white feather! mane to the wind!"[88] Hussar, Dragoon, or Cuirassier, Cavalryman Destouches of the "1st Specter," Colonel des Entrayes.

Born *à rebours,* in some ways. Yes, "in reverse": Harras's words, on the last page of *North,* even as a chariot, a chariot of women, a chariot of children, disappears into the East, led by Isis. The shepherdess and her herd, Isis the Gatherer ...

Harras notices ...

"You see, my dear Destouches, the Russian retreat in reverse ... return! return! *ooah!*"

Göring interrupts him ...

"Oh, excuse me! excuse me Harras! forgive me! they never took that route! never!"

"Ah, well, I thought!"

"But no! but no! dear Harras! don't think! ... very few came back through Stettin! ... a handful!"

"Yet! ..."

"Oh, no, Harras! I'm stopping you! ... I know ..." [...]

"It seemed to me, Göring ..."

"Don't let it seem to you! wait, Harras! ..."

Sitting in the snow, he's going to get it . . .
"Not Stettin at all, Harras!"
His head in his hands . . .
"Insterburg . . . yes! and then Elbing! and Gumbinnen . . . Thorn! . . . there
they went through! . . . and then Plock! . . . Landsberg! . . . that was their
stops! . . . Neuenkirschen! . . . Stettin practically none! . . . Neuenkirschen! . . .
lots of sick men . . . Neuenkirschen! there were still souvenirs! . . . you know,
in the hospital! I served there, assistant M.O. . . . names in the wood, in
the beams, carved names, right? . . ."[89]

Where does this softness come from, all of a sudden, calming the
wound of all these carved names? What reparation is it a sign of? Is it
finally to reunite the dispersed members of the great battle corps that
Céline follows the Great Army step by step? . . . This is something we
will never know. The enigma remains intact. The same, at the end, as it
spelled itself out in the beginning, at the very beginning of the novelistic work, with the frail quatrain of *Journey*.

> Our life is a journey
> Through Winter and through
> Night,
> We are seeking our passage
> In the Sky where nothing
> shines.
> — Song of the Swiss Guards (1793)

Everything has been said about these few lines; everything that had
to be said.[90] In 1793, there is no more Swiss Guard, not since 1792. Unless we imagine that, slaughtered at the Tuileries, they have been resur-
rected; have risen from the grave to be reborn in the white plain, at the
dawn of Modern Times; ghosts mingled with the Grenadiers of the Swiss
Regiment of the Great Army, taking up the first stanza of the *Beresinalied*
(the very one, word for word, whose sadness freezes us at the threshold
of the book, even before attempting the *Journey*), the song of the Beresina
that was, at the foot of the bridges, "their farewell to life, their salute to
the homeland."

The Passage of the Beresinas in *Death on the Installment Plan*, after
that, was inevitable. A logical follow-up, or rather an eternal recommencement. Céline's work lingers at the bridges of the Beresina . . . And without the cannons of Austerlitz, no doubt would have fallen asleep there.

1812 ... 1807 ... 1806 ... 1805 ...: "On December 2, at four o'clock in the morning, the action began in a fog that was soon dispelled..." AUSTER-LITZ ... This is not yet what we want ... we are looking for a man among our own, of our blood, of our race, closer to Semmelweis: Corvisart...! Corvisart...

He isn't in the plain on this great morning of fire ... Where is he? Doctor of the Emperor, this is his place!

Why has he remained in Vienna, at the General Hospital, where nevertheless no orders retain him? [...]

During Austerlitz, during the most decisive hour of his time, he relieves himself of his responsibilities, weary, no doubt, of assuming them, to translate, with a great deal of difficulty, moreover, a major book: *Auscultation* by Auenbrugger.

Old progress! Old with fifty years of silence!

Corvisart resurrects it, lends his voice to it, and this becomes a very pure and very beautiful act in the career of this man. Could he have put to any better use the formidable authority conferred upon him by his marvelous position as Epic doctor?

Homage to Corvisart! Homage a little, perhaps, to Napoléon![91]

Céline is certainly dragging us back and forth, between Vienna and Austerlitz, and by dint of it, losing us. Where is Corvisart, finally? Here, a little; but also a little there. One ear on the cannon, while he is training himself, initiating himself into the subtleties of auscultation ... Certainly a highly imprecise figure, still — I willingly admit it — but one that, in its imprecision, is nonetheless a brilliant anticipation of technical solutions that will not impose their necessity on the writer till much later. Céline, essentially, in writing, will not relent till he himself has become, in turn, and in his art, a sort of Corvisart. Just as it is only from having had his ear exposed to the cannon that Corvisart can apply himself to capture the thousand vibrations, the quasi-imperceptible whispers of the living, so is it only from the explosion that Céline's sentence, little by little, will learn to draw its resources.

To the point, ultimately, of no longer being able to do without it. And we have then Céline's text in its final state. *Braoum!* ... First, the onomatopoeia; the seed of the onomatopoeia, seed of thunder. Then, but only afterward, music; what Céline calls his little music, all in embroideries of waves and laces of silence. And then, once more, *braoum!* ... and, once again, music. And so on, without stopping. Left ear, right ear.

Céline limps in one ear (like a horse). But at least he is moving; at his pace, at his rhythm. At the rhythm of the pendulum that makes the sentence go and the sentence swing, a flying bridge, from this left ear to the right. Between the two ears, the sentence is a bridge.

↩

The explosion fertilizes. Hence the flashback of the thesis, its return to the mythical cannon of Austerlitz. On this first attempt, nothing less was needed than thunder itself. And thunder again in *Journey,* but "then one of these noises like you'd never have thought existed. We had so much all at once in the eyes, the ears, the nose, the mouth, immediately, of noise, that I sure thought it was over, that I had become fire and noise myself..."[92]

Transverberation of the narrator. On the Flanders road, the noise *visited* him. But "the noise stayed," moved in for good. A troublesome tenant, always moving his furniture about, banging this, banging that, and roaring and bellowing, such a noise! a din! It's Hell at home. But the trace also of a subterranean labor, of some obscure work, which Céline listens for, suspended, all ears, attentive to what is brewing. So strong is certainty that there is no noise that doesn't open onto something and, finally, doesn't lead to something; no noise that doesn't give a signal for departure. Hence, and as if to better convince himself, Céline soon thinks of assimilating the racket inhabiting him to the locomotive (noise made machine, machining noise). He has a train in his head, a thousand trains in his head, all of them maneuvering, an entire marshaling yard. *Death on the Installment Plan*: "fifteen hundred noises, an immense din [...] it's the midnight train pulling into the station... The glass roof above shatters and collapses... The steam shoots out of twenty-four valves... the chains leap to the third floor... In the wide-open coaches three hundred wino musicians tear into the atmosphere forty-five scores at a time."[93] *North*: "for me and men in my situation the trains will never stop whistling."[94] *Faerie*: "I pick everything up [...] the freight trains... two... three!... everything maneuvering at the Batignolles... and under the Pont de Flandres."[95]

The bridge of Flanders, as it should be... It's very close to Ypres, on October 25, 1914, that the maréchal des logis (sergeant) Destouches, in liaison between an infantry regiment and his brigade, falls under enemy fire. Grievously wounded, but wounded in the right arm. As for the head, nothing. Nothing, in spite of Céline's reiterated assertions. "I took a bullet in the ear during 14–18."[96] "I took a bullet in the head."[97] And, this head, you're lucky if he doesn't shake it for you the way you ring a bell. "He nods his head again. There's a bullet inside. We feel, very impressed, that we could nearly hear this bullet rattle around inside."[98]

Drelin, drelin... "It's the tinkerbell dingdonging,"[99] the tinkerbell tied to his work. Since he missed out on the amputation, so successfully pulled off by Cendrars in 1915, let him at least have that. Even if *that,* he has to go steal it from Apollinaire. Jealous of his bandage (doesn't every poet, today, need a bandage to staunch his wounds?), he too therefore claims the privilege of having been trephined. A new fable. But, just like the other one, which it doubles and improves, the fable of the trephination wends its way through people's minds. How many testimonies, indeed, eyewitness, *earwitness* testimonies, can it not summon to its defense? The testimony of Henri Mondor, in the foreword of the first edition of Céline's novels in the Bibliothèque de la Pléiade, in 1964;[100] the testimonies of Marcel Aymé in the *Cahiers de l'Herne,*[101] of Milton Hindus, who notes in his journal, on July 22, 1948, that at the place Céline has been trephined "he has a steel plate, which provokes all sorts of noises in his head."[102] The testimony finally of Robert Poulet, who, sketching in the following terms the portrait of an aging Céline, puts the final touch to the thing: "His face, more and more sculpted, worked by suffering. His left eye, the eyelid drooping, the pupil extinguished, an impression of exhaustion and of nobility, the calm of a martyr saving up his last forces. His right eye, open, burning, piercing, hard [...]. A nose dissymetrical at the top; joined higher on the left than on the right. *By a sort of bridge. Perhaps a trace of the trephination...*"[103]

I am the one who has underlined, who has added the italics to what would nevertheless have leaped to the eye. The trace of the bridge can now be deciphered in the features of the physiognomy itself. The Miracle of the Holy Face, which suddenly renders pathetic the ritual *ecce homos* Céline (a Céline Outraged) harasses us with in the fastidious toccatas of his long German fugue. It is enough, basically, for him to show himself barefaced.

"I was stiff and cold, I was a bridge, I lay over a ravine."[104] Kafka's dream come to life.

∽

Extraordinary success! G. Groddeck himself would have applauded. But what is it, however, compared to the masterpiece Céline was preparing, at the same time, in the secrecy of his Danish jail? When he was writing *Faerie*...

The masterpiece (and it certainly is one) consisted in relating to each other the vomiting he was subjected to, the balancing problems he perpetually suffered from, and the whistling, the buzzing, the ringing located in his ear, which our modern otology classifies under the term *acouphens*. By thus establishing a correlation between three symptoms that nothing a priori suggested to connect, not only was Céline obtaining the clinical picture he needed to explain to himself the cause of his ills, but he was also solving a problem of art. From there on everything held (the nausea, the vertigo, and the aural hallucinations), just as the different parts of a landscape, long separated, suddenly gather to form a whole. It might indeed have seemed to him that by acquiring all at once this symptomatic coherence, the sickness was at the same time handing him the identity of the god hounding him, the triple god of the Passage. Which is no doubt the reason why Céline yells its name to us, in *Faerie*, with the same accent of triumph Archimedes must have had when Archimedes hollered his famous *Eureka!*

At that precise moment (and for reasons that do not matter here), Lili, his ladyfriend, is posing nude in the studio of a sculptor. She is there, on an iron bed, exposing herself, thighs open, to the livid gaslight dispensed by one of those mantles once planted like burning bushes all along the Passage of the Beresinas, thanks to which you couldn't cross it without worrying about the deceased whose presence this double row of flames betrayed, even if you couldn't see him... This time, you see him. Impossible not to see him. It's "Lili spread under the green Welsbach burner."[105] Lili's corpse, but a corpse in the position of a woman giving birth: an all the more unbearable sight. Time to hit the road. Ferdinand, consequently (unless it's Céline, if not Doctor Destouches himself: such distinctions, by this time, hardly matter); the narrator, let us thus designate him, retires. He leaves the studio, leaves the morgue, the workroom (here, too, we're not sure which) and finds himself in the street. Alone in the street, to witness the simultaneous and reflexive triggering of the three symptoms just discussed.

> I vacillate...one step...another...I catch myself!...and *wouaf!* I puke!...It catches me there...not far...twenty meters from the door... I see the sidewalk, that's all...and nothing else...I puke all over the sidewalk...on all fours, then!...all fours...in the gutter, if you please... because it's an alarm! Am I buzzing or sirening?...It's an alarm!...I vomit like a drunkard, me! I know! and I don't drink! Never! Never anything! It's the vertigo! [...] I'll cross! I'll cross anyway! To the archway all the way across!...yes, to the archway!...to the archway!...Sirens!...not sirens!...I vomit, yes! I vomit!...but the sirens? following the edge... the edge, you hear!...the gutter!...It's enormous a gutter of a sudden!... It's a gulf!...a gulf rising...and sinking!...raising and lowering you!... the vertigo!...the Eiffel Tower! a gutter seems!...down at the bottom a little hole, the sewer!...and then immense and then giant!...an immensity!...all of Paris!...the sewer...at the bottom of the sewer!...me, I know!...I hang on!...a thousand little lights!...candles!...the edge!... bravo!...I puke!...I puke into it!...I'm buzzing!...the vertigo! it hasn't got me, the vertigo! Ménière's vertigo, it's called!...the houses spin! and then!...rise! leave! and then! the buildings in the air! "Ménière! Ménière!" the sidewalks bulge!...I can hear you laughing...No! No! No! I'm hanging on and I will cross![106]

Ménière's syndrome: the classic identification, in pathology, of the otalgia affecting that part of the inner ear called the vestibule.

Nevertheless, vestibule, vestibule...Medicine uses such words! Medicine uses such names! Ménière...And why not *Memel,* while we're at it? Memel's syndrome. It depends on one's ear. Either you hear it or you don't.

2

STEPS

It's about to go up, have you noticed? Only just rising over Céline's literature. And it hasn't even capered about two or three times before it's already too late. It's immediately obsolete. The century belongs to the airplane. Heavy twentieth century, given over body and soul to the heavier than air, as if even in its first starts it had had to surrender to the laws of its own gravity: Caliban even there, "more and more Caliban, more and more" (Céline to Pierre Dumayet).[1]

We are still only halfway there (why, yesterday Ferdinand was just leaving England), we know nothing, hence, of the *Génitron,* of Courtial des Pereires, and thus even less of his chimera, of the immense windbag, his pride and joy — and already the first champion aviators will have rushed to burst it in advance. Those whose photographic portraits adorn Édouard's room, where Ferdinand has sought refuge, next to the princes of the steering wheel and the kings of the pedal. The automobile racer Rougier, the French pilot Louis Paulhan; "Petit-Breton, steel calves [...], Santos-Dumont, intrepid fetus."[2]

What, in comparison, and to spin out the metaphor, does it mean to speak with Céline the language of the obstetrician (the only language that gives the words to say the Passage, if not the passwords)? What is Courtial's project, his great project of demonstration flights, of educational ascents? An aborted project. No sooner formed than aborted. Nipped in the womb, we might say.

But, in this, the balloon is no exception to the common rule. It undoubtedly only knows how to age. But it's like everything else, like all the things in this world. Have they ever known the bloom of their first freshness? And what is more, do they even begin, are they even born, Céline's things? Only one thing is certain: that they last. And last interminably. Last beyond their own duration. Basically, they no more end than they begin. The amazing thing, actually, is that as old, as demeaned as they may be, "they still find, who knows where, the strength to age."[3]

It could be Armide's enchanted realm, in the Tasso's dream or Lully's opera. The things grow heavier in their sleep, the things fallen under the charm, removed from time by Armide's magic, just like the Christian knights, just like Renaud in Oronte's island . . . The Orionte of *Death on the Installment Plan,* by assimilating Oronte to the Great Nebula of Orion, certainly one of the most beautiful in the entire firmament; Orion the sextuple-starred, whose last lights shine ("Up there Orionte was gone . . . I didn't have any landmarks left in the clouds")[4] in the last of the night skies inspired in Céline by Flammarion — himself a flame from the gigantic bowl of punch where he liked to get drunk, and which eventually went to his head: priding himself, at the end of his life, on bearing a name that came to him, he said, from *Flamma Orionis.*[5]

Indubitably, the illustrious astronomer was already no longer of this world. Carried away by his passion, just like Courtial whom the Great Nebula of Orion soon draws into its sphere of influence; rewritten *Orionte* by Céline, who wanted to leave us this hint, if he couldn't convince us that the ballooneer and his balloon had both gone over to "Armide's side." Which, however, is the very side the family tradition, in its obscure science, had always located at the end of the night: on the road beyond Choisy.[6] From the name of the relative who lived in that area, Aunt Armide, who though she had seen the entire century go by her door nonetheless persisted in remaining, and, in the midst of every end, in the midst of the ends of everything, refused to surrender to the end, giving us by her stubbornness a hint of the sort of impasse death itself, in her mind, could not fail to lead her to. "In the dark, behind the aunt, there was everything that's finished, there was my grandfather

Leopold who never came back from India, there was the Virgin Mary, there were M. de Bergerac, Félix Faure and Lustucru and the imperfect of the subjunctive."[7]

Like an imperfect of the subjunctive, half-expiring: and with Lourdes as a horizon, Lourdes and its miracles; near the beautiful Madame Steinheil, between Cyrano powdered with stardust and the La Lune spaghetti: the monstrous bibelot of Courtial des Pereires!

⌇

Bibelot, yes. But in the image, quite simply, of all the objects cluttering our lives. Today's objects as well as yesterday's. For that is what all of them, to different degrees, are destined to become: the knickknack is universal.

A radical point of view, but one whose excessive character doesn't escape Céline's notice, who at least tries to justify it, and to explain it notably by the extraordinary vivacity of his memories of his grandmother's antique store, rue de Provence. Every childhood thus has its reserved territories, these vital spaces midway between Ali Baba's cavern and an allegory of Memory. For Giono, it's Mademoiselle Alloison's grocer's store; for Michel Tournier, a pharmacy. For Céline, it's his grandmother's antique store. To which, for this reason, he returns mentally every time he has to account for the "unreality unease"[8] he feels at the sight of his fellow men and, in particular, of the spectacle of their great unpackings...His opinion, in fact, has been definitively made up ever since he was a little boy: the shop being given, there is no leaving it. The shop is everything, contains everything; what exists, has existed, will exist. If the worst came to the worst Céline might concede us the back shop. The annex, if you prefer, the outbuildings. Better to leave it vague. No one knows exactly what its limits might be. The only certainty one might have acquired by dint of reading is that the whole wide world must be housed. And that everything, somehow or other, must fit in. Riches from every country, from the furthest lands, "the hundred thousand travel souvenirs."[9]

Hundreds and thousands, absolutely, and hundreds of thousands. All the "cheese of the picturesque";[10] strangeness, exoticism. Enough to think that the Célinian being only knocks about from trading post to trading post. Try changing places; it's as if you'd only moved from one room or from one warehouse to the next. As far as the eye can see, nothing but heaps, shambles and jumbles, bazaar and bric-a-brac; from Jules's studio, in Montmartre, "his painting bedlam,"[11] to Sosthène's London room, "full of knickknacks all around . . . curios everywhere."[12] And, to reign over an empire whose frontiers are in no case greater than the limits of their business, "the men of Capernaum."[13] Men who know the art of warehousing the entire universe, the art of fitting the five parts of the world between the four walls of an entresol: all the knowledge of the day in the boxes of the *Génitron* and "enough to make all of London dance, accompany an entire continent" at Titus Van Claben's, the music-loving fence of *Guignol's band*.[14]

Men, furthermore (if it is often in fact the same men, it is in any case never others), who have found a way to skim off the top of time itself. Oh! not, of course, to hold it back. Time, with Céline, rarely flows on its own. Time stagnates, on the contrary; it deposits. And it is even these deposits that foul up the normal course of things. What is required, then, is delicately to gather its dross; the thin film, the impalpable powder that is the properly ephemeral part of time, its flower. The precious flower that may well have been discovered and acclimatized one fine day by the winners of the Perpetual Movement Contest organized by Courtial: two flea-market dealers, whose skill would certainly have deserved a reward if the finances of the *Génitron* had still allowed for one. Entirely worthy of being paid the price, so rarely elegant was their invention. They "had mounted with hair, matches, on an elastic 'twist,' three violin strings, a little compensating system with collar-mounted drive that really seemed to work . . . It was the hygrometric force! . . . The whole thing fit in a thimble! . . . It's the only true 'Perpetual' that I've seen work a little."[15]

The prize, in all fairness, they certainly deserved it, these cunning hairsplitters! For an antique dealer is that too. The trade demands muscles, strong biceps; it requires, what is more, truly nimble fingers. One must certainly heft heavy burdens; but also, like that young lady from the railroad company, be able to decompose the water of the Seine "with a safety pin." She had set herself up at the level of the Pont-Marie, not far from the Washhouse, and consequently right smack in Impressionist country; and there, her little finger upraised, with a seamstress's grace, she "recovered the essences as the current flowed by"[16] . . . Nothing can be more subtle, as has already been hinted, than time going by. That which in time goes by is at least something subtle, the minutes that have flown, the tiny, miniscule wing of the seconds. Such a time, that is certain, can only be caught, if it can be caught, in a fly trap. In the affair concerning us here, it is therefore to the lightness of the device that our praise goes. To the pair's spidery work, the cluster of threads and waves that, under the heaped ruins of the past, create, as it were, corners of delicacy and open to the reader's imagination a whole pompadour ambiance, which the reader's imagination immediately hurries to furnish with the thousand appropriate little nothings, fans and zephyrs, butterflies, bits of ribbons, lace frills . . .

Always a Suzon, always a Lisette to keep watch at the back of the shop, in the clutter of dead things; a Céline[17] awaiting her mistress, the Marquise, the Countess, who is taking her sweet time to come . . . The eighteenth century is certainly dear to his heart. In case we had forgotten: Clémence's pride, Passage Choiseul, was a pedestal table, "a Louis XV, the only one we were really sure of."[18] A little powder table in *Progress*,[19] but still Louis XV. The powder table went one All Hallows' eve. To serve (who wouldn't swear to it?) the cunning artifices of some fine ghost. Speaking of which, isn't that La Pérouse (Louis XV, Louis XVI, what difference?), the ghost of La Pérouse leading the sweet people of the dead in one of the most fanciful pages of *Journey*?[20] He has planted his peg leg on the roof of the Opera, like an amputated Lully; like Jules, like Nelson, "the sidewalk artist," the Nelson of *Guignol's band*,[21] like Mille-Pattes, all the artists, basically; and his peg leg has become the axis around which the dizzying ballet of the specters organizes itself. Let us not lose sight of the fact, though, that before La Pérouse took his watch up there, captain for a night of this *Terpsichore*, the dead were "passing right over the Galeries Dufayel."[22] Which is the same as to say that they were flying over the heart of the commercial city. The Palais Dufayel was, in the 1920s, the temple of commerce. So that little by little everything falls into place, and we end up wondering, finally, if it isn't the world of the shop itself that has entrusted La Pérouse with its redemption. And that has placed its trust in him as in the most emancipated of beings, a shipwrecked ghost relieved by the waters of the

weight of his corpse, and having thus acquired but a little more vague-
ness of the soul, the perfect wraith, essentially, a pure emanation of a
century that was, par excellence, the century of lightness.

↬

Same flight of the ship of Paris, "the fine vessel" of *Death on the Installment Plan*.[23] In one leap, with its cargo of shades, bounding from "Dufayel to Capricorn."[24] From the earth to the highest of skies. The constellation of Capricorn is the penultimate zodiacal constellation.

All the way to the far reaches of the Southern Hemisphere, then, but
from Dufayel. And thus proving that though Céline's deliriums may constitute the most powerful of all elevatory machines (and, from this point
of view, all deliriums are equal), they nonetheless remain grounded in
the most basely material preoccupation of small business. It's the shopkeeper who's rising, he alone who is dreaming of rising, Courtial from
the depths of his basement, the antique dealer in his lair. And, no matter what appearance to the contrary, sinking, the former into his memory without recollections, into the sort of night he must regularly make
and from which he emerges, as he says, "dazzled";[25] the latter, into the
contemplation of a powder table.

And what a fine piece of furniture indeed, this dressing table. A fine
word to say the past. To suggest its eminently crumbly character, its
slow frittering away, a promise of lightness; of a lightness patiently won
over the natural gravity of things, but also already announcing a very
near change of state, a metamorphosis that will cause the powder to
sublimate itself and become volatile. For such is the chemistry, such are
the physics, such are the metaphysics of the past that there comes a
moment when, by dint of accumulating so many years, things finally
cease to age. Suddenly, they no longer are old things; they are other
things, things from elsewhere, which seem to come from somewhere
else and, as it were, from beyond. Things of heaven, at bottom. Given
that there is a heaven for things — there is, after all, a heaven for men,
and it's surely the same one. With, to get there, the same road things already take. So that, following it in turn, men are only speeding things
up. Out of impatience, projecting themselves into space. Such a hurry
are they in to put between the world and their dear person a little distance, this distance things can afford not to worry about, since it is, so

to speak, already given to them and all they have to do is let themselves slide into it, at their own rhythm. A precious advantage over men who do not know how to age, how to enter time other than with abrupt veers, somersaults, and great leaps backward. From Dufayel to Capricorn, for instance; a great step back, about a century and a half long.

For as to this point, no error possible, and here we can be rigorous. The date (date that would fix the term of the journey) is inscribed in the stars. And we can decipher it without any difficulty whatsoever on the maps of the sky offered to us by Flammarion. Maps that let us observe that in the direction of Sagittarius, but contiguous to Capricorn, right under the belly of the Goat, rises a little constellation. This constellation, whose utterly incongruous presence incidentally disturbs the antique simplicity of the place, is the constellation of the Aerostat, drawn in 1798 by Lalande, "as a souvenir of his own ascents." The drawing is precise. Everything is there, the globe and the rigging, the nacelle: an authentic balloon.

Truth forces us to say, however, that we didn't expect to find a balloon amid such venerable figures as the figures of the zodiac. Flammarion will be the first to wonder at it, and to take issue with it, "even if," as he concedes, "a balloon quite naturally has its place in the sky."[26]

But all the more naturally, then, it will perhaps be admitted, in one of Céline's skies, where, more than in another sky, the balloon had its place. Being henceforth where it ought to be: at the height of its glory, barbed with rays and with starry spikes, a veritable opera prop.

That opera is finally what this is all about is no longer, thanks to the distance we have today and the recent publication of Céline's letters to his chief editors, a suspicion, but a certainty. The "Opera genre":[27] the genre in which, and against its own rules, Céline, ever since *Journey*, has indeed sought to excel. Not to mention that Courtial des Pereires's aerostatic experiments, given this, couldn't have presented themselves under better auspices. Witness this confidence to Milton Hindus: "My inventor Courtial des Pereires perfectly existed; his name was Henri de Graffigny. His (innumerable) books are still sold in the little Hachette collections. The *Génitron* was called the *Eureka*. Located Place Favart in an entresol in front of the Opéra-Comique in Paris."[28]

A few lines earlier, Céline was still busy confessing to Hindus his un-failing attachment to dance and to female dancers. "It is impossible for me to live far from Dance ... Nietzsche writes, I believe, 'I'll only believe in God if he dances.' Louis XIV only believed also in ambassadors if they were perfect dancers..."[29] And it is following this sentence, after the re-minder of the Nietzschean profession of faith, after the evocation of those blessed times when a king, to imitate the gods, dared put wings at the heels of his envoys—it is immediately after that that the mem-ory of Courtial des Pereires imposes itself on Céline. As if, projected into his memory, the shadow of the dancer took there the shape of his balloon!

It is true that the language, maliciously, made it possible to confuse balloon and ballet. The two words are neighbors. This neighbordom, however, is nothing, compared to the chance that brings face to face the offices of the *Eureka* and the Opéra-Comique. Thanks to a simple closeness in space, what is pointed out to us is a proximity of an en-tirely different nature, infinitely tighter and much less circumstantial: a profound community of interests. To the point that the connections even grow tighter, stronger in the fiction than they were in reality; or, if not stronger, at least, as we will see, more necessary.

In becoming Courtial des Pereires, Henri de Graffigny changes address. He must relocate from the Place Favart to the arcades of the Galerie Montpensier. Thus dictates the book. A book in which the expanses of-fered to the gaze by an open-air space indeed have no place. A world without extent or depth, the world of *Death on the Installment Plan*. And, furthermore, with a low ceiling: you bang your head, just as you live cramped. Any place whatsoever, at least from the moment that Fer-dinand decides to occupy it, is a place that immediately closes up; a place that shrinks, and in all three dimensions at once; in its length, in its width; in height just the same: cul-de-sac, mousetrap, dead end, only opening into another dead end ... But opening into it, nonetheless. And which is probably why Céline still calls these kinds of dead ends passages.

Yet these dead ends are only passages by virtue of properties that elude all common sense, and in conformity with the laws of an entirely imagi-nary topography. Laws that for all that could be no stricter, and that impose on entire cities the configuration of a single place. For one place, here, rules over every place, one site over every site. And this seat, this Mecca, not a reader of Céline who doesn't already know it, has taken, in the work, the appearance of the Passage Choiseul. To which, consequently, rather than to Niagara Falls, might be more accurately applied, in all the ambiguity of its formulation, the famous line of Chateaubriand: *it wipes everything out.*

Yes, everything, absolutely everything. In front of it nothing holds; not the streets, not the plazas, not even the houses, unless they are rushing into it, are spilling into the abyss.

What is the Paris of *Journey,* for instance? Entrances, bridges, toll barriers... In short, the Passage multiplied. Not to say spread out, transposed to the scale of a capital, if we are willing to take into consideration the fact that the Place Clichy, symbolic heart of the Célinian city, is, furthermore, the great interchange of the work. The hinge of the book, with its two whores, at so much per trick; these women Apollinaire, the poet of *Zone,* so marvelously calls the *attentive ones.* And with its general, waiting for the cossacks since 1814. Montcey and his valiant troop. All the students of the École Polytechnique, their ghosts, let us say, closing ranks, opposing the rampart of their bodies to the vanguards of the disaster overwhelming Paris. A hundred and twelve years they've been holding like this,[30] and for no other reason, apparently, than to bring us back, *manu militari,* to the Passage of the Beresinas, which indeed opens up (astonishing shortcut of History) at the feet of the statue of General Montcey. Meaning at the geometric center of every recommencement, at the very place where the story, after each one of its episodes, comes to recycle itself. To go in circles, just like Bardamu,[31] prisoner of the Passage, which, wandering in the open air, out in the plaza, he continues to pace up and down, with the mechanical steps of the prisoner who, during the afternoon walk, reinscribes in space the limits of his cell. As if Paris, yes, all of Paris (infinite power of metonymy), were but his exercise yard.

And London, after Paris, in the Piranesian perspective of its docks, cut off at the horizon, nothing new under the sun, by the trench of the Passage Choiseul.

between Wardour and Guilford I had spotted, a long time ago, from my first weeks in London, a whole jumble of shops that were really like a museum in the travel souvenir department, curios, maps of the world, chromos, antiques from every country, etchings of sailboats, compasses, stuffed fish, albatrosses . . . a bric-a-brac of adventures like I'd never seen before . . . between Wardour and Guilford Street . . . And then it was pleasant, no water to catch, all covered, glassed passages running into each other . . . You could wait under cover for the downpours to pass . . . spare your soles a little . . . it reminded me of ours in Paris, as a passage, but then a lot more fun, a lot cushier too, not a low-class crowd, a people sewer like ours . . . nothing but colonial stores [. . .]![32]

The same, then; he spells it out. The same, but better stocked. A select clientele, as choice as can be, and merchandise especially, so you don't know which way to turn. Céline has always had the imagination of stocks, a fabulous imagination. To stock space, to stock time . . . The dream, really, the ideal would be to have them both in store before even opening shop: the dream of the Passage Choiseul. Passage Choiseul in which — or so it might retrospectively have seemed to Céline — time and space have been given to him from the start, have been waiting for him forever, warehoused right there, at home. So that, as far as he's concerned, he just has to live off his stock, without a care about tomorrow (space and time are easy items to sell, they have a high turnover) or a worry about supplies. He has been at peace on this point ever since his lucky star whispered to him the idea, not so much of making of the Passage his sole point of view on the world, as to make of the world itself the infinite, the voluminous expansion of the Passage.

So that the world indeed comes out of the passage, and never tires of rapidly and continuously flowing out of it, a flow that could easily lead one to think that its reserves must be inexhaustible. Why doubt it? It's in this obscure passageway that Céline has located the womb of the world. *Anus mundi.*

Between the arch of the universal conservation and the feminine porch of fecundity. Yes, the two together; and the two, contradictorily. Less a childhood memory than an imaginary realization, the shops of the Passage are the product of this contradiction.

— Seen from one side, the world, through the Passage, will appear to be an enclave, an ark lost in the midst of floods. Complex of Noah, which

Céline seems to share with Giono,[33] would actually share with him were it not that Giono, in the figure of Noah, is only interested in the ark. As far as the spectacle of the waters unleashed is concerned, the master of Manosque turns his back, and, like Saint Jerome in his cell, retires. Remembering perhaps, along with Cendrars in *L'homme foudroyé*, that the writer must never set himself down in front of a panorama, especially a sublime one; remembering, to tell the truth, what writing is, and that writing is but "a view of the mind"[34] . . . Whereas Céline, on the other hand, has every intention of going back to the Flood, to the biblical myth in which the cataclysm is nearly contemporaneous with Genesis.[35] Certainly the Flood evokes the image of the ark; but this image, with Céline, is not an image of refuge, or only rarely. It is rather, above all, an image of chaos becoming conscious of itself. A point of view on chaos, if one insists, but not at all exterior to chaos. What could be, anyway, outside chaos? Chaos is general. Because the world is finite — finite ever since the world was world; because the centuries are consummated — consummated ever since the beginning of centuries; because our time is the time of the abolition of times. Hence the strangeness of our behavior, and this way we have of existing in inexistence. "You're extra," the narrator of *From Castle to Castle* tells us,[36] and it's to the point. It is only too certain that in persisting in our being we are in excess; that we are involving ourselves in an infinite duration. Is not death, after all, the measure of all things? Our time, this time after death imparted to us, is thus a time without measure. A time whose term we cannot conceive, whose term it is even highly likely we have gone beyond simply by being born: *off-limits,* from the very moment of the first cry. The inevitable character of this going beyond: that, too, is one of the meanings, in Céline's text, of all those antique dealers, those thrift-store owners vegetating like travelers in the middle of mounds of luggage, anxious to leave, to set sail for Cytherea, gazing out at sea, "waiting for their Watteau."[37]

— But, seen from the other side, everything is strangely reversed. And it is then at the picture of a world in labor that the palingenetic spyglass of the Passage seems directed. A world at term, with the shopkeeper as midwife. The very one who, a short while ago, was ensuring the conservation of the world in the temporary space of his shop, in that improbable no-man's-land with the most precarious status, "half Quarantine half operetta,"[38] and who is now the one nursing things along, speeding them up.

Thus Courtial des Pereires, Courtial at his counters: at the sign of the *Génitron,* a Céline company. The sign says it all, shamelessly announcing, proclaiming, that here we deal in fertility. Except that if we were to look a little closer, we would see that everyone, in Céline's work, jewelers and bandage sellers, haberdashers, traveling and door-to-door salesmen, brokers in this, brokers in that, never deal in anything else; and that sex is the true object of their dark speculations. How can we be surprised, under these conditions, that they always feel at fault, that a sentiment of guilt accompanies them in the exercise of their enterprises? A theological version of the business license, it's, alas, the price they have to pay. The merchant is born guilty. Which is the reason the merchant goes to ground; the reason he is so careful to transport the stage of his activities all the way down interminable corridors, into cubbyholes, recesses, places — in a word — whose existence we wouldn't even suspect.

To which it could be objected that, placed as it is under an unforgettable — and oh so eloquent! — sign, Courtial's business is nevertheless conducted in the full light of day. And the objection would in effect stand, if we didn't remember in time that the offices of the *Génitron* are located under the arcades of the Galerie Montpensier: hardly prime real estate. Who, hell, would think of trying to find them there? To be there, is it really to be anywhere?

Entering Céline's book, not only did Henri de Graffigny change his name and become a character in a novel, but he passed irrevocably onto the side of the *fictitious,* the only side from which there is no return; henceforth out of reach, a ghostly inhabitant of the parallel city that doubles the main thoroughfares of Paris with a network we could nearly call underground. An occult network, at least. Passages, tunnels are to Céline's work what attics are to Kafka's. And it is but a step from these suffocating basements to those overheated garrets. In this respect, as in so many others, the Célinian world of commerce is extremely close to the Kafkaian world of justice. Which isn't the justice of the Palace, the justice in red robes, but rather, as the author of *The Trial* specifies, the *other* justice. And isn't it also of the *other* commerce we have been talking, for some time now?

⌒

For too long, no doubt...Enough is enough. We have, with Kafka, reached the required degree of *unrealism*. And are finally ready to witness the reversal, the complete inversion of signs, that the text of *Death on the Installment Plan* had in store for us.

We had left the publisher of the *Génitron* in his hole: he was there a minute ago; and he still would be if magic hadn't put its two cents worth in, snatching him off the earth, halfway through the book, to an air in double time. Yes, an air, and a dancing air.

— But the Place Favart? But the Opéra-Comique?...

— That's really what we're still talking about! The offices of the *Génitron* will be under the arcades: that is a done deal. Courtial's home, on the other hand — for Courtial doesn't live in Paris, he lives out in the suburbs — his home will be called La Gavotte.

O Vestris! O Rameau!...Along with the minuets, with the rigadoons, with the passepieds, the gigues, and the chaconnes, the gavottes made the gallant Indies dance under the ceilings of Versailles. What could be added, if not that the ballooneer has simply taken up residence in the most Versaillian (meaning the most dazzling, but also the most French) of all the *opéras-ballets*? The choice of a house in the vicinity of Paris and the name he confers on it bear witness: to be the equal of Rameau, that, obviously, is what he seeks.

Of Rameau, and not of Pilâtre, not of the Montgolfier brothers... Unless they are all in league; unless the two questions, of dance and of the balloon, are in fact one and the same. All the more easy to confuse, it is true, that with Céline, a few leagues apart, they both deal with the same thing...With a thing that is the thing itself. How else could we name this "sex" thing, indicated by the sign of the *Génitron* in an enigmatic gesture that both points at it and gives it the finger. Final sale, it seems to say. Everything must go, and let nothing more be said. Let us finally be free of this weight, the specific gravity of things. For things only weigh on the stock, things only weigh on the conscience inasmuch as they bear with them a little bit of the secret that has been harassing the son of the shopkeeper, ever since he learned what a shameful commerce mothers must carry on in this world.

And which is why, in the final evaluation, things weigh out the same.[39] All of them, solidary. Feather or lead, there is no longer a noticeable difference. This straw hat, for instance, Ferdinand's boater, it'll run a good "two pounds."[40] At the very least. Note that with lace, it's even worse: these frills, these little nothings that a gust of wind would carry off, finally add up to a very heavy gear. "All that crap sure weighs," notes Uncle Édouard . . .[41] The perception of the mass of things is, with Céline, independent of their physical properties. An ingredient mingles with the matter things are made of, an ingredient that, it seems, is not itself matter. A sort of heavy substance, uniformly divvied up between all things. As if they had all been kneaded in it; as if they were all stained with the same foul mud, their original defect.

A hereditary imperfection, so to speak. The defect is the weight of a lack. A weight that is added to the proper weight of things and that gives their gross weight. We did not say, alas, their net weight. The net weight of a given body can only be obtained, precisely, by subtracting the defect. And, as for the question of the subtraction of the defect, it is my thesis here that this is the very question Céline is confronted with; that it is the eternal question, the question that constantly poses itself for him, tangled up as he is, line after line, and at each new page, in inextricable problems of weighing, of balance. Problems, it is only too obvious, whose givens escape the sciences of measurement. But they only have to borrow from their languages. To make us believe in the objects it speaks of, literature does nothing but borrow from languages. Just as it never opposes to these languages anything but other languages. What would the point be, otherwise, of tossing in the scales, as Céline does, a dancer, a balloon? They would, after all, have to be two weighty arguments indeed.

I

Considered as such, the argument of the ballet doesn't take much place in *Death on the Installment Plan*. But little as it may take, it is nonetheless entirely there. Its contents hold in one word: *Montretout*, literally "Show-all."

Every day, in the evening, his offices closed, the publisher of the *Génitron* heads for the village of Montretout. Gare du Nord (north is up), a short trip, a few kilometers on a suburban line (he hardly sees them go by: *Facilis* ascensus *Averni*), and there he is. In his "home": his Gavotte, as he calls it . . .

The reader, of course, is smiling. The allusion is as plain as the nose on the face. Montretout, Montretout, Show-all . . . More antics. Incorrigible Céline! The reader can see him coming. Courtial at Montretout, like Bardamu at Fort Gono, Bardamu on the *Amiral Bragueton,* Bardamu on the *Infanta Combitta* . . .[42] The reader, this time, could have spared himself the trouble. Because Céline puts in it (puts in the word) that which isn't there, that which shines by its absence, shines to the point of dazzling us, by the very fact that it should be there. We will grant to the reader that such a name, a name the likes of which one could only find in the Célinian geography, we wouldn't have spontaneously thought of looking for it on the Carte de Tendre. Where, however, we would have found it: Montretout-sur-Lignon.

The name has a history in Céline's work. It's an old story, and it's a short story; part of a scene in *Progress*. A funny story, too. Like all funny stories, the story of Montretout rests on a misunderstanding.

Berlureau has just been asked if he knows an address:

MRS. PUNAIS: Now! you are a bachelor, Monsieur Berlureau, you told me?

MR. BERLUREAU: *(with a sigh)* Oh, yes.

MRS. PUNAIS: Well, then, you must know where bachelors go . . . where bachelors go . . .

GASTON: I am, Madame, totally embarrassed.

MRS. PUNAIS: It is too late to go back. Please let me continue. [. . .] The moment is ripe, I want to know . . .

MR. BERLUREAU: Madame Punais. At your service.

MRS. PUNAIS: Where, for instance, Monsieur Berlureau, you would go? . . . *(One or two usherettes pass from the auditorium to the stage and laugh as they listen.)* Such as you are.

MR. BERLUREAU: Such as I am . . .

MRS. PUNAIS: If perchance the desire struck you . . .

GASTON: Bachelor that I am . . .

MRS. PUNAIS: To go without being known . . . ? *(Through the left and right doors stylized and typical characters enter: maids, concierges, mailmen listen to the confidence.)* A spring afternoon, for instance.

GASTON: *(happy)* After five?

MR. BERLUREAU: *(astonished)* In a garden?
  Everyone on stage makes a sign and whispers: "No." Bowling?
  Same stage action: "No!"
  (bantering) Well, to the merry-go-round . . .
  Same stage action: "No."
  . . . To the café? I don't go there . . . *(He thinks.)* . . . the concerts haven't started yet, that's later! . . .

GASTON: That's not it! He knows!

MR. BERLUREAU: I don't know! After five? *(lower)* In winter I'm afraid.

GASTON: And not alone?

MR. BERLUREAU: To my sister's in Montretout?

MRS. PUNAIS: Bachelor... come on... that gives you rights.

MR. BERLUREAU: I prefer music... I don't vote...

GASTON: His sister lives in Montretout, ta-da.

MRS. PUNAIS: That isn't enough... what he wanted... was the name of a place — where you would go sentimental.

GASTON: If I was a bachelor.

MR. BERLUREAU: *(suddenly enlightened)* Ah! you want to go to the boston! What an infamy! and for Madame Marie what a betrayal!

GASTON: I am punished!

MRS. PUNAIS: *(rapidly)* It isn't for him. It's a strange favor to take some Americans I know in my business.

MR. BERLUREAU: Well, then, if it's for business, that's quite different, I'll give the address. *(He whispers it into Gaston's ear as all the characters filling the stage try to hear some details.)*

GASTON: *(having heard)* It isn't expensive.[43]

Boston is put here for *boxon*, brothel. Intentionally, or else (it's possible) by mistake. After all, it could be Céline's slip, a typist's error, or a publisher's typo. The manuscript of *Progress* isn't sure; no more, actually, than its transcription. But, as things stand, it hardly matters. Chance, if that's what it is, is on our side. By putting this pun in the mouth of the innocent Berlureau, it brings him to tell the truth; at least to utter this truth, and in this case really the only one that counts, that the waltz (the Boston is a slow waltz) is simply the atonement of the pleasure taken in sex, its winged offspring. For a waltz has wings the way a ship has sails. So that Céline, when he tells us "dance," isn't saying anything different from what sailors say as they head out to sea: "Raise the jib! All is paid!"

This truth, however, has its flip side. Change one letter, and the name of the waltz rings unpleasantly to the ear. The dancer is now in the brothel, like Jesus amid the doctors. Gospel Truth. And a truth that the somewhat laborious jokes Berlureau's sister has been the butt of will have prepared us to receive. His sister from Montretout. If that isn't a promise... A promise kept. The word of the revelation will be accomplished. The truth of the thing will be entirely revealed. Nothing, absolutely nothing, will be concealed. It's very simple, we will see her naked. *In Naturalibus Veritas*: tableau!

It's the third scene. A brothel, somewhere in Paris. There is Madame, there are the maid, the girls, the customers. Ah! as for these latter, nothing but voyeurs; and what is more, frustrated voyeurs. Impossible people waiting for God knows what. Do they even know? They are shown this one, that one ... Even the new girls won't do. These gentlemen want something different. And on that they're categoric: something novel, something never seen before; a complete surprise or nothing, a miracle. They are hoping for a miracle and will not leave till the miracle is accomplished.

Heaven has heard them, Heaven that is watching them. For God doesn't miss a thing of what goes on on earth, that place of ill repute. He has even had a telescope set up, so as better to see, from his cloud, "a great enormous cloud,"[44] the comedy of *Progress*. A comedy-ballet, it is true. God can take a look at it without compromising himself too much. The danced parts of Céline's works present themselves, to whomever catches sight of them, as nothing more nor less than a sublimated version of the sexual commerce. The sanctification, let us venture the word, of the exchange between the sexes. Three times sainted is the dancer, because the dancer has power over the hell of the body and its bestiary. Because she alone can overcome the beast with two backs ... There is no doubt that Céline's God, from his vantage point, is busy cooking up a new heresy for us. His eye on the spyglass, and entirely absorbed by the show, he is wondering if dance, in the end, might not be the wave of the future. In any case, he finds that the dancer is a fine invention and that she should be put to better use. "I am going to use these even bodies a lot in the centuries to come to light up lust; I want to make it beautiful, it's a step toward me."[45]

The dancer's step is a step toward God. Her spin the arc of a compass. Searching space, seeking the golden number. The section, the ratio that the monk Luca Pacioli di Borgo called the divine proportion.

So God, who has a sort of natural sympathy for voyeurs, being one himself as we have seen; God who could never resign himself to abandon them when they are so far along (isn't it to contemplate the divine presence that in the depths of their heart and in secret they aspire?); God sends them a dancer. One of those angels in short skirts; one of those "finds of harmony,"[46] to be made to vibrate with a dulcimer, "with the diapason between [their] legs,"[47] a note so right it is impossible to hear it without crying out, like the author of *Trifles*, "It's God himself! Quite simply."[48] Or, if not God in person, his monogram; the name of God imprinted with each step, written in the clouds, in the air it illuminates, by the radiant body of the dancer, this body become sign, a semiotic and even sacramental body, the body of the new Eucharist. It is indeed the other host, the one you only devour with your eyes ... So that when she appears, when, fallen from the sky into "the pale and swollen meat of European prostitution," she removes her clothes piece by piece, and, finally stripped, as naked as one can be, delivers this inspired speech to us, it's nothing less than the *Hoc est enim corpus meum* of the Catholic dogma that in all humility we should receive:

> The desire of men, you see, Monsieur of the most loving people on earth, it's powerful and vague, and you have to realize that, you see? ... it's yes? it's four hours of work a day, marked there, work like this *(She does movements to music)*, not in "my flesh" but simply in the muscles ... there ... that one ... the quadriceps ... you see ... and balance ... there ... and then this too ... nothing is easy to obtain ... work ... firmness ... touch ... do you feel? ... the day when women will be dressed in muscles only ... and in music ... so many fewer sentences ... when soft and pink thighs will finally be reputed disgusting ... when rachitis, atrophies, badly placed pregnancies will no longer be what they are today, delicacies that are boasted of and that aesthetes appreciate and paint, Monsieur, but degenerated natures indeed, on that day, Monsieur, will the world still live of words? Will it believe that beauty is a mystical gift, or that it is simply made of gold and rest and sun, the slaves either were not beautiful in Greece, Monsieur ... To be beautiful, you have to do nothing else and want. *(She disappears, dancing, into the darkness. Gaston remains alone.)*[49]

Thus speaks the dancer. For the first time. The first, and, basically, the last. Oh, certainly, we will still hear a lot about her (God knows!), but we will never hear the sound of her voice again. Forever mute ... To the point that we might even think she had been struck by a spell, a curse, if we didn't soon see that her forced muteness is, on the contrary, her luck, and that by forbidding her all access to speech, a good witch, her godmother, is forcing her to deploy herself in the only space she belongs in, the space of the poem. For Céline, who has read Mallarmé,[50] knows that dance is poem, but he also knows, furthermore, that in order to compose "the most nuanced poem in the world,"[51] this corporal writing, unlike the other kind, has no need of *devices* ("the term of the 1914 war!),"[52] no need whatsoever, in other words, of the crutches of language. Even offstage, when they aren't dancing, the true, the born dancers shine. They broadcast themselves, they propagate themselves, they emit from afar, come to us on waves. Thus, to converse with their fellow dancers, do they not use words, but their hands only, "the fingers . . . a gesture, a grace . . . that's all . . ."[53] And we have Virginia, the adorable damsel of *Guignol's band,* we have the little Tourbillon, that "spirit."[54] A delicate and exquisite model, on which are built, in the work, all the Arlettes, all the Lulus, the Lilis; and, in life, Céline's women and his distant loves, Lucette Almanzor, Karen Marie Jensen, Inès from the Tabarin, Irène Mac Bride, Margaret Sande ("Radio City four shows a day"),[55] and, "especially miraculous," Daphne Vane and Kathryn Malowry of the School of American Ballet;[56] not to forget the first, but also the most beautiful of the gifts of America, where "the beauty of women is immense like the rest,"[57] Elisabeth Craig, the unforgettable dedicatee of *Journey,* a charming mind, very fine, and who "understood everything before you'd said a single word"[58] . . . And on the same model, although in another realm, but a neighboring one, the actress Suzanne Bianquetti, "the screen artist she was! and her vaporous gowns against a 'blue soft light' background! 'moonlit' . . . what a sublime artist, perfectly silent, not a 'talky' . . . the verb that kills! . . . the woman who talks makes you go limp, we only ever had good hard-ons with the 'silent'! . . ."[59]

For Céline's passion for dance has no equal but his passion for the cinema. But the unique, the irreplaceable silent cinema; the cinema of his childhood. From the time when his grandmother, herself not a very talkative woman ("she didn't talk much and that already is enormous"),[60] took him there for the matinees. It was at the Robert-Houdin, every Thursday. "We'd stay for three shows in a row. It was the same price, all the seats at one franc, 100 percent silent, no sentences, no music, no letters, just the purring of the mill. It'll come back, people get tired of everything except of sleeping and dreaming. It'll come back, *A Trip to the Moon* . . . I still know it by heart."[61]

A film by Georges Méliès (alas! "where are you, Méliès?"),[62] *A Trip to the Moon* dates from 1902. It was a one-reeler; the film only lasted sixteen minutes. But what minutes! Sixteen minutes of infinity. Sixteen minutes that in seeing, that in seeing again and again virtually continuously, the child multiplied into as many times as an afternoon could contain, to the point of making them an eternity at his measure, an eternity of silence.

Céline's answer to a survey by the review *Arts* (this survey followed the launching, on January 2, 1959, of the Soviet satellite Lunik):

> I am a specialist of the Moon. The Sun? I don't understand. When I was seven, I would go three times every Thursday to the Moon with my grandmother. It was at the Robert-Houdin cinema (which has since become the Musée Grévin) around 1907. You'd go up in a shell. It cost fifty centimes (in *heavy francs*). You'd reach the Moon, and you'd start again. It was a lot of fun. I did it hundreds of times. Whatever happens to the Sun leaves me indifferent.[63]

To go to the movies or to go to the moon? From *Death on the Installment Plan* to Céline's answer to the survey of the review *Arts*, lies only the distance separating a wish from its accomplishment. And a distance that suddenly vanishes as if by magic. The show over, you would climb in a shell, and that was it. For what it cost extra... The moon at that price, it's a steal. Fifty centimes is a modest sum. At least till further notice. Meaning, in fact, till Céline's parenthesis. And then, what a fall! "*Heavy francs.*"

Why, in full flight, must the thought of the fall suddenly clip our wings? Because it's an old man who's speaking, all exhilaration dissipated. Because it's a writer preoccupied by the crudeness of the means that literature, to elevate them, puts in the service of men. And the fact of the matter is that if it's still a question of cleaving the air, there probably isn't, in the whole world, at least when compared to the childish simplicity of the shell, a more inappropriate machine than a work of the mind. The *Véga of the Stances*, for instance, certainly is, in *Guignol's band*, the great book of dance.

— You could even say its in folio: never was a term more adequate... Like a single sheet unfolding, spreading out as you read it — a loose sheet. Catch it! Just in time.

— Yes, let us close the book. The dancing book. A whole "miniature ballet [...] details and finesse a fly's prick."[64] A goldsmith's work. The jeweler Gorloge, it's quite simple, couldn't have done better.

— Nor, alas, heavier. For such is the irony of the thing that, the book closed, you are left with a rather heavy brick on your hands. How hard it is to move, you don't realize: the equivalent of "two great phone books," and "bound mastodon."[65]

— It's nothing though, next to Céline's great move of his collected works. In *Cursed Sighs*. In Montmartre, the place of his martyrdom; Montmartre under the bombs.

— Everyone gets the Golgotha they deserve!

— Christ of the Butte, indeed. And carrying his cross, the instrument of his torture on which his genius will nail him. Let us understand "eight ten twelve legends one more sublime than the other,"[66] but which turn out to be kilos and kilos of paper. You can't imagine "how heavy they can be, winged poems so-called."[67]

— You can't imagine it because you haven't thought about this enough, that the weight of books only comes from what you put in them. *Words, words, words...* The proof is the ease with which the little Tourbillon, suddenly appearing like the Angel of the Lord, relieves him of his burden. Without a word, as it should be (what would be the point otherwise of being a dancer?): "just her finger in the string."[68] And yet "some fucking heavy junk [...] the damned bundle."

— As crushing as you like: it will have been enough for her to oppose the counterweight of her silence to it... Give Céline a fulcrum, and, in turn, as he'll immediately swear, he'll lift the world. Using only the lever of silence. The celestial mechanics are unaware of this principle? It's the mechanics that are in the wrong, and it's the proof that there is nothing celestial about them. Enough said; back to the movies.

Back to the museum whose enchanted premises we should never have left... Once a movie theater (who doesn't know it?), the Musée Grévin is a museum of waxes, full of the simulacra of the great prattlers of this world. False appearances, yet so faithfully rendered that, as people like to say, they only lack speech. But the fact that they lack it is obviously, here, what is so inappreciable about them. And isn't it also, on their part, a moving hint? As it were a wink, a trick of destiny that would come confirm, in this comical manner, the deep calling of this place for silence. As peaceful today, cluttered as it is with its vain figures, as it used to be, when the beam of the cinematographer flickered nonchalantly in the darkness of the theater and obscured everything, bathed it in a sort of lunar clarity. A grey light, a soft light, but soft! so soft you could die... You immediately went, you lost your head. Yes, you were mooning.

And so far from the sun! Noon the just, terror of all worried souls... As much as the night star delights Céline, as much as it transports him and puts him out of his mind, the day star, on the contrary, crushes him, weighs on his shoulders: a leaden sun.[69] No less unbearable to Céline than Auguste's interminable speeches are to Ferdinand. Which is why his name is Auguste. With his boasting, with his deadly chatter "of an old bored king,"[70] he presents every sign, the most indubitable marks of his solar ascendancy. Auguste, Augustus, son of the sun; whereas Céline would prefer to imagine himself Knight of the Moon, to dream himself, in the arms of his sylphid, waltzing the Brown Waltz,[71] without music, without anything, in the serene night, the oh so comfortably calm night of the very first dark theaters.

For, it must be repeated, if Auguste belongs to the sun, it is only because he speaks, and speaks, and speaks, to the point of making you dizzy. And then gets carried away, and then bursts into threats, rages like an artificial sun. An all too perfect imitation, in his delirium, of the other sun, the real one, the drunken logos that, for Céline, will always incarnate the hysteria of speech... Were it the pure logos, let us nonetheless note, the sun would seem no less suspect to Céline, who would still oppose its illusory nature to a link, in his eyes, far more fundamental, a link made beyond, or rather before, words. For there is no doubt that the need for silence the Célinian being is perpetually suffering from betrays his nostalgia of an original relationship, an absolute relationship, and as such anterior to language, the relationship of the child king, the divine child, to his mother.

And which is why, returning from the Moon Theater to our star dancer, we seem to be, all of a sudden, in a better position to comment on the astonishing striptease of *Progress*; better prepared to grasp its meaning.

At least are we starting to divine that it was a restoration ritual that we have just participated in. And that nothing less was at stake, then, than the reestablishment of the mother into poetry.

To reestablish her, that should be obvious now, *beyond words.* Isn't Céline himself already inhabiting his language as an intruder? A stranger in the house of the Father, he has chosen to become *Parigot,* the way he could have chosen to become Belgian, to become Swiss or Creole; he talks argot, slang, and he has adopted the accent, consciously exacerbating the conflict, and dissociating himself from a language whose vaunted transparency, in becoming an affair of state (the famous French clarity and the barely concealed will to integration it expressed at the time), also ostensibly manifests its lack of memory or its ignorance of Babel. And Babelism, this can never be emphasized enough, is one of Céline's temptations, as he puts into his books more and more English, more and more German, at the same time that Cendrars, and for reasons that are perhaps not too different, puts into his Russian, Greek, Portuguese, and even Bulgarian... Eternal foreign-language students, communing with the same linguistic nomadism, they are both, evidently, camping *extra muros.* At the doors of the cities that are also the doors of the languages; beyond the limits of their respective enclosures.

Eternal students, eternal wanderers, they are, like their brethren, placed under the protection of the Virgin; Our Lady Beyond Words, whose cult brings them together in a common adoration. Ardent apostles, the one and the other, of a religion that, though it may not be a religion of speech, nonetheless already has its martyrs. Actresses, for Cendrars, whose lips are scarred by a nasty fly; embalmed female saints muzzled with the root of a fennel; infibulated queens, their mouths sewn shut; cooks with their tongues cut off... And, for Céline, the procession of the talkers who are the ritual targets of his profanations. Bigoudi, Angèle, old lady Henrouille, Bébert's aunt, and especially Clémence, the inexhaustible Clémence, a real chatterbox.

Faithful, as far as that goes, to her model, if one is to believe the family story: Marguerite Guillou, according to her relatives, didn't have her tongue in her pocket. Some have even leaped to the conclusion that the oral dimension of Céline's text might have come from there, his spoken style as it is too often, out of laziness, referred to. Céline, inciden-

tally, didn't like the expression much. And one must in all fairness recognize that not only is it bad, but it is out of place. Unless, of course,
one means it to signify Céline's relentless struggle against that which
speaks in language, his relentless attempts to make it puke everything
in it that is speech, and therefore bad, and therefore maternal.

A relentlessness, short of being able to describe it as therapeutic, that
we will call stylistic. Actually, the comparison with medicine was inevitable: to confront speech, for a practitioner, is it so different from
having to confront death?

No matter what, it's with this question as a backdrop that rises the
mirage of the dancer. A mirage apt to satisfy in Céline both the doctor
and the writer. For, if the dancer exposes an irreproachable anatomy,
she especially offers us a glimpse of what the body might have been before the first sin, of what the maternal body of language was before its
fall into a given tongue. Because what is ultimately given to us to see,
between the admirable arch of her thighs, that triumphal arch, is indeed language itself, but language reduced to its formal aspect of pure
syntax, language raised in all its splendor, sustained and standing, in-
contestably evident. A golden phallus.[72]

Golden, then, is language, just as silence is golden. The talents, the ca-
pabilities expected of the actress who will play the dancer in *The Church*
(Céline's second but also his last play; from then on, understandably,
he will prefer mime to the theater): "it must not be the lines that act on
the public, or the patter all those mediocrities who claim to be beautiful are usually surrounded with [...] I want, on the contrary, for the actress herself to have a 'sex appeal,' a biological attraction that it would
be entirely useless to praise."[73]

In short, the same goes for the dancer as for those things "that must
be, on the stage, obvious and not demonstrated."[74] Now the obvious immediately imposes itself to the mind through its certain nature. It implies the notion of a truth so perfect that this truth needs no further
proof and no further clarification. There is nothing left in it to clarify.
It is clarity itself. It only has to show itself. Enter Elisabeth Gaige, in the
second act of *The Church*: "She's a pretty girl who proves it by getting
undressed."[75] And promptly. This is the *Quick Theater*. Which is to say
how fast things go (faster than the speeches) and how the truth no longer

bothers with circumlocutions. Not only will the truth not disguise it-self, but it will only allow itself to be discovered in the instant. Like Phryné, in Gérôme's famous painting; Phryné before the Areopagus, and whom the painter has captured at the very moment when Hyper-ides, to defend her, giving up on the power of words, strips her naked before her judges.

Céline will never tire of delving deeper into the mystery of this light-ning flash of the revelation: repeating, from ballet to ballet, Hyperides' gesture. Here, it's Virginie possessed by the demon of dance, Virginie "tearing off her clothes";[76] there, it's the first subjects of the King's Bal-let, it's the little troop preparing itself for the revels: "They get un-dressed...all of them..."[77] Whereas in the Palace of Jupiter (yes, God himself! God who is certainly *progressing* by leaps and bounds), the cur-tain rises on a "half-naked" Juno.[78]

⌐

They bare it all, all of them. Because they are all beautiful and beauty "hides nothing." The sentence is Bardamu's, in *The Church*,[79] and it is a cruel sentence. It hits little Janine straight in the heart. Not that she too, in her own way, isn't a pretty girl. But it is certain that she bears lit-tle relation to those walking beauties that already enchanted Baudelaire (a feast for his artist's eye) before being glorified by Céline. The fact is that little Janine would only be able to seduce at rest, having to conceal the disgrace of a slight limp...

Bardamu's cruelty, however, is aimed not so much at the young girl as, through her, at "the limping under-man"[80] whom we always carry with us like a remorse, our childhood companion, and who is perhaps in the image of this childhood itself, or of our, to say the least, difficult relationship to it.

Search the memories of your contemporaries: the devil if you don't find some little gimp, the Aleijadinho (in Portuguese, the little cripple) who will have carved out the baroque edifice of the seat of their thoughts, of their interior castle, of the fortress they all retreat to...How long will it have taken the Bardamu of *Journey* to uncover in Sergeant Alcide's past the atrophied leg of his little niece? The buried thing whose presence obsesses him, to the point even of having little by little upset his entire existence, to the point of having made it into a life entirely subservient to the imperious necessity of salvation. Having gone to Africa so as to provide for the little cripple's needs, was it not written, then, that to skirt the coast of Hell, he was condemned to move in with the angels?[81]

To evolve, in other words, in the sublime. Except that, let us beware, the sentiment of the sublime cannot be exclusively measured with the gauge of devotion. So much generosity, of course, demands respect. It is very beautiful, but it is also only very beautiful. Of him who seeks to reach the sublime, no matter what meaning you give the word, other qualities are required. Infinitely rarer, a more subtle alloy...

Qualities, no matter what, that our sergeant had; qualities we notably see him display during those absolutely exceptional moments that, in the depths of his Gehenna, he has the art of hatching like very precious flowers, when, every morning, he leads the exercises of the native militiamen placed under his authority.

> At seven o'clock sharp, every morning, Alcide's militiamen went to exercise. As I was living in a corner of his hut, which he had let me have, I had a ringside seat to witness the fantasia. Never in any army of the world have there been soldiers of better will. At Alcide's call, while pacing across the sand by four, by eight, and then by twelve, these primitives exerted themselves enormously by imagining bags, shoes, even bayonets, and, even better, by seeming to use them. Barely issued from a nature so vigorous and so close, they wore nothing but a semblance of short khaki trousers. Everything else had to be imagined by them and was. At Alcide's peremptory command, these ingenious warriors, dropping their fictitious bags, ran into nothing to inflict, upon illusory enemies, illusory thrusts. They created, after pretending to unbutton their uniforms, invisible stacks and on another signal threw themselves passionately into abstractions of musketry.[82]

The uniforms are a pure fantasy, the weapons ideal. Besides, no one uses them. They only appear to. And it's the appearance that counts; the appearance, on every level, that ensures here the triumph of the fiction. A triumph that would have transported Baudelaire with enthusiasm, he who so admired the genius of children in bending the most modest object, a chair, for instance, a simple chair, to every whim of their imagination...

Sergeant Alcide must necessarily be a great child, if he isn't a great poet. Actually, in the absolute, it's same thing. Except for the difficulty, for the poet, of having to recapture the divine faculties of childhood, a difficulty that should not be underestimated. Baudelaire himself, in his whole life, never once concealed to himself the insuperable nature of the task that, in the name of this equivalence, he had imposed on himself.

The ease, the perfect naturalness with which Sergeant Alcide acquits himself of it might therefore seem astonishing, if the nature of the principle guiding him wasn't soon revealed; if this principle itself couldn't be seen at work in the pantomime show he treats himself to day after day, and whose performers' only salary is a few cigarettes: paid in smoke, meaning in the only legal tender in the realm of faerie, realm some of Céline's texts will soon spirit us away to, once Céline gets the idea of writing for the Salle Favart.

If he wasn't already dreaming of it at the time of *Journey*. A more subtle reader, even unaware of *The Church* as the reader of the time necessarily was, might have guessed, from the brio of this fantasia, that he was dying to try. For, if plucking the rigadoon is one thing, devising these "exercises of the imagination," to use the title the good sergeant himself has bestowed upon them, is another, which requires just ever so little that he become an improvised choreographer.

So that the character of Alcide, in this new role of the ballet master, was perhaps meant to celebrate the return among us of the Gallic Hercules. Priding himself on adding, to the twelve labors the myth has retained, a new exploit, the righting of the original wrong of lameness. Dear soul, you were limping . . . well, now dance!

An undeniable enriching of the myth, had the work not thereafter denounced it as an imposture. A work in which the persistent presence, the repeated presence, of lameness beside dance comes to feel a little disturbing. All the more disturbing in that it indeed seems to be the rule. With Céline, if some cripple isn't dragging himself in the dancer's footsteps, it's the exception. Behind Virginia, "frisky young girl with muscles of gold,"[83] here comes, for instance, on London Bridge, Sosthène "hobbling around."[84] Who was nonetheless a fine dancer once, in the time of his splendor, when he would go into his "great magical rigadoon."[85] That was when you should have seen him, and not now, when he is but a shadow of his former self . . .

— A shadow, a shadow, that's easy to say. Is limping, then, so far from dancing? In *Birth of a Fairy*, doesn't old Karalik dance the witches' dance with a limp?[86] And what about this corps de ballet brought on stage by an improbable machine; by a great berlin that leans, that leans, and, finally, collapses, an axle broken...[87] Not to mention the farandole of the stevedores, in the ballet-mime *Hoodlum Paul, Brave Virginie*. "They advance with great difficulty... But always dancing, pitching, however... weighty as bears... They are leaning on heavy canes."[88]

Everything thus seems to indicate, as we can see, that lameness is the hidden motor of the faerie. After all, the first one to dance, in the first scenario collected in *Trifles,* the first one clumsily to venture a few steps, even before the entire corps de ballet comes crashing down on stage, is old Karalik.

This may be worth stopping at. *Birth of a Fairy* is a story of origins. The fairy is none other than the dancer herself. How dancers are born: this, in the clear, is the argument of this interesting choreography.

And of all of Céline's choreographies, to tell the truth. With him, it's the only theme anyone ever dances on. If anyone is even dancing... It is no secret that Céline's ballets are ballets to be read; that they were no more meant to performed than, in their final conception, Musset's plays. Ballets in an armchair...

Ballets without music, just as well! And music, one should reread on this point the conclusion of *Trifles,* is the wing of dance. "Outside of music everything collapses and crawls."[89] Is that clear enough? Do we not know, now, that a ballet without music is a truly lame business?

As for the reasons that condemn the danced parts of Céline's work to this disability, they are perhaps less anecdotal than might seem at first. We know the theory Céline ends up settling on: if, with a single voice, every composer and every musician refuses to collaborate with him, it's because in France, it's because in Russia, it's because everywhere in the world the opera is in the hands of the Jews.

No doubt that of all the bad reasons he could have invoked, this was by far the worst. It is a good thing we do not have to deal with it here.

Especially since it may allow us to think that such bad reasons might conceal other ones. Reasons of an entirely different nature, less exterior. Intrinsic, so to speak, to the very constitution of the choreographic object.

In this hypothesis, it's the object itself that would draw from within itself the strength to renew, at each attempt to materialize it, its capacity for resistance; it's the object that would have been conceived in such a manner as to remain a pure virtuality... Let us simply consider the fact that if, as has been said, the dancer is a fairy, it follows logically that her mode of being is a way of not being.

What could be more inaccessible than a fairy? More elusive? It is possible, therefore, that the invention of dance, in Céline's mind, may be mysteriously subordinated to the certainty of its impossibility.

And not a merely technical one, that should be obvious. The technical impossibility only manifests a more essential impossibility. Some irremediable defect. Of the sort, for instance, of the one we have been designating under the name of lameness.

For, if lameness precedes dance, lameness, alas, outlives it. It is first, it is last. First, like a reminder of what there was before dancing, Karalik limping amid the lame; but last also, and like a prefiguration, then, of what cannot fail to return (Karalik again...), once the dancing is over, once the dancer has flown away:

> She has turned into a fairy... The Poet is disappointed... but still in love... Forever in love... more... always more... with his Evelyne turned into a fairy... Evelyne leaves very softly, pulled along by her little friends... She disappears... dissipates... chiffons... thicker and thicker toward the back of the stage... becomes more and more unreal... spiritual... diaphanous... She disappears... swallowed by the haze of the set... chiffons... The Poet is alone now... Old Karalik turned into a toad! jumps, wriggles, will from now on forever escort the whimsical swarm of the mocking spirits of the forest... The Poet on his rock... at the edge of the water... desolate... unrolls his great manuscript... He is going to sing... he will always sing his ideal, poetic loves... His impossible loves... Always... always... Curtain.[90]

The faerie evaporated, and as a counterweight to it, we have this rock, with all its mass; a rock, we soon see, on which are condensed all the gravities of that always singular practice, literature. But all the more singular if the term writing must henceforth only be applied to those operations that seek to redress, in a sort of frantic overcompensation, a compromised equilibrium. And it should be obvious, in a page such as this, that the function of writing is no more than to fill the void in which the dancer, by her departure, has dumped us. Or, if not writing, at least, and to be more exact, style. The discovery of the necessity of style, in Céline's thinking, does seem to coincide with the acknowledgment of failure that caps his choreographic research, his choreographic speculations.

The proof is that this coincidence leaves its mark on Céline's style, that it determines it in the minutiae of its form, and even in his idea of it — the idea that, little by little, he comes to have of it, progressively renouncing the idea of the "beau style," of good writing, in favor of the idea, itself a little twisted, of a style that would go all sideways. The sentence, he dreams, is a door you pull off its hinges; the sentence is an axis you bend, a stick you break . . . And we ourselves, reading Céline's poetic art, find ourselves wondering, asking ourselves if it isn't just the licentiousness of a lousy worker we are being invited to witness.

The fact of the matter is that Céline is spoiling things for others and spoiling it gaily. To break things down, that is his business, to narrate helter-skelter, "according to the spasms,"[91] and to put everything cautiously askew. To transpose, as he says in his language. But his language never says exactly what we think it wants to say. His language trips, and he himself, if it wasn't tripping, would deliberately catch his feet in it. With that acute, absolutely exceptional sense he has for the *necessary clumsiness,* a sense that causes him to find charm in the blunder, whose mastery he will vie with Rimbaud or Verlaine for: as envious of Arthur's knee as of poor Lelian's, so afraid is he of not being clumsy enough and of being unworthy of the rank he feels he can claim, by virtue of his double quality as the orphan of a dancer and the son of his mother.

His mother in whose person, and for the purpose at hand, Céline will have attempted to resurrect the figure of Asmodeus. And thus of Le Sage's devil, who is a limping devil, inasmuch as in limping he denounces in passing everything lame in this vale of tears . . .

But did Céline's mother truly limp? We know, thanks to his biographers, that she had a somewhat weak leg, probably the aftereffect of poliomyelitis. But a cured poliomyelitis, after all: Marguerite Guillou had been out of danger for a long time.[92] Thus if her walk, as she went about her business, might have seemed slightly lopsided, it was without offense to the eye and nearly imperceptible: completely out of proportion, in every respect, with the fantastically jerky walk Céline saw fit to attribute to the Clémence of *Death on the Installment Plan.*

Who doesn't see, though, that in choosing, by way of a fiction, to become the son of a bandy-legged mother, it was his entire work that the writer had thus decided to rest on shaky ground? First, that which shakes does not fall, as the proverb goes. And, to prove the proverb right, it would be enough to consider — as Céline considers, incidentally, madly fascinated — the cradle of the great dynasties. We would see, for instance, how it oscillates, how it vacillates, the castle of the Hohenzollerns, "skew-whiff! crooked all over!";[93] and how it challenges all the laws of equilibrium, firmly clinging to its rock, its split stone, set way up there, as History proves, to hold for centuries and centuries. Enough to wonder if the most wobbly situations aren't at the same time the most durable. As far as Céline is concerned, at least, there is no point in denying any longer that the question deserves to be studied. Lameness, with him, founds. It's on the bad leg of the mother that the work rests and must lean even in its greatest flights of fancy.

Lift the train of delirium and you can touch it with your finger, that atrophied limb, dry, knotty. As surely as when Clémence pulls up her skirt and sticks it under you nose. For Céline attributes this habit to her. She must always be showing, must always be exposing herself, and, through her lack of shame, must always be reawakening the disappointment we felt the day when, as children, we discovered for the first time that under the skirt of the puppet that seemed so full of life to us, there was nothing but an awful piece of wood.

— But an entire work built on this discovery?

— That is what I am suggesting, yes, arming myself with the only secret the work itself betrays. A fool's secret, for that matter; always known to everyone, and even rendered public, unwrapped on the stage of *Progress* in its very first scene.

MARIE: You're a lucky one, you, to be able to go walk like that! . . . me, it'd be nice if I could dance.

MRS. PUNAIS: You can't?

MARIE: You know.

MRS. PUNAIS: Your leg still hurts? *(Marie nods yes indeed, a little.)* It hurts again, then?

MARIE: A little bit — and especially too it looks like it got a little thinner. *(She shows her legs to her mother, the light forms a halo around her legs; the mother bends down attentively.)*

MRS. PUNAIS: The left one? *(Marie nods yes.)* Show me my sweet. *(She touches.)* You don't limp?

MARIE: A little bit.

MRS. PUNAIS: How long's it been since you noticed?

MARIE: A good three months.

MRS. PUNAIS: You didn't tell me. *(Marie nods no. Mrs. Punais looks closely and then tries to reassure her, but she is worried.)* Oh, you know, you look so much, you end up worrying for nothing!

MARIE: Well, anyway you know.

MRS. PUNAIS: Gaston, what does he say? *(Marie indicates that he doesn't say anything.)* He noticed? *(Marie indicates that probably.)*
The maid has come in, she looks at the scene, she listens, Marie suddenly notices, lowers her dress embarrassed — the maid stays there, she is thinking.

MRS. PUNAIS: *(to the maid)* You want to see my behind?

THE MAID: No! *(She leaves.)*

MRS. PUNAIS: *(emotional)* Ah! I sure thought you were completely cured. That's what he told me, Doctor Ratier, he told it also to Madame Doumergue. It won't come back. You're sure, my sweet, that it's a little thinner? Show me again? *(Same halo, they bend over and both look anxiously and attentively.)* Maybe you didn't rest enough. He told you, the doctor, you remember, you'd still have to rest from time to time... *(She feels.)* There, you see it's a little less hard than on the other side, it looks like.

MARIE: Ah! ah!
At that moment, following the maid, the women of the house slowly enter, the maids, the concierges, workers; they look at the scene and remain silent and attentive, fabulous in the half-light, mutely taking part

in this little feminine aesthetic drama, and then exit, whispering into
each other's ears, silently talking.[94]

People hurry, run in from all sides . . . One last effort, and Céline was summoning the entire planet to the shameful exhibition. All these people, indeed, so that no one will remain in the dark; so that no one, after that, can say that he didn't know, he hadn't been told, he wasn't aware that, if everything under the sun was going so badly, it was because Marie, it was because Céline's mother had one leg shorter than the other. My mother limps, therefore everything limps; things, of course, but men too. This is so true that ever since, in Céline's text, every individual is a *pilon*, a peg leg: *pilons,* the passersby; *pilons,* the shopkeepers, the customers, the tenants in their buildings. "It's a crisis in the entire joint . . . All the peg legs come to the skylights . . ."[95]

She limps.

She talks; it's one and the same.

Clémence's chatter proceeds directly from Marie's confession of her inability to dance. If we will only remember that dancing is associated with silence, we will find that it is because she can't dance that the mother talks so much: to conclude, not unjustifiably, that her lameness is the scandal of the speaking body.

Whereas the corps de ballet is the reparation of this scandal. At least it is in theory, and it would be a fortiori in practice, if all the speculations, all the progressive daydreams that Céline brings to the question of dance didn't make it exclusively a utopia.

Utopic? Dance is even doubly utopic. A conception of an ideal society (and this is the utopia in the classical sense), dance is, furthermore, a conception that has condemned itself to remain in the state of a project: a conception, let us settle on this formulation, that seems hardly interested in its own realization. Not only will Céline's sweet eclogues, his lyrical suites[96] never be given the chance to be put on stage, but they even barely, literarily speaking, maintain a semblance of existence. The story of their publication, in this respect, speaks volumes. A few ballets did make it into the bookstores, but in such a confidential way, and at the cost of so many difficulties, that even the least informed reader couldn't help but suspect that it was Céline himself who, each time, found a way to guarantee the project's failure.

As if, in his mind, a ballet couldn't constitute a work in its own right, certainly. But, for all that, it isn't even allowed, or so it seems, to insert itself in a vaster whole where it would naturally find its place. Why, otherwise, would Céline have published three of his principal scenarios in the first, not to mention the most violent of his racist pamphlets? It is hard to imagine a less fitting support than those "Nostradameries";[97] given the circumstances, one hardly sees what they might have prophesied, other than a pathetic fall. The editorial helplessness such a desperate gesture betrays is a marvelous illustration of the impossibility encountered, when it came to ballets, by their author. Deprived of any autonomy and unable to integrate themselves anywhere, we will have to get used to the idea that a ballet will never be anything more than patchwork. Just like these prostheses that, far from correcting a limp, make it, on the contrary, all the more noticeable.

⌒

Hence it is no accident if the last of the ballets of *Trifles* squares off the genie of dance with the demon of lameness...

The scene is a warehouse, a world animated with a disorganized agitation. People enter, exit, come, go, run, fly...

And, leading the dance, the illustrious Van Bagaden.

At first it is just a name. A name that exemplarily provides this curious entertainment with its title. But which thereby immediately fills our ear with a god-awful falling noise. *Bagadam! Badaboum!... Patatras!* The whole kit and caboodle...

And it would indeed be nothing but an expressive onomatopoeia if it didn't have, in addition, the implacable precision of a chisel. A portrait, it's simple, wouldn't have painted the man better. Powerful by his fortune, staggering under his riches, the gout laying him low has made him into what his name tells us he is: the great soft thing we will soon discover, elephantine and asleep, the image of one of those idols through which Oriental religions incarnate the mystery of passive causes. The same mystery that is being celebrated in this theater, where it is Van Bagaden, nailed as he is to his wheelchair, he who could never even dream of setting one foot in front of the other — it is the merchant in person who, with his heavy cane, puts things in motion, sets the tempo for the little people of perfume girls and cigarette girls who turn, who whirl, who flutter before his eyes, but who are under his orders, because he is the master: master of the house and ballet master.

That the ballet master is but an impotent old man forms a rather nice allegory. And nice not only in and of itself, but in consideration of the lesson it delivers. For we are in effect meant to understand that dance is one of those things of which it is said that, without performing them ourselves, and simply by watching them be performed, they cut the ground out from under our feet; meant to understand this and recognize, at the same time, the idea, here implicit, that the company of dancers alone can diminish us physically; the idea that dance performances are dangerous to remain in front of too long; performances where we always risk losing something: whether we lose the use of a limb, as we have just seen, or whether we lose the limb itself.

Such at least is the terrible contingency in which the character of the artist, the unspeakable sculptor of *Faerie for Another Time,* will find his most immediate sanction. His name is Jules; but, in the text, he's "the" Jules. The reader gets the point: this Jules is a John . . .

Fascinated by little dancing girls, to the point of lying in wait for them as they leave their lessons, he solicits on the public highway. He can't help it, he has to have his little dancing girls. And he would be unable to continue living if he couldn't constantly touch them, finger them, and feel them up, if he couldn't at any moment take the greatest liberties with them. Every day that God has made finds him organizing, in the secrecy of his studio, all sorts of blue movies. But the most surprising thing yet is the ease with which, one after the other, they answer his call and let him seduce them. As if, in one glance, they had recognized their master in this poor man's Casanova.

A stub of a man, it's a fact, a sort of runt: compared to these big girls, he's knee-high to a grasshopper. To cut things short, since one thing explains another, Jules has no legs.

Admittedly, a legless man is not a lame one. But it's a question of degree, not of nature. The difference between a legless and a lame man (and this, of course, is what is so atrocious about it) can be expressed quantitatively. The man with no legs accomplishes, completes what the lame one had only started. For whereas lameness, as has been suggested, diminishes you, the fact of having no legs radically amputates you by half. The subtractive operation the gimp is submitted to is pushed, with the legless cripple, to its ultimate consequences.

And this is how, obviously, from the dancer's point of view, the legless man is far more interesting than the merely lame one.

The interest she shows in him is closely akin to the interest we all naturally feel, from the consciousness of our integrity, for those beings who have lost it. The interest of all whole things for those that no longer are. And the dancer's body (must we repeat it?) has the plenitude of a dream body: it is smooth, it is dense, it is untouched.

A closed form, impenetrable, whose resistance love itself could not overcome. Isn't it remarkable, in this connection, that to get a dancer pregnant, one has to do it, so to speak, behind her back? Without her noticing, and, especially, without the living citadel she opposes to the other's desire being broken into.

Thus, in front of Virginia outraged, let no one hasten to cry wolf! It would mean to have badly read the text, where the scene of her defloration is filtered through the prism of delirium. Not just raped once, the poor girl, but hundreds, thousands of times.

And the number, in its exaggeration, immediately betrays the implausibility of such a supposition. When the responsibility is shared by all, when it is unanimous, it is anonymous. One then speaks of an inexplicable misfortune. Virginia's motherhood, all things considered, is just such a misfortune.

Without rhyme or reason. Nor much reality. If she finds herself pregnant, the morning after her mad night at the Tweet-Tweet Club, a return from Hell in some ways, it must therefore be the work of the devil. The great Anonymous One, he whose name is Legion, and who is thus everyone, and who is thus no one.

Virgin and mother, yes. It's been known to happen.

A long time ago . . . And so what? The Spirit blows as it pleases.

Not to mention that we might well be allowed not to deal with these subtleties at all. The dancer's interest in the legless man, to switch registers, is also, far more trivially, the mother's interest, for instance, in her child; the interest, at least, that the pervert dreams of in his fantasy, when, to improve his relationship to woman, he aspires to become a child again, to be, like Jules, a fat babe in arms that the young ladies pass back and forth with greedy looks and great disgusted airs.

Because he is dirty, the artist, foul, revolting! To see him in his box, all encrusted with colors, all smeared with matter, you would think it was an awful piece of flesh thrown on the garbage heap. Which, however, is the thing the dancers have made into their thing. And so passionately that we soon find ourselves thinking that this unnameable thing could only have issued from them.

Struck by this thought, we are extremely close now to touching what is probably the very essence of dance; or, if not its essence, at least its paradox. It is indeed somewhat paradoxical to claim, like the stage directions of *Progress,* that the dancer is *whole.*[98] For, as we are starting to suspect, she is only whole, in reality, in proportion to what she lacks.

Not that she misses it, or is thereby deprived of anything whatsoever. She does very well without it and all the better in that she retains the use of it: far from having separated herself from it, she has, so to speak, unloaded it onto a third party.

The fact remains that in all rigor the dancer can no longer be said to be whole unless she has been put in presence of this third party: gimp, cripple, or legless man, but, in any case, a third party included in the system. The system they form together, and in which the cripple's function is to bear, in his disability, all the weight of the dark share, the accursed share perhaps that the dancer had to amputate from herself in order to show herself to us in her most beautiful light, to gather up all the lines of her body, to put on her Sunday body.

Thus we have Mimi, in *Normance*; Jules and Mimi posing for posterity, with the Butte as a pedestal and Paris at their feet, "the two up there in the air, the one naked and the other legless."[99] The perfect couple, in short, as if the cripple, as if that little runt of a man had drawn out of himself, without having to be taught it, the truth that he alone could be "the term that allows woman to be in harmony with herself in her craving for wholeness."[100]

A consequence of the same paradox we had mentioned earlier but can now spell out in these terms: what the dancer's body is lacking, that body with its vaunted wholeness, the cripple's body — a diminished body if there ever was one — has in excess, and even has a hundredfold. The place he takes up in the work is incidentally in proportion to this excess.

A greater and greater place, as if there could never be too many cripples or as if the cripples themselves were never crippled enough. We will not have failed to note, in this connection, the gradation that has led us, since the beginning of this discussion, from the lame to the bedridden, from the bedridden to the one-legged, and from the one-legged to the legless. But shall we say of this gradation that it proceeds in increasing or decreasing values?

The angle from which Céline forces us to consider the question obviously determines the answer. The more Céline progresses in his work, the more important the character of the cripple grows, the more thickness, the more relief he gains, the more he stands out. To the point of creating a vacuum around himself. In the image of Jules, precisely; Jules again, immovable under the bombs of *Normance*. A rain, a hail of bombs, whose coming he himself hastens by bouncing around in his box, by thrashing about like the devil himself: rainmaker, Apocalypse maker. The world of men collapses, falls into dust, goes up in smoke; and, with it, vanish every mirage and every illusion. The test of the real, if you like; a leveling, a radical unveiling . . . So that we can finally see exactly what holds, what resists. Nothing, of course. Nothing except Jules. The only one to come through it, and to come through intact, enhanced by the trial. Apotheosis of Jules.

But in breaking the enchanted circle of the dancers, significantly absent from *Normance*,[101] to grant Jules his apotheosis, Céline was simultaneously consecrating — a Céline after the fall, it is true — the triumph of the stump over "Mistingo's legs."[102] The triumph of the principle incarnated by Jules's disability. An odious principle, certainly, and one that Céline took a long time to submit to. For wasn't the same principle already hinted at, in veiled terms, by the "little aesthetic drama" in which, in *Progress*, were caught up mother and daughter? Because try as the mother will to minimize the thing, and try as the thing itself will to wrap itself in mystery, the spectator's attention is nevertheless entirely focused on the circle of light that suffuses it in an unreal glare; the halo that exalts it and in this exaltation seems to display it in its principle.

MARIE: It still bothers me that the maid saw, you think she saw?

MRS. PUNAIS: Oh! she didn't understand. *(Marie indicates "yes," "yes.")* But you know if both legs were the same, it'd be very elegant, this one isn't too thin.

MARIE: Ah! you see that one is thicker than the other, don't you?

MRS. PUNAIS: *(embarrassed)* No, no, my sweet, it doesn't show at all like that—it's because you told me—when you look close. *(Marie cries, Mrs. Punais comforts her.)* I promise you, my sweet, it doesn't show.

MARIE: Yes, yes, Mother, it's disgusting.

MRS. PUNAIS: Disgusting? Of course not, come on, Marie, it isn't disgusting at all! You are crazy, my sweet!

MARIE: Yes, yes, Mother, for men it's disgusting.[103]

"It's disgusting..." Whereupon, in *Death on the Installment Plan,* Auguste chimes in: "It's revolting."

> She's tripping around so much she can't stand on her pin no more. She has to climb back on the sack...She collapses...She pulls everything up, all her petticoats...She reveals all the thighs, the lower belly, the slit and the hairy...She writhes in her pain...She rubs herself like that very softly...she's bent in half...
>
> "Ah! come on! cover yourself! will you cover yourself, it's revolting!"[104]

Denoël, Céline's first editor, demanded that Clémence lower her skirts a bit. He was willing to grant the writer the belly, but he categorically refused the rest. Yet "belly" is vague. And precision here was necessary. In the very interest of the cause that had to be defended, and that just happened to be the cause that Céline was defending. To wit, that sex is evil: the opposite of good, but especially that which isn't right in us; or rather which is off-kilter. In its brutality, this encounter between the pin and the slit locates the point where are articulated the two questions of lameness and sexuality. Lameness of Clémence, lameness of the species... We all limp, because we are all sexed beings. A single defective part, a single sick organ, and the human machine no longer runs straight.

—But what about the others, the machines that aren't human?

—Ask the man of the machine, ask Édouard who is "mommy's brother." Auguste, for one, doesn't understand the first thing about them.

It's already enough that he has to knock himself out on his typewriter! One reaches the mechanical through women, who are "persons of the sex," as they used to say, *les personnes du sexe*. But then also, and for this very reason, we cannot expect, as far as engineering goes, anything more than some fine heaps, Fulmicoach,[105] cyclopumps,[106] "mazing cans"[107] — Édouard's *pétrolette*: "The tricar, it would buck first and then it collapsed back down on itself... It would kick two or three more spasms... Awful cracks and hiccups [...] So then we heeled over."[108]

Just like the boats. And it's normal. The boats that go on water (right, mommy?), the boats have legs.[109] Hence the fact that boats, necessarily, are always off-kilter, hence the fact that they are always threatening to sink. And the *bateaux-mouches* on the Seine, and on the Thames "the whole boatish brood,"[110] and "the great steaming steamers,"[111] the liners, the cargos, the sailboats — and Paris. The ship of Paris, to which, in the very first pages of *Death on the Installment Plan*, Céline moors his daydreaming; Paris that sails, Paris that flies, but is soon in a dickey, is soon listing. The ship no longer obeys the rudder. The ship is scraping the bottom, bumping into the statues, the monuments... While Céline, wrenched from his meditations, gets tangled up in the logorrhea of maternal admonitions; lectures and more lectures to weigh on his dream, lectures thanks to which the dream of the boat, his fine dream, ends in shipwreck. *Mergitur*...

And rises, reappears... Saved from the waters. "That's all a miracle is!"[112]

We cry miracle when an event seems in contradiction with the laws of nature. But a ship, considered from this angle, is a miracle every instant: a permanent prodigy.

The emotion Céline derives from the sight of these "dainty monsters,"[113] of these great *navigots,* "potbellied upstream collossi, boiling propeller maniacs,"[114] is an emotion akin to the one the invention of the heavier-than-air must have provoked in its day. If not an even greater one; an emotion increased by a method Céline abuses of, which consists in laying it on about the apparent weightiness of the things meant to fly on the waters, or, not so different, meant to fly in the air. These sorts of things, with Céline, are not just heavy, they are dense, they are clumsy, they are awkward. No doubt, in this respect, that in Baudelaire's place it would have been enough for Céline to have noted that

Ses ailes de géant l'empêchent de marcher

[Its giant's wings prevent it from walking]

(that and nothing else) for him to have drawn the conclusion that the albatross was indeed the prince of the sky.

And since we are on the topic of ridicules, we might as well state it clearly: there are forms of grace that, far from being weakened by ridicule, find ways to adorn themselves with it, to draw new charms from it. The strange machines men employ to go on the sea are laden with this sort of grace. To the journalist who was asking him what he put into his books so that his books would go the way they went, Céline, at the end of a long enumeration, added this answer: "The deformed leg of the little cousin must also fit in, and the sailship boat so wide open to too many winds."[115]

The leg in the book, the ship on its keel.[116]

For how could we not think that it's the deformed leg, a woman's leg, that, in its oscillating movement, rather mysteriously sets the ship's course? Oh! a bizarre course, strangely rolling—enough to fear the worst, if the ship didn't, on the contrary, seem to lean toward it on its own. For if, in order to advance, it is enough here to defeat the fall, first must you trip! Anyhow, everyone knows this, and I'm not saying anything new. Other than perhaps this: in getting the idea of correcting lameness one would certainly be falling into an error. It's Auguste's error, as he grows indignant over certain nautical difficulties. He wants all the lyricism of docking, and nothing but the lyricism; the lyricism without the burlesque of wrong moves. Yet this mixture of lyricism and burlesque is the very essence of the Célinian poetry:

> the whole tub on the same ramp!... to keel over!... who who has fun without disorder?...[117]

Wherefore Auguste's error is only repeating, though less seriously, another error. I mean the error of dance—of dance from which faery so-called, from which pure poetry amputates the real. For now we can see all too well just what the dancer is in the absolute: the mother minus what makes her limp, the mother operated on to remove her sex. So that every time the dancer lifts her leg—to reestablish the balance, we have to visualize Clémence lifting her skirt. *In parallel,* Verlaine whispers to us . . . An answer to the ideal striptease, maternal exhibitionism underlines its cost. The dancer can, of course, bare it all, but only on condition that the mother, on her side, hide nothing.

It would obviously be another thing entirely to make the mother dance. But the utopia of the ballet doesn't go that far. Which is why it is only a utopia. Either, as far as we can tell, the mother isn't the one dancing, or, if the mother is dancing, then we have to admit that she doesn't know how to dance.

We can always dream that the mother is the one dancing and that the mother knows how to dance. But we can only dream about it.

II

The argument of the balloon, in comparison, offers an immediate advantage. Its superiority over the argument of the ballet lies in the fact that it is, apparently, immune to the objection of lameness. As proof, to go quickly, we have "the Gambetta in his nacelle."[118] Simultaneously the objection, lameness's objection to the very fact of the balloon, and its finest refutation. The balloon rises, and rises all the faster that it is bearing away into the clouds, to an operetta refrain, as it were, that ghost of a leg: Gambetta, *la gambette*. Legs, legs, legs!

Céline is exulting, then a prisoner in Denmark, Céline at "the bottom of the pit."[119] Which is, of course, the irony of the story. Did he know, for instance, that it was in a tavern, a little café named the Caveau,[120] that the brothers Robert and Charles launched the subscription that allowed them to built their aerostat? "Crypts, cellars, volcanoes," as Patrick Wald Lasowski has shown, "the hearths from below vomit dazzling balloons toward the sky..."[121] We already shiver at the effects Céline might have drawn from this splendid thought, if he hadn't had, at the time, other things on his mind. Still having, after "the Gambetta," to put Sarah in the same basket — "Sarah Bernhardt one-legged,"[122] as he says. Which says it all.

Yes, everything has been said; and, in one move, the beans have been spilled.

For this piquant allusion to *la divine* suggests to us that it isn't so far from the balloon that runs through Céline's work to the Montgolfier that, on a morning of the winter of 1784, amazed the good people of Lyons. It was very cold, very windy that day. In spite of the cold, however, in spite of the wind, they decided to go. One Madame de Flesselles had been given the honor of putting the spark to the bonfire. But the poor woman limped, and, as the device in its crossbars was rocking under the gust of wind, one of the onlookers let slip a witticism, quite to the point: "After all, the godson should resemble the godmother!"[123]

The same satirical trait, by ricochet, hits Courtial's balloon. Even sharper, though, even clearer and even more precise. Without even a sentence. Just a name. The name given to his first spherical, an enormously wide "captive": all the better target for the epigram.

Which, consequently, hits the bull's-eye. Baptized the *Archimedes*... And never, or so it seems, was a name worse chosen. At least if we stick to what Archimedes represents, Archimedes whose name remains associated with the invention of the science called statics, which is, properly, the science of equilibrium.

What can be said, then, of Courtial des Pereires's aerostatic experiments? It is possible to say nothing, but how not to laugh!

> I never saw it take off straight...It was limp from the start...We only blew it up, for many reasons, with the greatest reservations...So it'd skedaddle sideways...It waddled over the roofs. It looked with its patches like a great colored Harlequin...It frolicked in the air waiting for a real gust, it could only puff up in a full wind...Like an old skirt on the cord, it was calamitous...Even the most yokel hicks realized the thing...Everybody was in stitches seeing it go stagger into the roofs...[124]

Waddling, staggering, and skedaddling sideways... The drunken balloon, putting the lie to its name. If, however, it truly is lying in invoking the patronage of Archimedes, and thereby connecting with the reading a philosopher such as Michel Serres proposes of the *Arenarium*, of the book *On Spirals*, or of the treatise *On Floating Bodies*; Michel Serres who demonstrates, in his *The Birth of Physics*, that what matters to the scientist of Syracuse, all told, is not so much equilibrium as the loss of equilibrium: "Archimedes, the inventor of statics," he writes, "defines less equilibrium than the angle of inclination [...] this is the subject of Archimedes' first discourse. He is always talking about compensated inequalities, or, on the contrary, of uncompensatable ones."[125]

In a word, Michel Serres again: "Everything proceeds from the balance, but on condition that it tilts."

Archimedes, then, and all the more so the *Archimedes* of *Death on the Installment Plan*, says the lameness of the beginning, says the leap, the sideways step of the balloon, by which it is connected to, by which it is angled on the question of the origin. Whereas, in comparison, the dancer's step, although also a step sideways, is only a step beyond; a step that makes the dancer stray from the question, that makes her skip over it, makes her spring over it in a leap that carries her straight to the sky.

I have already pointed out the utopic nature of the aspiration to the beyond expressed by the dancer's step. The classic paths to the beyond are rarely practicable. So that it is all the more meaningful that the metaphor of the balloon (a metaphor that not only takes for a time the place of the metaphor of the ballet, but also transfers its effects to a completely different stage and for entirely different reasons) brings Céline to reconsider the first principles of his all too classical metaphysics. Which is why, wherever he once wrote *au-delà*, "beyond," Céline, ever since this other scene (and this other account), will henceforth write *outre-là*.[126]

No need to invoke, in order to explain it, God knows what quirk of the pen. The word once ventured (if I am not mistaken, it appears in 1941),[127] Céline will resolutely stick to it. Although this resolution, in an inconsistency that deserves to be cleared up, in no way modifies the apparent landscape of the Célinian pastoral. The dancer dances no less, and that is a fact; although, symptomatically, she does dance other figures. Figures that are no longer quite the conventional figures; less and less positive figures, as the movement of decay first announced by the ballet *Hoodlum Paul, Brave Virginie* accelerates; a ballet specially written, but against the tide of the official celebrations, for the World's Fair of 1937. If we examine, one after the other, Céline's subsequent productions (and therefore *Scandal in the Abyss*, whose scenario was being printed when he hurriedly left Paris on June 17, 1944; but also the synopsis of the ballet that he wished, in 1945, before his arrest, to produce at the

Royal Theater of Copenhagen and that has only reached us amputated of its title; *Thunderbolts and Arrows,* furthermore, a mythological fantasy in the manner of Offenbach, begun in March 1945, though only completed in March 1947; and, finally, *Arletty, Young Girl from Dauphiné,* a vague project that he never followed up on and that we know nothing about, other than a letter he wrote in 1948 to the famous actress),[128] we are forced to note that in each one the star dancer, a fallen angel, has made a faux pas, a wrong move: Arletty kills and robs, Pryntyl prostitutes herself, Erythre steals Jupiter's thunderbolts; as for the lead of the "untitled" ballet, whose action is set at the turn of this century, she too is just a bad lot, the girlfriend of a respectable gentleman whom she leads into debauchery, to the savage rhythms of a "Negro" music . . .[129]

The source from which Céline drew the freshness of his inspiration has, it seems, dried up. But not the flow of his soothing speeches on dance, which seem to swell in proportion! Letters to Milton Hindus, to Albert Paraz, to Jean Paulhan, to Georges Geoffroy, to Roger Nimier . . . statements to the press, which he ceaselessly floods with his passion, but in a somewhat too reasoned form, as if it were an object that had suddenly become external to him. Like a man henceforth convinced that, no matter the efforts you make, you are never the contemporary of your own desires. Living, through his marriage, *at the side* of a dancer, rather than living with her.[130]

So that by borrowing, to examine in turn the question of dance, such and such of the statements we have just mentioned, often public statements, and especially subsequent to *Death on the Installment Plan,* it is clear that we have proved nothing against Céline's determination in favor of the *outre-là.* Even had we wanted to, we couldn't have. The poetic invention of the balloon, in Céline's work, marks a point of no return. You don't come back from the *outre-là,* were it on the wings of dance.

∽

The Célinian *outre-là* plays on the French language's confusion between two *outres*— *outres* that in English are clearly distinct. For there are indeed two *outres* in French: the *outre* that comes from *ultra,* which in Latin means "beyond" (as in "ulterior" or "ultraconservative"), and which Céline sometimes writes, archaically, "*oultre*";[131] and the *outre* that comes from *uter,* which in Latin means "belly" (as in "uterus," the same *outre* that the *Robert & Collins* translates as "goatskin, wine or water skin"). So that in this language you are allowed, when it comes to *outres,* to enjoy two for the price of one.

But, when we talk about permission, it must be perfectly clear that it isn't the language that allows. Obviously, the language neither obliges nor allows. It does, however, leave everyone the freedom to bind himself linguistically with all sorts of obligations that have been formed outside of it.

The hypothesis is thus that Céline is *binding* himself. We don't yet know what he is binding himself to; but we can state that we know the linguistic form taken, as far as he is concerned, by the obligation in question. An obligation, in short, that would be expressed through the confusion the French language has allowed itself between *uter* and *ultra.*

Between the belly and the beyond; even though, a priori, the belly seems better suited to welcome notions such as those expressed by the *en-deçà,* the before, the hither. Don't all the suppressed, all the swallowed things naturally find their place there? The belly has long sketched out for the imagination a space of intimacy, being the seat of the most secret functions of the body, of the heart, even, eventually, of the mind . . .

Thus, at least, the dominant trend of thought, and the path this thought has traced. But it is not at all, in our hypothesis (need it be said?), the path down which Céline will send Courtial's balloon, and, behind this balloon, his entire work to come. Another path apparently interests him, a neglected path, though it did exist in the field of the language, in the unconscious of the French language, not to say the unconscious of a great many European languages. "If we consult the history of the language," writes, in this respect, Suzanne Allen, "we can see that the word uterus originally functions in a doublet with the acceptation of *outre,* which draws its resources, through the Greek *udria,* from the Sanscrit *ud,* which means both *water* (everything aqueous) and *out of. Ud* is very pertinent, as far as the analysis of an unconscious of the language goes, inasmuch as it combines in 'outre,' in its lineage, the double metaphor of the water-bearing object made out of goatskin and the *en outre,* transgressor of limits."[132]

So that no matter which side of the horizon of the language we gaze at, the same possibility seems offered to us; a technical (lexical) possibility simultaneously to think the *en outre* and the *outre,* if not to include the former (the *en outre,* transgressor of limits) within the limits of the latter. So that in saying *outre-là* Céline, basically, is designating a beyond that would run through various dead ends.

                        ↶

Is a genesis of the *outre-là* possible? Probably, since the text of *Death on the Installment Plan* allows us to witness the birth of the idea. And itself becomes fascinated by it, to the point of corrupting the reader's imagination. To the point of arousing, through a rather perfidious sort of maieutics, to the point of giving birth in the subjugated reader to an irrepressible desire to deliver himself of his own mind.

This art of giving birth, maieutics, we know that Socrates held it from his mother, a midwife. Midwife: such was also the profession of the worthy wife of Courtial des Pereires, before she had to abandon it to help the great man prepare his ascents — a "first-class diploma holder,"[133] a student of Pinard "who had delivered the czarina,"[134] herself a midwife and a placer of cupping glasses.

The belly of the pregnant woman, the bell of the cupping glass, and the envelope of the balloon: all this holds, all these globes englobe each other...

But let us return to Socrates, by way of Alcibiades' portrait of him in the *Symposium*: "I say, then, that he is exactly like a Silenos, the little figures which you see sitting in the statuaries' shops; as the craftsmen make them, they hold Panspipes or pipes, and they can be opened down the middle and folded back, and then they show inside them images of the gods."[135] As statues reproduce themselves, so do great thinkers: on their own. Palingenesis of the philosopher. And of Courtial, therefore.

A Courtial *d'outre-tombe,* from beyond the grave, caught, on the pebbles of the path, in the half-light of a Lazarean dawn. It's the morning after his desperate gesture, after his suicide. An end he had dreamed in the Roman style, but which he will have blown like everything else, rushing it with a hurried shotgun blast. Barrel in the mouth... An ordinary death, a six o'clock news item. It won't be easy to lift this one back up to the level of delirium. Even hysteria and all its theater will hardly be enough. At least it can give it its best shot. The grand finale . . . The burst head is only a gaping wound, when the wife, distracted with grief, the wife who knows what she's talking about, takes it upon herself to show us the thing. The thing that is there, but that we don't know how to see. "A placenta! . . . ," she cries. "It's a placenta! . . . I know! . . . His head! . . . His poor head! . . . It's a placenta! . . . You see, Ferdinand? . . . You see? . . . Look! . . ."[136]

The obstetrician delivered. In the image of those sculptures, the figures with their figurines, simulacra with their secrets, described by Alcibiades . . . Why conceal it any further? I might as well come right out with it: I hold Courtial for a new Socrates. For a Socrates whose Plato would be Céline. The portrait of the man is a good likeness, at least faithful to the tradition. The satyr and his flute, a big-bellied Silenus, with a curved forehead, a pug nose, bulging eyes. A great drinker, who grows animated when he speaks. Athletic, a gymnasiarch. Sometimes laughable. Zeno, who didn't like him much, called him "the jester of Athens." Others even saw, in his physiognomy, the marks of debauchery, of fatuity, and of anger.

All things that make of Courtial, already, a possible Socrates, if not a likely one. But there is no likely Socrates. The image we have of him is a confused image, often contradictory, fragmented, degraded; yet, by this very fact, an image amazingly similar to the one left behind, in the third part of *Death on the Installment Plan,* by that reasoner, that somewhat rotting enchanter, Courtial des Pereires.

A burlesque Socrates, for a book that could also be, in the same burlesque mode, a Platonic dialogue; dialogue that in imitation of the *Symposium* or the *Republic* we would be tempted to call the *Balloon.* Just as we have the *Phaedo* . . .[137]

Just as we have the *Phaedo,* we will thus say the *Balloon.* The *Balloon* or *on the soul:* maieutics of the *outre-là.*

⤸

And the *outre,* to begin. The *outre* in the feminine gender, the "goatskin." The *outre* itself, to say it all, "seven hundred kilos of furbelows."[138] Far more than the poor Clémence could ever carry, in her errands, in her hunt for the customer. What, however, are seven hundred kilos, some fifteen hundred pounds, compared to the "enormous heap of lace" that Céline's mother, for her entire life, had to fix every day; "the fabulous mound," as he recalled in a letter to Lucienne Delforge, "that always hung over her table — a mountain of work for a few francs. [...] I had nightmares about it at night, she too. It has stayed with me. [...] Like her I always have on my table a huge heap of horrors pending, which I would like to patch up before I'm done for."[139]

Always, always... There has always been, between them, this bale, this enormous heap, this fabulous mound.

Mother and son have this in common: both of them, they repair, are associated in the same mending routine. And perhaps caught in the same fabric. Because, if we think about it, do we really know what mending means? Is it to put some devastated place back into shape? Or is it, on the contrary, through an even greater devastation, to introduce the supreme lightness into this place? The fact is that the thought of lace, for Céline, cannot be dissociated from the thought of havoc — whether it is applied to the lace itself or whether it is applied to writing, for which the lace is then but a metaphor. It is only when Céline's text begins to fray, splinters, tears itself to pieces, that Céline's text swells, and, filled with air and suddenly lightened, tears itself off the ground and takes off before our eyes.

For every takeoff, its tearing-off. One must remove by force, vanquish at all cost the adhesions. To mend, in this sense, is to rend; and to splice is to slice. All-powerfulness of a paronomasia, whose reason is founded outside of Céline. Reread Cendrars, whom he doesn't like, or better yet Vallès, whom he does.

There remains Céline's avidity, his appetite for air, which, for once, is rightly his own. Ready to leap, always... Whereas Proust hesitates to breathe, whereas on the verge of suffocation he still rations himself, judging that every new inhalation draws him a little further from his mother[140] — Céline, on his side, quivers at the least breath. The slightest flutter, a breeze, "a gust of wind, he escapes."[141] All too happy to go gambol, to go wallow in the bed of all the winds. Better to be a wisp, gossamer than son of your mother, when mothers breathe down your neck and smother you under a glass bell... No doubt the mad idea of the balloon is rooted under this bell. The Bell of the Passage... So that to rise it requires gas, that same pestilential and heavy gas suffocating the shopkeepers in the rear of their shops.

Which, in passing, betrays Céline's ambition: to suspend Courtial's nacelle under the Passage bell. For it's the bell that flies, the bell that flutters and plays the fool in the abyss. Having, by this extravagance, the extravagance of its aspiring to fly, become unrecognizable.

This explains the balloon's shape, or rather its lack of shape. Its inability to keep any shape whatsoever. The higher it rises, the more pieces it loses, the more it dislocates, scatters itself. With the reservation that the scattering, here (we have given the reasons), bears witness to the flight and to the cost of the flight. To the point that, in Céline's language, scatter is used in an absolute sense to signify flight. "Laughs scatter!...Dances of joy!...rounds bear away."[142] And soon *scat,* by apocope. Céline having gotten the idea of adding the example to the rule, the effect to the cause, and of scattering the word itself. Scat and sparkle, are, in the end, the same thing. But a fragile thing. Fragile as a butterfly.

With Courtial's balloon, we obviously only have a farcical version of this fragility. Outrageously farcical. Yes, an object that by itself goes too far, goes beyond all reason. A perpetual exaggeration.

It was no little pause to sew back up, darn, patch up the ugly envelope, cobble together pieces that couldn't hold anymore...It was an endless bother...Especially since to better look closely I used an acetylene lamp... Like that in the basement, it was extremely imprudent...near the adhesive substances...which are always rotten with benzene...It ran all over the place...I could already see myself a living torch!...The envelope of the *Zealous* was a perilous affair, in numerous places a real sieve...More rips! More tears! always again more terrible ones each time we went up, each time we came down! On the landing drag through the plowings!... On the backside of every gutter...In the rows of dormers, especially on the days with a north wind!...He'd left pieces everywhere, great tatters, little debris, in forests, after branches, between steeples! Battlements... He carried off tin chimneys! roofs! tiles by the kilo! weather vanes at every sortie! But the most treacherous guttings, the most atrocious rips, were the times he impaled himself on a telephone pole!...There often he split in two...[...] In spite of an infinite guile, my great ingenuity, I very often despaired over that bitch envelope...It really couldn't take anymore... For sixteen years it'd been taken out in every circumstance, at every opportunity, every tornado; it only held anymore by the overcast seams, bizarre cobblings... Each inflation was a soap opera!... When it came down, when it dragged, it was even worse... When a whole strip was missing, I'd go take a graft from the old skin of the *Archimedes*... That one was nothing but pieces anymore, big tatters in a closet, in a jumble, in the basement... It was his first balloon, a completely crimson "captive," an enormously wide windbag. It had lasted twenty years, every fair!... I sure put some meticulousness into reglueing all this, end to end, intense scruples... It made for some curious effects... When it rose at the "castoff," the *Zealous* above the crowds, I could recognize my pieces in the air... I could see them pucker, gather up... It didn't make me laugh.[143]

Us, yes! Laugh at finally being there. For we are finally there; and up to our necks: "in the thing."[144] To go to the fact, or better "to the nerve" (watchword of the new aesthetic), is to be engulfed.

Little chthonian god in his lair, here now is Ferdinand, and here we are with him, drowned, buried beneath the folds of the envelope. For, as we have seen, whereas at each landing Courtial is extracted, or better ejected, from it ("He'd spurt like a puppet"),[145] the boy, on the contrary, goes back at it every night. *Regressus ad uterum.*

—But what about the thread? The needle?

—Well, it has to be sewn back up, this belly ruined by its multiple pregnancies. This torn pocket, whose seams are bursting... *my mother's cross!* A cross the son takes on himself, and of which, staggering in turn beneath the burden, he relieves the sainted one. No doubt the invention of the balloon also figures as the symbolic coin of this exchange. Heavy cartage of the species, fabulous mound, Clémence's bundle and the Passage bell—the balloon in its pouch carries them all along: making it all into one package.

↜

There is something rather amusing, after that, in witnessing the incomparable Courtial struggling every Sunday toward the blue, in demonstration flights that would like to be pure feasts of the mind. Such, of course, is the official reason for these Sunday exhibitions: to support a pedagogical enterprise whose avowed goal is to raise the reader to knowledge. The *Zealous*'s role is to help the man of science reawaken the sleepy ardor of the ignorant masses, activate their zeal. In a way, he is giving the impulse to a momentum.

Well, momentum, that is a big word: "it would slump, unhappy thing, at the takeoff even, rather than rush to the skies."[146] Without neglecting the fact that, when it comes to ascents, Céline's text especially lingers on the stunts, on the tumbles of our acrobat. To the point of making us wonder if aerostation isn't purely and simply a physics of the fall. To the "flying skeleton" Mille-Pattes, "the virtuosic magic, the true prowess of the atmosphere."[147] But, for our acrobat, who has yet to enjoy the prestiges of "*outre*-catacomb,"[148] there is nothing left, for now, but to fall. To fall from on high, perhaps, but with the firm intention of falling lower, always lower. The progress is in the descent. Courtial's machine achieves the prodigy of a *descending* balloon.

> So I had like that to go pick him up in perilous situations in the four corners of the Seine-et-Oise, in Champagne, and even in the Yonne! He scrapped with his ass every sugar beet of the northeast. The beautiful rattan nacelle, it hardly had any shape left in the end...On the plateau of Orgemont, he stayed two good hours entirely buried, stuck in the middle of the pond, an enormous pool of manure! Moving, frothy, prodigious!... All the yokels of the area were splitting their ribs laughing...When we refolded the *Zealous,* it smelled so strong of all the matters and the juice of the pit, and Courtial also actually, entirely padded, miry, coated, soldered in shit paste! that they never let us into the compartment...We traveled in the luggage coach with the instrument, the riggings, the junk. Back at the Palais-Royal, it wasn't over!...Our pretty aerostat, it still stank so bad, like that even in the depths of the basement, that we had to burn, and for nearly the whole summer, at least ten pots of benzoin, sandalwood, and eucalyptus...reams of Armenian paper!...They would have expelled us! There were already petitions...[149]

And with this nosedive ends the career of the *Zealous.* At the end of a mad run that will have led it, belly to the ground, to sink into the cloacal body of matter...

—It's beneath everything, Courtial's balloon!

—Absolutely, and that is actually its merit. It gets to the bottom of things.

—To the bottom?...All the way to the bottom?...But one never reaches the bottom, the very bottom. Deep down, under what we conventionally call the bottom, isn't there still something?

—Thus, to go deeper, to reach (who knows?) the bottomless bottom, must we switch machines. And thus, in the fruitful mind of the founder of the *Génitron,* is born the idea of the diving bell. A challenge to the looters of the abyss. Courtial is waiting for them all in the gulf beneath the seas, in the depths of the oceanic canyons, on the embankment, so to speak, that serves as the base of the plateaus of the continents, where lie, mingled with the pelagic deposits, the sunken treasures of all the armadas. Immense project, vertiginous project! Yet isn't it obvious that this new project inscribes itself in the logic of the preceding project, and that the diving bell relays the aerostat? Archimedes, from whom the archballoon, the mother balloon draws its name, and from whom the son of the balloon, the *Zealous,* draws its resources, taken strip by strip from the old bag of that sort of inexhaustible womb; Archimedes, all things considered, would also have deserved (it should even have been realized a little earlier than it was) to give his name to a submarine. "Any body sunk, etc." Everyone knows the famous theorem. But does everyone know that before being concerned with floating bodies and with the behavior of solids sunk into a liquid — does everyone know that Archimedes was fascinated by the things of the sky? Diving of his own volition from the abysses on high, and dragging us with him, into the abysses below.

But which way is up? Which way down? Our heads are spinning... The indecision the infernal sites of the work plunge us into, as far as our situation in space is concerned, is not the least of the illusions provoked by the structure of the *outre-là.* Let us consider, for instance, how Mille-Pattes's mad gambols at the Tweet Tweet Club, "endless cabrioles between ceiling and floor,"[150] put to the task the most hardened sense of orientation. And not just simple observers but the dancers themselves — who, as is pointed out to us, "were getting ill."[151]

Without subjecting the reader to such extremities, and if we may be permitted for a moment to extrapolate, to ask the history of science and techniques to continue Céline's book in a manner worthy of it, there would be some pertinence, perhaps, in recalling that the bathyscaphe of Professor Auguste Piccard, that deep-sea submarine named, very much to the point, the *Archimedes,* transposes underwater the principle of the free atmospheric balloon. The gas is replaced with gasoline, the ballast is formed by steel shot held by an electromagnet . . . So that the reasons that cause the balloon to rise are exactly the same as those that cause the bathyscaphe to descend.

The amazing coherence of Courtial des Pereires's itinerary goes that far! Beyond the book, so to speak, but with its permission.

Courtial, meanwhile, sure of himself, and going his way, is flying from fall to fall, sinking a little deeper with each catastrophe. This new affair ends as disastrously as the affair of the balloon. A silent partner who changes his mind at the last minute, and it's the abyss; an unfathomable gulf that precipitates the ruin of the enterprise, and lays low all the projects built on it. Where the offices of the *Génitron* once stood, there is now a gaping crater. The frustrated inventors, pushing in their rage one of the diving spheres against the building, have completely devastated it. The only things saved from the disaster will be a few maps of the sky (cosmogonies on "Alfa" paper), a miniature altimeter,[152] and a great scrap of balloon, "a whole yoke of the Archimedes"[153] that Courtial's wife manages to extract from the hole. With infinite pains, but she absolutely wanted it. Displaying the energy of a woman who always gets what she wants, even if she has to turn everything upside down to get it, knock the world topsy-turvy, put the zenith at the nadir. For where are we, after all, that we always need a balloon? And all the way down to the thirty-sixth circle of Hell, will we still have to convince ourselves that the journey is following its course, and that we are still rising?

In saving from the debacle a debris of the *Archimedes,* the midwife has given us the proof that the *Archimedes* will not allow itself to be forgotten, that whether extracted from a hole or pulled out of a closet, it hardly matters — the *Archimedes* rises from the grave and returns to haunt us. Like a lost soul, bound to our steps; an unburied corpse . . . No tomb for the *Archimedes;* no end that doesn't once again draw some new spasm from it, and thereby revive the insoluble question of its final destination. Which is how, finding ourselves one more time with its mortal remains on our hands, we thereby acquire the materials for the envelope of a new aircraft. An ultimate balloon for an ultimate stage?

This stage, the third of the book, we will refer to it, with Céline, as agriculture by radio-tellurism. The idea once again is Courtial's, who has suddenly gotten it into his head to apply to gardening the properties of terrestrial magnetism. Equipped with a homemade wave generator, he is confident he will pour over the vegetables the beneficial rain of electricity, as he likes to say. And we will gladly grant him the expression. But the balloon? As far as we know, a balloon has never been much use for plowing. The worthy woman nursing the thing (a thing, it is clear, that is the midwife's thing) immediately manifests her reprobation, and in the strongest terms: "You're always dealing with things, Courtial, that are none of your business!..." The thing that is his business, and that makes it its business to care for him, we, the readers, certainly know what it is. And she, then! the finicky guardian of the envelope. "His type," she edicts, "it's balloons! Me, I never budged an inch! I never stopped telling him! 'Courtial! your spherical! It's the only thing you know how to do! [...] It's not worth insisting! Your gig, it's ascents! That's the only thing that can get us out!' "154

Profound words, we are willing to admit it, but useless words. In her wisdom (which is, however, extreme), the midwife has not guessed. She seems unaware, Old Mother Sheath, that her good husband couldn't even do what she suspects him of wanting to do. It's true that, thanks to her status, she has an external point of view on the thing. The midwife remains at a distance from the *ustera,* to call it by its name. She is on the other side. But, on that side, she is alone. The world, in the final analysis, is divided in two: given the *ustera* (and if something in this world is given, it couldn't be anything else), there is the *before,* the midwife's station, and there is the *beyond.* Meaning everything over which the midwife extends her domination, and that we could collect under the general heading of hysteria. Hysteria, with Céline, defines what is. And what is, without exceptions.

— But, then, hysteria aside, other than hysteria what is there?

— This question has no answer; it has no meaning. For a simple reason, but conclusive in its simplicity: that there is no outside and that everything is inside, beings and things in the same bag.

— Except if we posit the midwife, as we just did.

—But even this, come to think of it, is of no help to anything or anyone. For even if we were to posit her, and to posit the hypothesis that she is outside, she wouldn't be there to help us come out, to get us out of the bag, but quite on the contrary to put us back into it. To stuff us back in the oven, as it were!

No sooner has Courtial's Irène (oh, the irony of this name!) come to suspect, in her husband, the vaguest urge to flee, that she sets him straight and sends him back to his balloon. Completely unnecessarily, as it turns out. Carried away with enthusiasm,[155] and firing himself up as he narrates the conquests he foresees, Courtial is already all wrapped up... And not in another balloon, which destiny would have maliciously pulled from its pocket, but in the very same balloon, his "spherical," which Irène had reproached him for abandoning, and which will soon, in his craving for horticultural glory, come crashing down on his head.

He has taken two radishes, one from the last cold frame of his own garden (an entirely electrified garden), the other from the yard next door (a vulgar garden). Holding one in the palm of each hand, as in the pans of an imaginary scale, he turns to Ferdinand.

"Compare, Ferdinand! Compare!... Compare! I am not influencing you! Conclude for yourself!... I don't know what she might have told you, Madame des Pereires! But just look!... Examine! Weigh!... Let nothing trouble you!... The fat one: mine!... With telluride! Look! His! Without telluride! Infinitesimal! Compare! There! I will say no more! Why confuse you... Conclusions only!... Conclusions!... what can be done!... What must be done!... 'With'!... [...] So, judge for yourself... Do you understand me? No?... You don't understand? You're just like her!... You don't understand anything!... But, yes! But, yes! exactly! Blind! And the big radish here! You can see it, no? There in your palm? And the little one, you can also see it, no? The puny one! the infinitesimal one!... That little runt of a radish?... What could be simpler than a radish?... No, it isn't simple? Well, you're disarming me!... And a very fat radish, Ferdinand?... Suppose an enormous radish!... Here, big as your head!... Suppose I blow it up like that, with telluric flashes, me! that tiny little ridiculous!... Well? Huh? Like a real balloon!... Ah? and that I make a hundred thousand like that!... radishes! Always radishes! More and more voluminous... [...] to take the radish as an example! I could have picked the turnip!... But let us take the radish!... The surprise will be greater! Ah, then! I'm going to take care of it!... Completely from now on!... Completely... you hear me... Do you see from here?..."

He's still gripping me, he drags me toward the view... toward the south side... From there, that's right... we can see all of Paris!... It's like an immense beast, the city, it's crushed on the horizon... It's black, it's grey... it changes... it smokes... it makes a sad noise, it roars all softly... it's like a carapace... notches, holes, thorns that catch the sky... He doesn't give a shit, des Pereires, he's talking... He addresses the scene... He straightens up against the railing... His voice goes deep... It carries over there... it swells over the quarries of landslides...

"Look, Ferdinand! Look!..." I widen a little more... I make a supreme effort... I really am tired... I wouldn't want him to start all over...

"Further, Ferdinand! Further!... Do you see it now the city? Over there! Do you see Paris? the capital?..."

"Yes! Yes!... Yes!... That's right!..."

"They eat, don't they?..."

"Yes! Monsieur Courtial!..." [...]

"Say, they eat, Ferdinand!... They eat! Yes, there! they eat!... and I, poor lunatic! Where was I?... Oh, futile valor! I am punished! Struck!... I'm bleeding! It's only fair! Forget? Me!... Ah! Ah! Ah! I'm going to take them for what they are!... Where they are! By their bellies, Ferdinand! Not by their heads! By their bellies! Customers for their bellies! I'm dealing with the belly, Ferdinand!... [...] Enough by the mind! Funerals!... With the guts, Ferdinand!... With the colic ferments! Ouah! With the dung! Oh! to wade! Pouh! But it's great! Challenge? Here I am! What kind of seeds do they think I'm made of? Courtial! Winner of the Popincourt Prize! The Nicham and all others! one thousand seven hundred and twenty-two flights!... With radishes! By the radishes! Yes! I'll show you! You too, you'll see me! Oh, Zenith! Oh, my Irène! Oh, my terrible jealous one!... Not an hour to lose!..."[156]

Radishes, then. In their green tufts. Little Montgolfières crested with flames: inverted balloons... "I could have picked the turnip," he says. But he immediately gives up on the turnip. His choice, for the purposes of the demonstration, has to settle on the radish. From the Latin *radicem*: root. A rounded version of the *raphanus sativus,* our pink radish is essentially nothing but a bulbous excrescence; a bloated root he'll just have to blow up with great telluric flashes, for the unbelievable wedding he dreams of to be finally celebrated. Wedding of fluid and matter, the union of the opposite principles of air and earth, at the end of which, however, it isn't matter that is lightened, but only the root that finds the momentum to go a little deeper than it normally would...

Just as the plant sinks its root, just as the root grows in the opposite direction from the stem, the balloon imperturbably follows its trajectory.

Which confirms the fact that the Célinian balloon is indeed the radical balloon. Balloon that comes out of the root, yet still goes quite a way with it. As if it were animated by a curious geotropism.

Geotropism also of the words with which the orator follows it. One of those flights Courtial has the habit of, but meant, this time, for the city, for that Paris lying way over there. Paris the Belly, yawning for all to see. Already, since *Death on the Installment Plan*, there was nothing left of the basins, the fountains of the Jardin des Tuileries, but a crater "all groaning with abysses and drunks"[157] — anality triumphant having soon found in the volcano a scene on its scale. To which it will thereafter stick, never to forsake it. "Once you're there," concludes *Journey*, "you're good and there."[158] The fact of the matter is that *Normance*, some twenty years later, is still there. Starting with its dedication to Pliny the Elder, which evinces its desire to exalt the city in its eruptive dimension alone. The Butte, the Vesuvius: same difference. Same foul vessel.

The chosen vessel, perfectly summarized, on a smaller scale, by the town of Blême-le-Petit where they have finally set up their "telluric bazaar." A small village, what they call a hole. That truly is, in fact, nothing but a hole, to which Céline immediately gives the perfection of a gulf. To dive into it is to hit bottom. When you have sunk too low, there no longer are degrees in abjection. The only effect of Courtial's infernal machinery and of its orgies of waves will have been, as we know, to provoke the anger of the gods. To awaken the Genie of Larvae, the Spirit of Decay. The earth, by their fault, has become corrupted, and they are mired in refuse. Only one place has been spared, the tavern of Salignons-en-Mesloir, a nearby burg. Which is where, periodically, the master and his disciple go to pick themselves up . . . At the sign of La Grosse Boule, the Big Ball. And the sign speaks for itself. How could it be more clearly stated that, if they are there, with their feet in the mire, they have kept their heads in the clouds? . . . Even at its worst moments, not once will the text have strayed from the line it had set for itself. We are always in a balloon, we are in it up to here. Yes, till the bitter end. Till the death of the balooneer, till his remains, which are still part of the flight plan;

included in the program, if not, more roundly (sold, wrap it up!), in the balloon itself.

⌐⌐

The body was found on a winter morning. Caught in the ice and the dirt of the path, as if it were already trying to reintegrate matter; as if death were but a birth in reverse. The corpse is even in the position of a fetus. But a headless fetus. The head has entirely disappeared under a hood of flesh, red, bloody, spongy. A placenta, the midwife doesn't doubt it for a second. Unless, in her delirium, she isn't imagining she has covered him with it herself, like a covetous mother trying, through this magical gesture, to reincorporate her product. Or to fill, at least, the great void, the abyss she sometimes feels yawning inside her, ever since they took everything out. "All of it 'bald' from one day to the next! . . . with a scalpel!"[159]

For the time has come to remember that Irène has undergone *the complete,* as they still say in the French countryside; meaning a hysterectomy. But here we should favor the popular expression, more evocative and more moving. Because in the fantasy of totality women thus ask us to share, like a secret, however, that we never asked to know, there is probably a little of what Lucette Finas names *the appalling feminine.* And which only has so much power over men's imagination because men, precisely, feel that it cannot be reduced to some simple mass of viscera. For them, it is always more than an organ. Perhaps it is not even an organ at all. It is something immense and vague at the same time, something deep: it is depth itself, unfathomable. And the frightening mystery of women.

Irène's hysterectomy is set at the heart of the book as its most secret operation. Take everything out of Irène, and suddenly everything comes together; the argument of the balloon takes shape, develops before your eyes . . . Starting with the balloon itself, Irène's ball and chain. Yes, the interesting, the oh so terribly interesting depth that woman conceals within her bosom, is also what she has to drag behind her. Irène's balloon is the counterpart of Clémence's bale; her *Archimedes* and her *Zealous* having both become, the one sustaining the other, a sort of uterus, an artificial organ whose pieces father and son tirelessly glue back together: a uterine fetish that she, on her side, devotedly worships, even

going so far as to gather the crowds around it on all those Sunday Sab-
baths she forces her husband to hold. Look, she seems to be saying, look
how it blooms, enormous flower of flesh; and look how it rises! . . .

But, given that this is a public celebration, it is hard to ignore the
fact that it doesn't rise so well. Impressive monument, big balloon, all
puffed up, swollen with its own importance, but even heavier for all the
hopes placed in it. The hope, or rather Irène's conviction, that motherhood is a reality that resists the wear of time, and that a mother, no
matter what is done to her, remains a mother; that in spite of the reversals, in spite of the disasters, like the *Zealous* she must always last. And
if Irène's conviction so easily prevails over Courtial's doubts, it's because
the road he is on, the path he is blindly following, bypasses through her
fantasy; because the balloon is just as necessary to him as to her.

I said the balloon; I did not say the airplane, that fake progress, that
unnatural infatuation. It's the balloon Courtial needs, the descending
machine.

As famous in its own realm, and for similar reasons, as the case, famous in the annals of medicine, of the female patient Doctor Mirmilleux
was once called upon to treat, "a total metritis, with a uterus that just
tumbled down, rotten, a sponge of pus."[160] The most beautiful example
of a prolapsed uterus ever observed, the most extraordinary womb descent! Enough to solidly found a reputation: "That woman," Doctor Mirmilleux explains to his colleague Bardamu, "made my success in three
districts." But the publisher of the *Génitron* doesn't solicit the favors of
the crowd any differently. The truth of the matter is that the fantasy of
aerostation only adds another chapter to the history of obstetrics, to
the history that Céline, ever since his doctoral thesis, considers the history of our damnation. Carved upon the pediment of the work like a
modern version of the myth of the fall, the question of motherhood
remains vigilantly on guard: Sphinx awaiting her Oedipus. Alas! there
are no more Oedipuses. A vanished breed. And without Oedipus, no
answer to the question, no solution to the riddle.

So that Courtial never claimed, when he was advertising his screwy
balloon, to be modifying in any way the normal course of things. The
fall is an irreversible movement. Against which we are therefore help-
less. Lucky if we can just barely give ourselves the illusion of anticipat-

ing it, of keeping a few lengths ahead of it. Humanity, for centuries, has thus been racing ahead of its fall. And it even dares glorify itself of this race, of this frantic race, under the name of progress. Hence, in resisting progress, in at least choosing the balloon over the airplane, Courtial is choosing to let himself be overtaken. Envelope of the spherical, bale of Clémence or bell of the Passage, no matter what you call it, the thing is gaining on him. The thing because of which we fall, but which is simply, all things considered, the fall itself, the interminable falling of the thing. And Courtial's chance. His chance finally to be caught, and for all the ambiguities of his case to be wrapped up.

⤸

Gesture of the bird-catcher pulling the hood back over his fine hawk, she has thrown over the body, as it is being brought back, a corner of her skirt; and then "her great Scottish coat to wrap his block better."[161] The midwife, however, with this double gesture, is far from having fulfilled her duty, which is to help the dead man be reborn, but be reborn, so to speak, backward.

Thus, barely home, she is already begging the gendarme: "Can I cover him?" As if he wasn't already covered. And cover him with what, anyway?

> I was wondering what she wanted to put on him? . . . sheets? . . . We didn't have any . . . We'd never had any in Blême . . . We did have covers, but they weren't but rags anymore . . . and absolutely rotten! . . . [. . .] The gendarme didn't want any of that! . . . He wanted her to ask the Brigadier herself for permission . . . But the Brigadier was snoring . . . He had sunk on the table . . . We could see him through the door . . . The other hicks were playing manille . . .
>
> "Wait! I'll go! . . ." he said in the end . . . "Don't touch him before I come back . . ." But she couldn't wait any longer . . .
>
> "Ferdinand! you, you go! Hurry, my boy! Go get me quick in my mattress . . . you know, through the slit . . . ! where I stick the straw? . . . Search! Deep with your arm toward the feet! . . . you'll find the big piece! . . . You know . . . from the *Archimedes*! . . . The red one . . . the one that's all red! . . . It's pretty big, you know . . . It'll be big enough . . . It'll go all the way around! . . . Bring it to me! there! right now . . . I'm not moving! . . . Hurry, quick! . . ."
>
> It was absolutely exact . . . I found it immediately . . . It sure stank of rubber . . . It's the piece she had saved from the depths of the rubble the night of the disaster . . . She unfolded it in front of me . . . she spread it on

the ground...It was still a good piece of cloth. It's the color that had changed...It wasn't scarlet anymore...it had turned all brown...She wouldn't let me help her to wrap Courtial in it...She did all that herself...She especially couldn't move him...She slid under the corpse the whole piece of fabric nice and flat...extremely gently, I have to say...She had more than enough yardage to wrap the whole thing up...And all the meat of the head found itself closed in too...The Brigadier was watching us work...The other had woken him up..."So," he was yelling from over there..."You're going to hide him still?...Huh?...You won't quit, then?"

"Don't scold me, mon bon monsieur!...[...] I beg you!...Monsieur l'Ingénieur!..." That's how she started calling him all of a sudden: Monsieur l'Ingénieur, Mister Engineer!...She was starting to scream again...

"He went up, Monsieur l'Ingénieur! You never saw him, you others!...You can't believe me, of course!...But Ferdinand, he saw him!...Huh, that you saw him, Ferdinand?...How well he went up!...You remember, don't you, my boy? Tell it to them!...Tell them, my boy!...Me, they won't believe me!...Mercy! Sweet Jesus! I'm going to say a prayer! Ferdinand! Monsieur l'Ingénieur! Mother Mary! Mary! Lamb of Heaven! Pray for us! [...] He went up, Monsieur l'Ingénieur, he went up, it was magical!...Up to eighteen hundred meters he went up!...[...] He went up two hundred times!...a hundred times!...I can't remember my love!...Two hundred!...Six!...Six hundred times!...I don't remember!...I don't remember anything!...It's horrible!...Monsieur l'Ingénieur!...Three hundred!...More! Far more!...I don't know!...[...] Three thousand!...Ten thousand!...Jesus! Fifteen!...Eighteen hundred meters!...Oh, Jesus! Ferdinand! Can't you say something?...That's too much!...Goddammit, shit!..." She was losing herself in the numbers again...[162]

As Courtial's only shroud, the famous yoke, the last scrap of the *Archimedes*...But as his viaticum too, to help him cross from this life to the next. Isn't death, after all, the "Cast off!" that the poor woman, for his only funeral oration, is desperately miming in her madness? Yes, certainly, the great leap. The leap to the stars. The very last pages of *Death on the Installment Plan* open to the infinity of interstellar space. "The sky was truly clear!...I think I'd never seen it so sharply...it amazed me that night how bright it was [...] A unique chance, exceptional." And then, as in a novel by Camille Flammarion, as in *Lumen,* as in *Stella*—the specter of Courtial des Pereires.

I recognized every star... Nearly every one, basically... and I sure knew the names!... He'd bored me enough, the other customer with his trajectory orbits!... It's funny how I had retained them without any good will too... it must be said... The "Canopus" and the "Andromeda"... they were there Rue Saint-Denis... Right above the roof across the street... A little to the right the "Waggoner" the one winking a little into "Libra"... I could recognize them all right straight... Not to mess up on "Ophiuchus"... that's already a little tougher... It'd be easy to take for Mercury, if there wasn't the asteroid!... That's the famous trick... But the "Cradle" and the "Hair"... you nearly always confuse them... It's on "Pelleas" that you screw up but good! That night, no mistake!... It was Pelleas on the button!... to the north of Bacchus!... Blind man's work... Even the "Great Nebula of Orion" was absolutely sharp... between the "Triangle" and "Ariadne"... So, then, impossible to get lost... A unique chance, exceptional!... In Blême, we'd only seen it once! during the whole year Orion... And we looked for it every night!... He would sure have been delighted, the child of the lens, to be able to observe it so sharp... He who was always grousing after it... He had published a book on "Asteroid landmarks" and even a whole chapter on the "Antiope Nebula"... It was a veritable surprise to be observing it in Paris... where the sky is rightly famous for its filthy opacity!... I could hear him jubilating, Courtial, in a case like this!... I could hear him going off, there, next to me, on the bench...

"You see, son, the one trembling?... that's not even a planet... That's just a lure!... It's not even a landmark!... An asteroid!... It's just a vagabond!... you hear me?... Watch out!... A vagabond!... Just wait maybe two million years, maybe it'll give a profuse light!... Then it'll yield a plate, maybe!... Right now it's just a finagle and you'll lose your whole picture!... And that's all you'd get from it... Ah! it's tricky, a "Vaporide," my little brat!... Not even an "attraction" comet... Don't let yourself be fooled, Jack! The stars are tarts!... Watch out before setting off! Ah! they aren't little white dwarfs! Now bite that! As a dynameter! Quarter second exposure! Burns your film in quarter tenths! Terrible they are! Ah! a real drag! Watch out, Ninette! Plates aren't cheap at the 'Puces'!... Ah, but no, my dear Bishop!...".[163]

A whole production, with its *stars* that shine for just one night, while down below the little whores are turning the men on, the ladies of the Rue Saint-Denis, all the oblivion merchants... They have beautiful names, the stars, it's true, but they're just assumed names, spangles for the stage, fool's gold. Come the day, nothing but Maries, Isabelles, or Louises. Besides, they are tarts, and also vagabonds. Daughters of Eve, just like the others. No more dancers in the sky than there are on earth.

And then, the sky: easy said. There is sky and sky. Where exactly will we locate it, Céline's sky?

Right, perhaps, where Jules Laforgue locates his: in the bosoms of the galaxies, a muddle of Milky Ways, a whirlwind of embryonic worlds, in the womb of all the yet-to-comes...Such is the place, "birthplace where we have no birth," "royal place where we have no seat";[164] such are the shores, the distant lands Courtial must have reached: a miraculously rejuvenated Courtial, as if he had swum the river of genesis upstream and was now but a seed amid seed, a germ amid germs. A Vaporide himself: a word that has to be invented, because there is no word to say that. Because it doesn't have a name in any language.

Of course it is probably just a hallucination. Ferdinand is on edge, Ferdinand is at the end of his rope...But a hallucination that is the anticipated realization of an impossible desire. We can feel the sort of passability it supposes before the ineluctable. Before the necessity of being swallowed in your mother's cloacal body, so that your own body can finally emerge, clean, washed of its uterine filth, of its cadaveric corruptions. Like the astral body of the occultists, barely a shade of being; something like a maybe, and which wouldn't even have acquired the property of registering on photographic plates. A light situation, "between death and existence"—the same claimed by the author of *Trifles* when he declares, at the end of his harrowing book, that he wants to "go ghost."[165] To Célinize (Selenize?) himself, that is really all he wants; and what his Cascade wants, and what all of his Courtials, his Sosthènes, his Silenuses want, when, drunk with desire, they go dancing to the moon.

The work we are dealing with will have been little more, when all is said and done, than the operation of this Célinization. Here, in short, is a work aimed at, if not the night star, at least its author's name: yes, the very name of Céline.

—In that case, he has reached his goal, forever in the sky. Céline on his cloud, starting with the first page, with the title page of his first novel.

—Certainly, he is there: how to deny it? But without being there. Being there only in thought, being there only in project. It is at that place, beside his name (beside, let us be clear, his grandmother's name; his mother's mother, and as such the only person with a valid claim to the work, as is attested, through the permanence of its initial dedication, maintained without any regrets or reticences for over thirty years, by Céline's faithfulness to a conception of genealogy all the more ideal in that, reversing the natural order of generations that will have us be our mother's sons, it eliminated motherhood), it is thus at that place, upstream, that Céline is waiting for Ferdinand, Louis's envoy, the envoy of the one who remained downstream, lost in his vale of tears. Waiting for Ferdinand to have completed his journey, if the word is still appropriate and we can call a journey the perilous crossing of the dark maternal continent. Céline, on the cover of his books, Céline waiting for himself, on the other side of his mother. *Outre-là* . . .

3

PASSAGES

Baraboum!

We are at the concert, and the artist is preluding.

Boro, to make room, he pushed everything back, to the right, to the left...
with great kicks [...] then he freed his piano but ferociously... to get all
the junk to collapse... everything cluttering him... the whole Capernaum!... *Baraboum!*... finally settled stool, everything wedged!... go for
the waltz!... Arpeggios, trills, the sauce!... and I know you...[1]

Baraboum! and go for the waltz... Let us make no mistake on the
baraboum. The aforenamed Boro may be fat, "a pachyderm as to weight,"[2]
but, once at the keyboard, he goes in for the nuance, goes in for the
arpeggio, "all acrobat, all stuntsman, all imp."[3] Fairy fingers.

The *baraboum,* then? Let us say a professional reflex. Boro is short
for Borokrom. And he was called that "because of his chemical knowledge, of the bombs he had made;"[4] and that he continued to make, tossing them here and there, when the mood was on him, to then go sit at the
piano when he had nothing left to do. To play between two explosions.

A real case, then, this Borokrom! But not at all... Far from being, to
the rule, the exception we would expect, the pianist of *Guignol's band* is
its most perfect illustration.

Let us change books, moving, for instance, from *Guignol's band I* to
its sequel, *Guignol's band II,* and we will hear the music being announced

106

by the same burst of thunder. "*Baradaboum!* [...] an appalling crash [...] a hundred thousand cauldrons! maniacs! [...] the atrocious uproar!... it sweeps crushes crams the windows! [...] ah! my poor ears! Ground my head! O scrap heap!"[5]

A bottle of gas that just exploded. Well, gas, let us be clear... Not the ordinary product of the distillation of coal, but a suffocating gas, a vesicatory, corrosive, and especially explosive gas, the most merciless, the most murderous of all combat gases, the *Ferocious 92*. Ferociously new— ah, you can say that; still, as far as we are concerned, less remarkable than its inventor, a sweet dreamer who "professed Botanics and the Harpsichord in Dorchester."[6] A musician first and foremost, who only deals in chemistry, his hobbyhorse, "in his spare time."

↫

From the musical bomb to the gas-producing harpsichord... Not to forget Marie's piano in *Progress*.

Marie plays the piano. She has barely begun when the maid comes in. The activity on stage starts up again.
THE MAID: I've come for the gas!
GASTON: The gas!
MARIE: That gas!
ALL TOGETHER: That gas!
GASTON: It's terrible, it's awful!
MARIE: What?
GASTON: But everything! the maid! that one! that! the gas![7]

For a long time, I wondered what the man from the gas company was doing in this pianistic interlude. But I finally remembered that in the Passage Choiseul, in that gas bell ("thousand of mantles"),[8] Céline declares having witnessed the end of songs. "In the beginning," he explains to Pierre Dumayet in a televised interview, "before the war of—'14—every time he came in...a shop girl...she would start to sing. She sang for the whole length of his crossing of the Passage. And then after '14, there was no more singing in the Passage. It's a sign of the times."[9]

Another sign of the times: nowadays, he specifies, "it's lit by electricity. No more gas."

Yes, cut the gas, and *finita la musica . . .*

We can, however, very well wonder now whether or not Céline was ever aware of the strange gramophone marketed, under the name *Flame-phone,* by a British firm in December 1922. It was a gas gramophone, which made use of the naturally amplifying powers of the flame. A power you can easily ascertain for yourself by holding a tuning fork above a lit Bunsen burner. The acoustic properties of singing flames have actually been known for a long time. They were put to use, for instance, in 1872, by Frédéric Kastner, from Strasbourg, with his pyrophone. A gas organ, this time, or a flame organ, and which gave its inventor such satisfaction that he even thought of applying its principle to a system of lighting by musical fixtures . . .

I can't help but imagine the emotion Céline would have felt in listening, thus relayed by the flames, to the voices of Caruso and Lucrezia Bori in the candle scene of the first act of *La Bohème.* Céline who, in *Normance,* will precisely manage to have two of his characters rehearse Puccini's lyrical work (a work first performed in France in 1898 at the Opéra-Comique, a step from the Passage Choiseul, therefore) — under the bombs and in front of a Paris in flames.[10]

᠆

— But what about the bombs?

— Precisely, "it didn't prevent anything, the bombs." On the contrary, "it shook the place up real good." And then, "it would bring all the fads back, all the great 1900 crazes, the world topsy-turvy, what an apotheosis it would be, France queen of the world, of the musette and the most Fine Arts."[11] Not to mention that bombs . . . Just look around you. Arlette, in Montmartre. "Before, she was bored, now she won't stop singing, even here she's crooning on all fours, still in costume and everything . . . under the showers of the R.A.F."[12]

Nothing like a bombardment to get your voice going, to warm up your skills. Or to untwist your fingers. In this connection, isn't a soldier like General Gebhardt, a cavalry officer in command of a panzer group on the Russian front, worth a President Truman? The former excelled in the ditty; the latter, under whose mandate occurred the terrible explosion of Hiroshima, had a strong penchant for the piano. To each prince according to his size, it goes without saying. Céline only concedes a small amateur's talent to the modest general;[13] he recognizes, however, a prodigious talent in the man who dared to unleash the nuclear fire on Japan, sitting him at (his own words) "Amadeus's harpsichord" itself.[14] We'll forgive him for the understatement!

Just as I will be forgiven, I would at least like to hope so, for the thunderous opening that the fable dictated to me . . . But that the fable, however, hardly explains. What does the fable say? It says nothing. But, saying nothing, it imposes upon the reader a certain image of the body. Always the same image, ever since the thesis—the introduction, the official act by which Céline sets up shop in literature—image set at the tympanum of all his works. Yes, this image is first. Inaugural and founding. Created, made of a piece, from the ear. The left ear, to be precise. But why still be precise? For who is talking about ears? It isn't an ear anymore, it's a gigantic convolvulus. And all the more gigantic because its dimensions increase in proportion to the "fifteen hundred noises" it not only collects, but, in collecting, especially seems to increase the power of: "an immense racket," "the organs of the Universe," "the Opera of the deluge." To use Céline's words, to use the language dictated to us, in its prologue, by *Death on the Installment Plan*.[15]

And thus the right language in the right place. Because in the very place where others display their noble nature, where, as they say, they speak heart-to-heart, Céline has chosen to expose his ear. His great horn of an ear, like the impressive louver-boarding from which will henceforth echo the *bam! bam! bam!* of the three knocks, which at the theater announce that the show is about to begin.

Certain psychoanalyses have invented a name to designate such organs. They call them hypochondriac organs.[16] These are organs that have the faculty of behaving within the body like independent bodies. Added bodies, whose growth the subject witnesses within himself, aghast.

Aghast, but not entirely powerless. Striving, quite on the contrary, against these foreign bodies. Working to expel them. Hence, perhaps, the dins Céline deafens us with, in texts more and more stuffed with onomatopoeias. And *brroum,* and *crrac,* and *vrang, dingg, pingg, vrromb, rra, vlaf, vrr, plaouf, paradaboum, bromb, broum, brang, firrt, vlooouf . . .* To stick to a few specimens, taken from a merely two-page-long suite!

There are a great many onomatopoeias in comic books, but nothing next to what is in Céline's work. And what is in the work is nothing next to what is in its author's head. In the head of the author of *Normance*. "If I gave you," says he, "all the 'brrooms' you'd be clocked, couldn't take it! flabbergasted, quibblers, prostrated . . . as dazed as I myself! you too would look for the table, run under the table! . . . You'd splutter for centuries: 'What? What? . . . vat!' I'm not inflicting one one-thousandth of the 'broumms' on you."[17]

But it's also because he values it so much, and because the onomatopoeia (or what the onomatopoeia is the symptom of, at least) has too much value for him not to soon want to put a term to his prodigality. We are touching here on something essential, which is that in the end Céline is just like every hypochondriac. That, just like them, he is far too attached to the organ he keeps complaining about for his ostensible efforts to get rid of it not to be doomed to fail. Oh! of course, he'll always be ready to play you the little tune; and, from book to book, to play it is as much as necessary: "a little shard in the left ear,"[18] "a little piece of iron,"[19] "a bullet inside . . . maybe two,"[20] "the bullet in the head and the big bell"[21] . . . No more bullet in Céline's head (must we repeat it?) than bullet in his ear. But a dysfunction — that, on the contrary, is certain — of the otolithic apparatus; one of those little ear stones, a loose stone sowing its wild oats, yet that he values like the pupil of his eye. Like the cornerstone of his work. An entire work built on this base, resting on it . . . A work, rather, that will never tire, as long as it lasts, of going *clopin-clopant*, of hobbling back, of regularly hobbling back to renew itself in the ear.

Actually, it's all one and the same. *Clopin, clopant* are both derived from the ancient adjective *clop*, which is formed on the late Latin *clop-pus*, which, in turn, with its double letter, the expressive twinning of its middle consonant, so characteristic of the adjectives designating a deformity, truly seems to be no more than an onomatopoeia evoking the heavy step of the lame. Compare it, for instance, to *scloppus*, whence comes *esclot* or *esclop* — the name in Dauphiné of a sort of clog — which, on its side, imitates the clicking, the loud lap you can produce by puffing up your cheeks and introducing a finger into your mouth. *Ploc!*[22] Émile Littré, after all, was perhaps not so far from the truth when he sought the origin of the verb *clocher* (to limp and to be cockeyed, to go wrong or not quite right) in the limping of the bell — the *cloche* — in motion. An error, according to etymology, but an error that Céline will take advantage of more than once, making the legless stub of a man of *Normance,* Jules, the John, Fanfan la Musique,[23] into a bell-ringer — but only after having depicted himself, it's only fair to recognize it, hopping and skipping in full peal: "it's like a bell that won't quit."[24] To the point that it is difficult to decide, when Céline, for instance, protests, "I'm deaf in the left,"[25] if he isn't at the same time complaining about his bad leg.

Clocher, in fact, is **cloppicare.* A fact, all things considered, that Céline, and even Littré, weren't so far from. The intuition of the lexicographer, if not the sort of sixth sense that the writer eventually acquires, puts them both on the right path. Besides which the ear, in such matters, is often a reliable guide. How many untimely, incongruous noises doesn't language thus remember, associated with the hesitant step, with the peg leg of the cripple? Mouth sounds, bell sounds, clogs scraping, here comes Lameness and its great traveling band: " 'labyrinthine disorders of Ménière' with orchestra."[26]

The lame, all on their own, the lame, limping, vanish into the deep landscape of hearing. Into the dark cavern whose vaults echo and amplify mysterious cracklings. Rather similar, actually, to the *little bangs* of our astrophysics, an astrophysics that has finally abandoned the hypothesis of the *big bang,* given up on the theory of a homogeneous and isotropic expansion of the universe... No, the universe was not made in one shot. But, from explosion to explosion, the universe is never done making itself: *brroum, crrac, dingg, pingg*... Thus Céline's work in its dynamic instability.

↫

Bombing, blooming: second after second. And, at each second, in tune. In unison, so to speak. Such is the rhythm, the process of this text. No matter which end you take it by, this end, that end, no matter. From one end to the other, you can read the effects of the dissymmetry that opposes, in Céline, an ear that crackles, that buzzes and whistles, to an ear that sings, vibrates harmoniously. A fruitful dissymmetry. As fruitful as the dissymmetry that can legitimately be credited to the ophthalmias the founding fathers of French realism suffered from.

What might have become of the real, and of its apparition in literature, without Flaubert's epilepsy,[27] without Maupassant's accommoda-
tion paralysis,[28] without Zola's myopia . . . I cannot even conceive it. All
I know is that from Céline onward the question is no longer the same:
having become, from a question of eye that it was up to him, a question of ear. The image of the body is radically altered. And, along with
it, literature's own representation of the world.

↩

Between being cross-eyed and being lame in one ear, there's a difference.
The difference, simply, that separates a Zola from a Céline. The sentence
of a Zola from the sentence of a Céline . . . What is a sentence, for Céline? Melody and racket, solidarily. It is rather rare, when all is said and
done, for Céline to grant himself the facility of offering a separate depiction of one of the two. When the flying fortresses fly overhead, he'll
also go turn on that gramophone, "three horns," a fantastic fanfare machine, in a carpenter's shop: full speed, everything at once, "the records,
and the saw, the Diesel and the bombs."[29] Or else, one night, during an
alarm, and like a new Edison, winding up a little nightingale that "sends
out its triplets barely the sirens are over."[30]

And everything, here, is in the adverb. *Barely* has the screaming, the
wailing of the siren ceased (Céline's classic recourse to extreme timbres,
to the "high caterwauls":[31] sharp fifes, rancid fiddles, strident brass, unusual instruments he shares a taste for with Satie), than the nightingale
immediately warbles. Without there being the least solution of conti-
nuity. And as if the one were merely taking over from the other. As if
the one and the other, putting our senses to the lie, partook of the same
nature.

A question of appreciation, obviously. But when you have an ear it
comes by instinct. Consider that bird of ill omen, Jules, nightingale of
the Apocalypse. The way he too has of improvising tender tunes on the
bugle, "to a counterecho of sirens."[32]

After all, how often, in Céline's text, don't noise and song thus vie with
each other in politeness, if not trade roles? The noise is in tune. I'm
taking it down for you, says Céline. And it is true that his sound effects
are a sort of musical notation. Or, to quote Cendrars, that as disruptive

as they may be, they remain, in spite of all, inscribed "within a harmonic scale."[33]

Which is how *Normance*, the book of bombs, will, in the continuum of its detonations, reveal itself as the most refined treatise on harmony ever written. Having reached the limits of deafness under the repeated hammering of the stereotypes, under the bass drum of the onomatopoeia, Céline's ear, first anomaly, loses nothing of its selective capacities. To the point that the reproaches he feigns to address to himself ("Well! well!... he could change tones a bit! *brang! broum!* how many pages already of his *broums*?")[34] hardly conceal the coquetry of an author less interested in making amends than in ironically underlining the immense delicacy of his sampling: a noise hunter, as much at ease before a din as an herbalist collecting simples. No matter how brutal the pounding may be, the characteristics of the sounds, far from being crushed into each other, as would have only been natural, exalt themselves in the singularity of their respective harmonic temperaments. Not an explosion that doesn't immediately become a musical object and that doesn't as such find its place in a graduated scale of timbres.

Because there is bomb and bomb, *broum* and *broum*: "one minute, it's thunderous 'boums'... and then after, it's trains,"[35] but "trains of melinite."[36] Come on, pay attention! clocked or not. And, in spite of the explosions and their anesthetic effect, please, distinguish! In spite of the saraband, "saraband all over the octaves! that it's a grinding of atrocious sounds."[37] And "the cannon in the distance! The tambourining...,"[38] the deep voice of the cannon that, regular and even, has been echoing at the horizon of the work ever since *Journey*; the "*blom belollom belom* that was a sort of millstone, in the depths of which passed the era,"[39] but that still lets you hear the music. A "rather sinister, rather Wagnerian, rather deep" music, but in which there was still something for the music lover: a "*berceuse rémoulette*," a "lullaby blended," if we may be allowed to apply to *Normance* the oh so suggestive expression of *Guignol's band*,[40] in which we also find *rémoule, rémoulade*, with the same intention of associating the blender to the hand organ grinding out its lament.

The image, in its polysemy, speaks for itself. It's when everything has been run through the blender, and thus ground and reduced to a pulp, that the properly musical operation can finally begin. And its dissociative action be set into motion. For, if bombs pulverize, music atomizes: it's a particle physics. "It has to turn! that's the great secret . . . never any slowdown, never any cease! to be strewn like seconds, each one with its little malice, its little dancing and hurried soul, but goddammit, the next one pushing it! . . . knocking it over with a trill . . . jumping."[41] No harder than that, after all, and it's the whole trick: "the great secret." Whether it's Borokrom — "rigadadoon!" — spouting his same old tune (since he's the one, whirling through the harmonies, possessed "by twenty little devils in his fingers,"[42] who was fluttering "on the ivories," playing it "blended" in the example I just cited), or the Allies — "rabadaboum!" — unrolling their carpet of bombs on the Butte. Just the one little detail, the detail that saves. In both cases. The "little malice" that can make a difference even in the undifferentiated. But this supposes an uncommon exquisiteness of hearing, to consider only the violence of the aggressions inflicted on the sense in question; an aptitude to compare thunders, to disassociate each one's acoustic qualities; and also, of course, the art of keeping their trace, the art of retranscribing them thanks to a particular notation, a *phonography*[43] — which, going the practice of the onomatopoeia one better in subtlety, engages it in an absolutely dizzying process of complexification[44] that consecrates, each time, and in extremis, the triumph of negentropy over entropy.

A triumph commemorated by the list below. A sort of ultrasound, although this is an expression that mainly belongs to the language of medical imaging. For, obviously, there is no more image here than paintings: *Normance* speaks, on the contrary, for the end of the picturesque, of "the pictorial genre."[45] Ever since the planes, in the sky of Paris, have overturned the colors and smashed the palette, it is clear that a page has been turned in the history of representations, and that the new page beginning here resembles the *sonorous* page that Blaise Cendrars, that the author of *Dan Yack,* was already calling for.[46]

Just a page; a few bars, for lack of the complete piece. At least this page goes to the heart of the matter: from the classic *boum* to its Célinian variation *broum.* Nearly, under his pen, a generic term. Wherever the usage would require the word *noise,* he puts *broum* or *braoum:* "I didn't start just yesterday with my *braoums!* . . . ," "*Brrroum! Brrroum!* it'd only

be 'brrroums' my story if I let myself be stupefied...but no! but no!...
details! precisions! I'm not losing you in the 'broums'!..., " "the bombs,
they know...but not these limp broums...and it's not over...the
'broum' of meat bouncing."[47]

Broum here, and *broum* there too. It's the noise par excellence, the
noise in the absolute. Uncomparable. A raw quantitative, defying the
imagination, as all nonmeasurable quantities defy it.

We can be all the more surprised, then, to see its material form vary
from page to page; at least not remain identical to itself, but, even if
imperceptibly, alter its appearance. Caught in the network, which we
could call inexhaustible, of its ornamentation: quavers, mordent, *grup-
petto,* appoggiatura (these are barely metaphors); and in the unfolding,
especially, of its chromatic values. A single blow of the bass drumstick,
perhaps, but never the same color, never the same timbre: such, here, is
the rule. An imperious rule, which holds that, under the reign of the
quantitative (must I insist on the intensity of the shock wave, the extraordinary speed of its propagation?), the qualitative must never abdi-
cate any of its powers of discrimination. On the contrary, it even seems
that they grow finer, that they are never as precise as when the discomfort of listening is increasing and, in matters of audition, the threshold
of tolerance has been crossed.

But so much delicacy in the midst of the hullabaloo: it's Dionysus Musician. The god of unsteadiness, the god of tripping, the god who makes
chaos sing. A music conquered from noise, compromising with it, open
to arrangements; and in that, concerting.

Céline is certainly not Bartók. Far from it. Nonetheless, there is, dis-
seminated throughout *Normance,* the first rudiments of a concerto for
percussion and celesta. All the materials are there, even if the book does
not presume, or does not seem to presume, as to their arrangement. Ex-
ceptionally rich materials; and all the more exceptional, let us repeat,
inasmuch as we are dealing, where they are concerned, with quantities
whose values are not fixed but constantly variable.

One will perhaps be convinced of it by examining the theoretical trajectory (it is, however, only a reconstitution, but an exemplary one) described throughout the book by the exploration of the harmonic possi-
bilities of a single, of a very basic, stroke of the kettledrum:

Boum (p. 45)

Rabadaboum (p. 45) *Paradaboum* (p. 101)

Badaboum (p. 255) *Baraboum* (p. 123) *Baradroum* (p. 125)

Baradrroum (p. 188) *Baradadrang* (p. 128)

Bataclan (p. 341)

Taraboum (p. 146) *Tarraboum* (p. 196) *Tarrraboum* (p. 113)

Taradaraboum (p. 55) *Trararaboum* (p. 180)

Patrabroumm (p. 140)

Broum (p. 16)

Brr (p. 224) *Brrr* (p. 98)

Brroum (p. 17) *Brrroum* (p. 17) *Broumm* (p. 98)

Brroumn (p. 11) *Brroumm* (p. 126)

Brrrroumm (p. 22) *Broooum* (p. 228)

Braoum (p. 11) *Brouam* (p. 135) *Braomm* (p. 113)

Bromb (p. 101) *Broomb* (p. 241) *Bromg* (p. 153)

Broom (p. 185) *Brrom* (p. 185)

Brrôôô (p. 110) *Brôôôô* (p. 89)

Brrong (p. 130) *Broung* (p. 119)

Brang (p. 192) *Brrang* (p. 130) *Brrrang* (p. 130)

Branng (p. 310) *Bramg* (p. 208) *Bram* (p. 207)

Brram (p. 146) *Brrram* (p. 142) *Bramm* (p. 119)

Blam (p. 282)

Bang (p. 190) *Bangg* (p. 204) *Bong* (p. 349)

Bing (p. 212) *Bim* (p. 254) *Bzzing* (p. 111)

Bzim (p. 255) *Bzzim* (p. 111)

Bzimm (p. 117) *Bzamm* (p. 117) *Brim* (p. 290)

Brag (p. 158) *Brrac* (p. 135) *Brrrac* (p. 56)

Blac (p. 282)

Bouah (p. 191) *Buâââ* (p. 227)

We hesitate to decide what to admire more: the landscape full of surprises offered to us by the *broum* in its posterity,[48] or the economy of means used to obtain it. It takes very little, most of the time — a doubled, tripled, or quadrupled letter, a diphthongization, a nasalization — for the physiognomy of the depicted sound to be sensibly modified. The modification may be slight, may depend on nothing: it seems all the more priceless. It is basically rather easy, for the sound-effects man, to reproduce opposite sounds; it is infinitely more delicate, on the other hand, to preserve the respective identities of neighboring sounds. To introduce diversity into uniformity. Which is what Céline nonetheless strives to accomplish, so unbearable does he find monotony. Monotony, however, reigns supreme; monotony that could pass as the simple application to the realm of sounds of the law of large numbers, the basso continuo of our terraqueous globe in the concert of the spheres, if it didn't appear that monotony, at the same time, had contributed to establishing this law — a law that Céline will have simultaneously and relentlessly fought on every front — experimentally. Monotony that the ear perceives immediately. Immediately and lastingly. To hear it once is to hear it always. Impossible to be rid of it. War itself and its savage parade couldn't produce a diversion: they only amplify it, raise it to the next power. A great deal of noise, certainly (bomb after bomb), but always as little relief. A very hollow roll of echoes, with no other intervals than those managed after the fact by the listener's talent; Céline's talent, consequently, Céline whose technical intoxication, in its very excesses, betrays to a certain extent the utopic horizon of his quest: carved out of the compact mass of the world into so many little individualities, each provided with beats, accelerations or decelerations, this quest for a new world, for a *new harmony* within which might resonate what Jean-François Lyotard calls "the enigmatic presence of the vibrating";[49] meaning a world in which "onomatopoeia" might finally be the name borne by the pure actuality of a sonorous event.

~

In tune, then, the noise; but off-key, the song. "Off! off! I yell: it's off! [...] Bombs no bombs, I can't let that by! ... she's butchering! [...] Brram! a hail! a stick of bombs! ... *brrac* ... *brram!* ... that I'm interrupted! out of breath! ... I start over and I'm off, off myself! [...] I'm singing off-key! positively!"[50]

Never in tune: it's the law. Always a quarter tone too high, if it isn't a quarter tone too low. And, this law, no one in the work evades it. Not the pastor Rieder, returned from a long and mysterious journey for the Rittmeister's funeral, but who, alas, "no longer sings true;"[51] nor Alphonse de Chateaubriant, whistling the Valkyrie — "the only tune! oh, the only tune!" — but whistling off-key, disastrously off-key, "croons ... even more off-key!"[52] It's everyone's lot. The pianist like the singer. Let the little girl, in *North*, play the piano: "off,"[53] we could have guessed it. So much easier does it seem, in such places, to be in tune with the din than to master your instrument. Céline, let it be said, has no illusions, he who only intends to exert his mastery over croaks and discordances.

But not in order to redress them, to correct them; and this is the strangest thing of all. Who will say what it means, this concern for precision, order, and equilibrium applied to chaos? For there is no question of ever leaving chaos. The music bathes in it as in its natural environment.

Better not to expect God knows what reparations from music. Torn to pieces, Orpheus. Cut, the cords of his lyre. The Célinian Orpheus is in the same position as Saint Cecilia, when, in the sixteenth century, at the instigation of Pope Leo X, who wanted to sanction the superiority of vocal, a capella music over instrumental music, she is depicted knocking over her little organ, a *positive* or table organ, whose broken pipes (see, especially, Raphael's painting at the Pinacotheca of Bologna)[54] litter the ground amid a devastation of violas, rebecs, cornets, and punctured drums. *Cæcilia in corde suo soli Domino decantabat*... On the ruins of music, invoking God in her heart.

Just like Orpheus, our Orpheus. Who, unlike the other one, the dismembered enchanter of the legend, is never done singing. Off-key or not, he doesn't care. As long as he can sing to the end. Sing at the top of his lungs, sing his head off. Till his last piece.

↬

It's from this angle that music suits Céline. What he likes in it is its power of separation. Which is the reason why, rather than airs (the melodies that link sounds), he likes notes, which detach themselves on their own, or can be isolated by analysis and saved from the rubble. Between several given masses, could there be a smaller common divider than the note? The sol-fa is to Céline what the operation called division is to calculus.

Yet, in all good logic, and so that the operation doesn't leave a remainder, we ought to admit that the mass can be divided to infinity. But the Célinian imagination of the note rests precisely on the postulate of an, as it were, inexhaustible divisibility. A limitless divisibility, whose power even increases proportionally to how it should, on the contrary, exhaust itself... Is France crushed, reduced to pieces? "La! fa! sol! la si do!"[55] And sharp, the "do": beware. A prevaricating note, chamfered, casual, devious. The love of risk, decidedly. But of the calculated risk. "Give it a chord! sharp! You've won!..." Only, for God's sake, "don't lose your nerve!...Hold to the [...] sharp! sharp! sharp!"[56] We've told you twice if we've told you once. Salvation lies in the semitone, the fine nuance. You either have a delicate ear or you don't.

If, in fact, it is only a question of ear...The minutiousness of the Célinian transcriptions is especially a function of the violence undergone, of the scale of the damage. The greater the disaster, the more subtle the score. It's because France was defeated, because France was beaten (one can also say pounded), that in 1941 Céline can cut his chords loose and, sowing notes, cascades of them, strew his arpeggios. And it's because Germany is in ashes that he sees trills whirling over the smoking stones of its ruins, swarms of sharps raining down. "*La! la! sol sharp!*": Sigmaringen.[57] Bombing of Hannover: "*sol sharp! sol! la sharp!...si!*"[58]

Four notes, and let's be done with it. Ultimately, we won't know if the city perished beneath the bombs or beneath the notes. Black magic, white magic: mad indeed who can tell the difference. Ever since *Guignol's band* at least, the decision has been out of our hands. Ever since the all-powerful onomatopoeia of the child king has been playing its part in the concert.

Besides, where do the planes harassing the Butte come from, the planes pounding it, grinding it, and chopping it to bits? From the very center of Paris, from the Opéra, answers *Cursed Sighs.*[59]

British planes, also. Not the same noise as the Luftwaffe machines "that are like a coffee mill." The R.A.F. engines "are all soft and continuous." Such a melisma! Cendrars again, the thing it is a question of and the word to say it. A connoisseur. The purring of engines holds no more secrets for him. Céline could have trained his ear under his guidance.

It's Kracht, in *North,* who ventures the parallel. But it's the narrator, in the final analysis, who concludes:[60] "Vas-y! *musik!*"

⌒

What fools and troubles the reader, what causes the reader, so often, not to believe his ears, is Céline's marked preference for light music, all "frilly,"[61] "little cheerful motifs,"[62] things that look like nothing, "three cents worth of couplets,"[63] "two notes, four at most,"[64] "slight noises,"[65] "flighty trills,"[66] "*pizzicati!* light!...light!"[67] Scratched out on a guitar ("The ultra of charm. You have that, you are a god.")[68] or plunked out on a piano, a harpsichord, a spinet, a virginal, a clavichord: no matter, as long as it clicks, as long as it crackles, as long as it hails down chords, as long as it sets your head spinning.

Tic. Toc. Choc... would have said Couperin, his master: the "Couperin of the 'Cuckoo'..."[69]

His singing master, his dancing master. His master especially in spells. No other word for it.

↜

Like the spell, music has the power to erase. Yes, of making things disappear. And even as radically, if not as rapidly, as the magic powder of onomatopoeias that Céline will sow like a glowing cloud over all the Sodoms, all the Gomorrhas of his German odyssey. Music, in comparison, takes its time. But slow as it may be, it always, finally, gets the better of things. The proof is that if you speeded them up — these things we are talking about — you would see them go like dust in the wind.

And this can be demonstrated. By the castanets, notably. An instrument that, at first sight, doesn't look like much. But there is none as devastating. You cannot imagine the terrible *memento quia pulvis es* it can become in expert hands.

> she takes out her castanets... Ah! the great challenge!... And hound!... she rages!... it's the dance!... the trance!... fingers full of nerves!... it's shivering in her hands!... crackles, rattles!... fine... fine... tiny... even smaller... grains, grains... mill... even smaller still... *trr!*... *trr!*... *trr!*... grainy... *rr*... nothing more... silence![70]

This nibbling, have we heard it well enough? The noise of shot, the hammering of the rain, like the materialization "of millions and millions of numbers, of decimals contained between the sonorous clickings [...], time cut up into millions of millions of infinitesimal fractions."[71]

Céline's music gnaws. Fine teeth, but what a bite! Gnaws and corrodes like the water called aqua fortis, as acid gnaws and corrodes. Music is a powerful caustic. What can it be compared to, in terms of causticity? To the art of the etcher itself, the only one, of all the arts of depiction, to have ever found grace in Céline's eyes. Insensitive to painting ("zero!... but then zero!").[72] To color ("it's not my strong point"),[73] to the image in all its forms: "a phobia of photos,"[74] a Muhammadan on that like Flaubert, "a resolute enemy of the effigy."[75] Against film, ever since it became an art for the masses, ever since humanity has been collapsing "in communal graves;"[76] that "Minotaurus of the Den"[77] who "gobbles" us and "sucks" us, who takes us by our weak spot, the eye.

The chink in the armor, the breach in the edifice . . . Let the planet heat up a bit — just a supposition — and "the termites would be the rulers of the world." Why? Because these little insects "don't see anything." Their strength! "The important things [. . .] the ones that last, are directed from within . . . It is our eyes that prevent us from reaching perfection." Yudenzweck, in *The Church*.[78]

Wise man's words, words to think about, words that in any case make it necessary to revise a few things. To the innocent, the full hands? No, not at all: to the blind. To those who keep their windows shut, who live behind closed doors, like Van Claben, the usurer of *Guignol's band*, in the middle of his spoils, "a whole cartload of clarinets, oboes, cornets, flutes, zifolos, a whole trunk of ocarinas, every amusement for the breath [. . .] there was enough there to make all of London dance, to accompany a continent, to rewind the thirty-six orchestras in the Horrible's closet [. . .]. He accumulated heaps of harps and trombones [. . .] that it clogged all the skylights."[79]

No opening on the outside. Total darkness. Midway between the dark chamber of hearing and the room of the crime. With that basement light, which adds to the subterranean dimension of the place and to the clandestine nature of the comings and goings, the business of its occupants. To the suspicious aspect of this instrument traffic they seem to carry on after dusk, with the precautions of conspirators. Handling a piccolo, a sax, a mandolin, as if they were handling explosives. And the fact is, they are explosives, and highly dangerous ones: infernal devices, assembled piece by piece, in preparation for the great night. What is brewing in the dark, under the gray cloak of the river's smog, is nothing less than the great plot of music.

Long before the metro, the revelation of the "Pigalle" station and the aesthetic conversion it brought about, Van Claben's warehouses, "his 'Pawnbroker' shop,"[80] are already the refuge of the secret headquarters from which proceed all the undermining saps, all the dark intrigues that Céline has never ceased to direct against the established authority of the "All-Film."[81] Against the visual arts, which are arts of the Surface.[82] Arts of the facade, undoubtedly deprived of hinterlands, as Giono would understand it; but what is worse, from a Célinian point of view, is that by only going skin deep they don't reach the *nerve*, the fount of vigor (Rimbaud's term) that alone can quench the genius of the poet-builders, the princes, the geometers, the founders of "splendid cities"; the nerve that is the vibrating string of the bow: *emotion*, "breathless emotion,"[83] the emotion that rattles you, grabs you from below, at the end of a progress that could remind us of the sapping tunnels that in 1914 went to catch by surprise the defenders huddled in their bunkers.

The emotional *charge* of a poem, a sonata: the expression finally means what it says, having been put back into perspective, reread in the light of the dirty trick fomented by Céline's text... Perish the cinema, its "similo-sensitive";[84] cinema and its cohorts, *paintering, daubing*,[85] *chromo* and company. Out the hatch, the so-called Fine Arts! The verdict has been pronounced and is without appeal. Not one will be saved — except for etching, worthy, on the contrary, of all our interest, and that Céline, as a sign of gratitude, associates precisely with the art (the art he prizes above all others) of combining sounds. Saying, in particular, of the etcher Jean-Gabriel Daragnès, whom he admires, "it's music paper with him, his touch, his refinement."[86]

And it's true that he couldn't have said it better. Except to say that music and etching are part of the same struggle. That both of them, equally, strip the real, show you its weave. Even the language feeds the confusion between the two, and more than once: "fishnet of crickets," "dotted semis"...[87] Are we talking about music or the work of the drypoint?

And take dance, also. Definition. The shortest one Céline ever gave. In a telegraphic style, so to speak. The required style and the required mode. "Music in flesh, there, in dashes, a tip!"[88]

It could look like a message, but a message in Morse code. And perhaps you like its rhythm. But have you ever even wondered what rhythm was? Life? Céline is categorical: "rhythm is stronger than life." The proof: worms. "They rhythm your meats [...]. Just look at their swaying, the hundreds, thousands, hundred thousands! the agitation, the shivering of the viscera... I've always marveled at necropsies... So, above all, honor to rhythm."[89]

Where we will have easily recognized the melodious carrion of one Charles Baudelaire... Music falls on the world like a battalion of larvae. And let nothing remain but the bones! And let the bone itself fall to dust! "Hazes and little dots!... the fine piece of work!..."[90]

↭

But what are we striving for here? To wipe the world off the map of the world? Men are already doing a fine job of that. The power of their bombs, these days, is expressed in megatons. The ultimate weapon of the poet is a joke next to that.

Insignificant, yes, certainly... If it didn't appear that it draws its main virtues from this very insignificance. For how can we doubt that Céline's *little* music — since that is how he himself draws his readers' attention to it — is the revenge of the small, of the infinitely small; the revenge of the note, that worm, that philosopher's mite; the revenge of the weak intensities, so to speak, over the strong ones? Let's say the bombs, to go fast. But not the bombs in relation to their destructive power alone. Let's say the bombs, now, while remembering (lesson of History) that they also generate rubble, that they pile ruin upon ruin, that they beget the mound and beget the heap: that they weigh down the body of things by increasing its mass. And that they provoke, thereby, a veritable deflation.

Such a pathetic collapse is the paradox of strong intensities. What a progress music is, in comparison! What an improvement! The ultimate weapon, as I said. Doesn't music avoid the deflationist moment of this economy? It certainly does, and this, ultimately, is what its true superiority rests on. Music, which is a true grace, finds here the mystery of its effectiveness; inaccessible to the common of the mortals, as mysteries generally are. And if its seat lies somewhere it must, consequently, be far from here. In a secluded place, *utopialand,* which the work locates in England, where *Guignol's band* had already transported us; that musical comedy Jean-Luc Godard will remember with his *Pierrot-le-Fou,* a delicate homage to Céline, and, perhaps for this very reason, his most musical film.

Instead of striking a light, instead of setting the keg on fire, as he does at the end — *baraboum!* — all that Pierrot, Jean-Luc Godard's lunar hero, who keeps repeating, even though his name is Pierrot, "My name is Ferdinand!" — all that Pierrot had to do was slip away, take English leave, so to speak, for the transposition to be perfect.

I

Take English leave: like Baryton, for instance. The Professor Baryton of *Journey*. A magistral exit. Disappeared, one fine morning, leaving no forwarding address. Vanished. Taking only, we are told, "a light valise, intending to reside wherever he went and in every circumstance, very mobile and very light."[91]

Not so much by whim, besides, as by a natural penchant. To follow the inclination of his genius, which had already led him, back when he was still practicing, to refuse to resort to the crude expedients of the medicines you could call heavy medicines. Hadn't he perfected a revolutionary therapy that consisted in resorting to the properties of fluids alone to reanimate the benumbed brain of his patients? Whether you were a mental defective or stricken with idiocy, Professor Baryton cured you with electricity.

Not, to be sure, with electroshock, which knocks you out cold, but with the rain of sparks that turns you into a will-o'-the-wisp . . .

And with film, a no less essential phase of the treatment, to Baryton's mind, who was simply, here, drawing on Céline's own experience. The experience he had acquired as a child in the darkness of the theaters, when they were showing *A Trip to the Moon,* at the Robert-Houdin, and he would stay for "three shows in a row."[92]

A one reeler, though; Méliès's film was barely fifteen minutes long. But how those few minutes would mark your day! What a parenthesis they opened in it . . . You would lose your footing, you would glide; literally, float, borne to the heavens. To such a point even that to the six or seven means imagined by Rostand's Cyrano to overcome terrestrial gravity, we would be highly inspired to now add the movies. With all due respect to Céline, and in consideration of what he sought at the movies. There, all the appropriate conditions having been fulfilled — highly mysterious conditions it must be said, conditions that *Death on the Installment Plan* doesn't shed much light on — the animated pictures delighting his eyes seemed to confirm for him, through a miraculous exception (in truth, the only exception of its kind), the universal law of the fall of heavy bodies.

Ever since then, the Célinian being, highly unreasonably, feels he has a right to expect from the movies the temporary suspension of the principle of gravity. To be proved right, in a word, over Newton!

Céline's peculiar attachment to the memory of the matinees at the Robert-Houdin cannot be explained in any other way. It remains all the more unshakable for being rooted in the hope that, in spite of everything and everyone, in spite of all the disillusionments, he had never ceased to place in the promises of a title. *A Trip to the Moon*: could there be a more beautiful definition, a more adequate definition, of the cinema he dreamed of? You flew without a machine; Ariel vanquished Caliban . . . Now that was the cinema for him. Chagallian, absolutely unreal, magical, to say it all. To say it as Céline says it in his books, where the word *féerie* ("faerie") usually serves to designate the ecstasy, the seraphic immateriality, that can only be reached outside of these books by the saints who, through fasting, prayer, and mortification, finally succeed in experiencing their own bodies, not as a ponderal mass anymore, but, on the contrary, as a volatile substance: the saints who sublimate themselves in God.

Just like the spectators during the film, who, in their own way, if we are to believe Baryton's theories, should experience something akin to this state. They may remain far from it, but they will still come close enough to prolong the benefits they have supposedly already received from the voltaic, the faradic aspersion they are submitted to daily by the illustrious practician, a man imbued with the principle that after a little electricity, a little film can do no harm. We can imagine the chagrin of the Lumière brothers, who, from on high, were probably none too pleased to see their invention recuperated within this medicine of effluvium, within this new Hippocratism that Baryton tirelessly preached against the Galenism of his contemporaries, before finally putting it to the test on himself.

But the definitive test, the radical cure. Baryton, in a Socratic gesture that will no longer surprise us, renews for his own use — just like, after him, all the Courtials, all the Sosthènes (and it will be, each time, furthermore, their masterpiece) — the art of drinking the hemlock.

An idea, in fact, that came to him little by little. Everyone around him could testify to that. Because they saw it coming. By his air. An in-between air, "a dreamy softness, completely equivocal."[93] And then his absences, more and more frequent . . . It was just as well to admit it: he wasn't really all there anymore. Always somewhere else, lost in his thoughts, having placed between the world and himself a distance that grew wider by the day. The situation was growing unbearable. It was about time, in truth, for him to act, to decide finally to disappear for good!

The confirmation of his departure was thus received with a feeling of relief. Confirmation in the form of a postcard, sent from England. Soon followed by several others, from Norway, Denmark, Finland finally. The last card, the last sign. You don't return from the ends of the world, from the Finlands, the Finistères. Past a certain limit, you don't exist for anyone anymore.

⤺

This limit, in Baryton's case, had been reached for quite some time. Ever since his mind had started wandering, and this wasn't recent. Always running after his shadow, always ready to fling himself onto the first occasion to wring the neck of a whim. And, in his line of work, there was no lack of such occasions. People had had plenty of time to get used to him. Baryton's outbursts no longer surprised anyone. No, it was only later, much later, that it all became clear. When he ended up wandering in the Far North.

The expression is Céline's[94] — an expression his heart would have spontaneously dictated to him (the North attracts him, magnetic pole of all his sympathies), if he hadn't also been condemned to it by the symbolism of the cardinal points, in whose distorting mirror the work, reflected, shows us a shrunken world, a world stretched along its axis. In conformity with a representation that knows neither East nor West, or that doesn't want to know them, and that, in this ignorance, res- olutely turns its back on History... If we accept, of course, that the course of things does indeed follow the traditional orientation. But how, oth- erwise, could we find the slightest justification for the geographical prej- udices of the author of *Journey*?

End of History, consummation of the centuries. Let us have faith in the work and its prophecies. Like John on Patmos, Céline from Mont- martre has seen the foul Beast. From the summit of the Butte, where the North-South line begins. And thus precisely at the point of origin of the movement that will lead the North to crash into the South. The terrible event Céline is waiting for, or rather, listening for, whose advent is announced to him by the roar of the *métropolitain*.

The metro of his youth. Of a time when the network was still of a... biblical simplicity. Two lines in all, no mistake possible. *Vincennes-Porte Maillot*, the first line, the pioneering line. Alas! a faux pas. Running from East to West, it was running in the direction of History. The wrong di- rection, consequently. To be avoided. The right one was the other one. The one that, starting at Montmartre, was built soon after, and whose line followed a North-South axis. And that thereby, though it may have have been the second line, chronologically speaking, became the first on the symbolic level. The line, this time, not to lose sight of. Not be- cause it showed the way, but, quite on the contrary, because it hinted at its perilous nature; because in the racket of the cars, every time a train passed the fatal platform, it beat the drum of the danger threatening us, a drum that Bardamu, in the depths of Africa, will regret not having heard. When the moment of truth rings for him, the moment to open the box containing the last word of the enigma, the key to his destiny. A first-aid box. "There was nothing left in it but some tincture of iodine and also a map of the North-South."[95]

Forget the remedy, it is laughable; count as certain, on the other hand, the diagnosis. For the map, the famous map, can be taken as a diagno- sis; one that sums up the patient's state, that explains it all. And notably, to make a far too long story a little shorter, that it was because he went down the line, rather than going back up it, that he has fallen so low.

Salvation is up, in the high notes, the high latitudes. At the octave or up North. In the land of pale suns, cradle of a race caught in a slow process of eclipse, and which, for this reason, is called the white race . . . A threatened species, about to leave us. And that would even long be gone, if the South, every day, didn't win a few inches more over the North. Existence over inexistence. Africa (generic term) over the Far North, where Baryton, for example, is bustling at this very moment; where Baryton is scurrying, as if he were in a rush to accomplish his transformations before the enemy could catch up with him. Hence the hurried end. Steps are skipped. Baryton goes: barely has he left and already he's but a memory. And a memory, Bardamu confesses, "that made us all a little ashamed."[96]

The shame felt by those who have remained in existence, who didn't have the courage to take the step. To cross to the other side. The side, as it so happens, from which the book we are reading has reached us. A novel,

> nothing but a fictitious story. Littré says so, and he is never wrong.
> Besides which anyone can do the same. You just have to close your eyes. It's on the other side of life.[97]

↩

This having been said, do we really know how to cross over to the other side? Obviously there's a trick. And, this trick, Céline boasts of having perfected it. Oh! it's nothing, don't expect marvels. As he warns Professor Y, casting a retrospective gaze over his entire work, it's just "a tiny little invention." But a practical one. Ah! absolutely. As practical as "the collar button . . . as the double cogwheel for bicycles." Besides which, first of all,

> there've never been any great inventions! [. . .] just little ones! Professor Y! nature gives, believe me, only extremely rarely the inventive faculty to a man . . . and even then she shows herself fucking stingy! . . . all those who go braying how they feel all bursting with inventions are just so many bloody jokers! . . . lunatics or not! . . . you'll note that when it comes to inventions, to speak only of a giant of the species, Lavoisier simply put numbers to numerous natural bodies that were known well before him! . . .

Pasteur on his side just gave names to all the smallest things he could see through his lens! . . . a fine story![98]

Fine, indeed. A genuine fairy tale, with its evil, but also its good genie. Because, come on, the names of Pasteur and Lavoisier didn't fall out of the sky. They've obviously been chosen on purpose, and chosen for what they represent. In the manner of the allegorical figures you can see in the old books of seaports, each one with its attributes and each one at its place, according to whether, on the map, it was meant to express the fears of the early navigators or to give a concrete shape to their hopes. Thus Pasteur, thus Lavoisier, who are to each other what the South is to the North. Pasteur, who, with his studies on fermentation, proves that everything that lives tends toward an uncontrollable development, whereas Lavoisier, with his analyses, extenuates matter, decomposes it into more and more subtle elements, until there is nothing left of the chemical bodies but a fine lace . . .

The yeasts all the way down, the lace all the way up: as it should be.

As it should be, too, Céline's desire to take his place beside such illustrious personages. To be a Pasteur, of sorts; a small-time Lavoisier. Yes, small if you insist. But the small — must it be repeated? — is in no way depreciated in the Célinian system of values. It is, par excellence, the weapon of the weak, the feminine weapon, but a weapon, at the same time, that owes its fearsome effectiveness precisely to its weakness, to its femininity. Consider Musine in *Journey*, Mélusine, the Doña Música of Céline, when, at the Armies, in the rear, before all the gathered cannon fodder, she *details* the sonata and the adagio. Victory of the detail over the mass; of the collar button, of the double cogwheel for bicycles, over those difference-crushing machines with which progress assaults our infinitesimal, our fragile, individualities. The whole secret of the Célinian parry.

⌐

A secret that Baryton is on the verge of discovering. Is at least circling around. One more effort . . . We do have to recognize that luck was on his side, the luck that put him in the presence of English. A key encounter. Enough to completely change his life . . . The reader must have already suspected that English, in *Journey*, is not a language like all the others. We had already been treated to Robinson's apprenticeship. Hardly conclusive, at first sight. It's the fault of the circumstances. A night shift, among foreigners. "You can't say it's the bad work we're doing. There's worse. But I'm not learning any English . . . For thirty years in cleaning, there're some, in the same gig, that only ever learned *Exit,* 'cause it's on the doors, and then *Lavatory.*"[99] As linguistic baggage, it is a little thin. Two words, no more, but then two words that by themselves perfectly sum up the situation: two words that say, We are in the shit and it's time to go!

Profound truth of this language, on whose certainties the city of New York was entirely erected. A city that, in place of a porch, a monumental entrance, offers the visitor its toilets, its public restrooms. But something immense, then, a whole underground expansion of space; "a sort of pool,"[100] from what we are told, and over which hovers, mingling with the smells and the sounds of water, the memory of the thermae of antiquity.

Such is the mandatory stop that the city of New York imposes on the neophyte, as if to relieve him of the weight that had up till then prevented him from rising to the level of its dream of stone. Without any further intention, apparently, but with a very sure science, drawn from the wellspring of the language itself, the English language on whose foundations the city rests, quietly assured of having thus completely grasped its spirit.

The propensity of Americans to take everything literally (such, at least, is the common opinion) was already great enough. Except that everything, this time, means excluding nothing. And thus including the suggestions of a language, that which in a language can be subtly persuasive; and the way, especially, that words have of depositing on the things they name a trace of their passage, of leaving some of their dust on them, which renders these things, as we assimilate the words, a little more foreign to us, and which disorients us far more than any trip would.

A change of scenery: this, ultimately, is what the Célinian being seeks in language. In his own, to start with, in his mother tongue. But also in the language of the other, the foreign language, where it's so much easier. Better reasons to set one's mind to it would be hard to find: they are excellent. Reasons that have done their time. And before Céline, even.

But we are still talking about Céline. Or rather, Robinson. For Robinson has finally gotten into it too.

"You can believe me if you want to," he would remind me, darning bits of memories in the evening like that after dinner, "but, you know, in English, even though I never had such great dispositions for languages, I'd finally gotten to where I could hold a little conversation toward the end in Detroit... Well, now I've forgotten nearly everything, everything except one small sentence... Two words... That comes back to me all the time ever since it first came to my eyes: *Gentlemen first!* It's nearly all I can say now in English, I don't know why... It's easy to remember, it's true... *Gentlemen first!*" And to try to take his mind off things we'd have fun speaking English together again. We repeated then, but often, *Gentlemen first!* at the drop of a hat like idiots. A little joke for us alone.[101]

We had *Lavatory,* we had *Exit.* The place and the word. The open sesame that was supposed to give the key to the passage, but that didn't open any doors, and we wondered why. No need to wonder any longer: now, we know. Thanks to Robinson's astonishing progress. A prodigious leap, leap that the concerned party himself might not have realized. But no matter. We can profit from it, and draw the lesson from the experience ourselves. For the lesson is clear. All the more so inasmuch as Céline's text, without being too explicit, doesn't try to hide the causes to which it attributes Robinson's failure in handling the English language. Suggesting in whispered words that what he lacked, in order to master its spirit, more than a light touch, was probably a certain delicacy of the soul. *Gentlemen first!* Decent people first, the noble-hearted only, the sensitive beings. It's for them that English is a viaticum, to them that it points the way out.

Not, of course, the English so prized today. Céline's English is a strange language indeed. Is it even a language? Can we say, for instance, of a language we can no longer use to communicate with our fellow men, that it is still a language? Such, however, is the English practiced in Céline's books. Or such, at least, the fantasy pursued under the name of English. Since what is paradoxically sought here, no need to hide it any longer, is a withdrawn space at the heart of the exchange, on its stage; a step back, an opportunity, as it were, to withdraw — while nonetheless maintaining ourselves within it — from language. To escape its obligations. Nothing else is expected of it, other — but this goes without saying — than the assurance after that of being able to spend many a happy day within it, of enjoying one's irresponsibility with a complete peace of mind. There is no doubt that English offers itself to the Célinian reverie as a refuge language. It's an island within an island, its superlative form.

The misunderstandings underlying Ferdinand's linguistic stay in England clearly demonstrate this. Intending him for the counter, Auguste and Clémence have found nothing more judicious than to send him across the Channel. The reason (must it be underlined?) being that, in the world of the shop, you can never know enough languages. An unanswerable argument, were the reasoning not completely unsound. Being shortsighted merchants, they have failed to consider that one might perchance come to love a language for itself. With a disinterested and nearly platonic love. To love it, in any case, without touching it, without even brushing one's lips against its cheek, resolved not to pronounce a single word of it. Rather die! "For three months I didn't blink; I didn't say hip! nor yep! nor youf!...I didn't say *yes*...I didn't say *no*...I didn't say nothing!...It was heroic...I didn't talk with anyone. I was jolly comfortable with it."[102]

— But this relentless muteness...Such stubbornness can only proceed from a vow!

— Or answer to a necessity. Satisfy, in the soul of the silent one, some inexpressible need. It seems, this time, that we cannot content ourselves with the explanations we gave earlier. We are no longer in Detroit, we are no longer in New York, the circumstances have changed. Yet, in spite of this change, it is clear that the feeling of strangeness that troubled Robinson so much in America has been preserved intact. A feeling that not only lasts, but that with Ferdinand, who nurses it lovingly, gaily proliferates, welcomed with open arms by the English language. A language that flatters, that encourages the desire we sometimes have, but that the Célinian being experiences on a permanent basis, to return to the happy days when a language could exert its charms without having to succumb, as it now does, to the pressing need to signify. How nice it must have been then to laze in it, to let ourselves be cuddled by all the graces with which it delighted our ear! A rain of sensations that fell on us like a spell of gentleness. We were comfortable. Ah! yes, "jolly comfortable." A child in his mother's belly.

↩

The pleasure with English is a pleasure of this nature.

— Incestuous, perhaps?

— Incestuous, surely. No true happiness but in crime ... No progress especially but in the return. Our future is behind us. As demonstrates Céline's language, Céline's idiom and its retrograde march; language and its becoming, its maternal becoming. As demonstrates English and its ritual anticipations of a homecoming that is taking its sweet time. A homecoming, let us note, that English celebrates in the appropriate manner. Lyrically, but also (regression *oblige*) in the foulest manner possible. If the work on language must be the work we have said, a work not so much of restoration as of rejuvenation at the carnal origins of language, and therefore a dirty job if ever there was one, at least here we will have the excuse of having done it as dirtily as possible. Without any kid gloves ... Isn't it significant, in this respect, that the road that leads to England is a road so obstructed with matter, so ignominiously fecal? Even more significant, the irony thanks to which the only view that the unfortunate passengers, who are at the end of their rope, have of the beyond they so aspire to, is from the head.[103] Through the hole, so to speak.[104] *Lavatory, Exit.*

No other alternative. It's either the staircase, the flight of pink steps leading to the catacombs of the city of New York, or else it's the boat. The ship of vomiting, in a modern version of the ship of fools. The same contortions. And the same jokers. Let us call them *opposites,* since they are people who do everything backward. They put the North at the South, the zenith at the nadir, and, as if they were in a hurry to be done, they do it double time. Look at them striving, spitting it all out as if to find, deep inside themselves, a noble soul. But nonetheless allowing us, between two spasms, a glimpse of what the major gesture of inversion would be; the gesture that would consist, for Céline, in redeveloping the entire site of the beyond under the name of *outre-là.* In turning the crossing of the desert, the long race toward the Promised Land, into a crossing of the body.

Of which this crossing of the Channel, in *Death on the Installment Plan,* is like a dress rehearsal. The mythical North-West crossing that for a long time will have made the work cross to the other shore, pass from French to English. As if, from one language to the other, it was the same distance. A distance expressed, for lack of being able to measure it, by the disaster of Monmouth in Macaulay's work, the *History of England* that never leaves Baryton's bedside: a lost battle, a mountain of corpses, "the immense agony of an army,"[105] an entire expanse to cover, to survey from end to end, and that gives its true dimensions to the mystery that the books to come would all strive to reverse, the way you reverse a pocket or reverse a glove: the mystery of incarnation.

In the shadow of which, being a doctor, Baryton is already entrenching himself. The first doctor of the work, if we exclude *The Church*; first in importance — at a time when the writer Céline had not yet had the presence of mind to integrate in his work the thesis of the doctor Destouches — Baryton prepares the arrival of one Gustin, the distracted listener of the "pretty legend" that, in *Death on the Installment Plan,* repeats, in the form of a romance, Macaulay's story. For the two texts echo each other: the historical narrative of a man posterity will hold as one of the most illustrious representatives of British imperialism, the promoter not only of a language but also of the values linked to it, and this Célinian fantasy in troubadour style . . . Perhaps it isn't obvious at first. And let us even recognize that, if the idea of connecting them does finally impose itself, it is not so much on account of positive resemblances as of affinities that derive, essentially, from the conditions in which they are read. A certain atmosphere, a climate, not to say a decor. What other word could characterize their respective frameworks, the choice environment that Céline, in both of the novels in question, inscribes them in? Here, a treatment room, one of the isolation rooms of Doctor Baryton's Health Clinic; there, a doctor's office. In short, the same place, where most likely lies the story of their common genesis. The deplorable story of the sickly flowers, of flowers that have grown in the shadow of the hospital, rooted in the same mass graves from which rises the complaint of Prince Gwendor, a complaint that lulls you to sleep, and then echoes the *lamento* of Monmouth, to whom Baryton lends his voice in interminable recitations. "He would read and reread the passage and remurmur it to himself again. [. . .] From that moment on, I can say it, he was no longer with us . . ."[106]

The result of repeating it over and over, and, to get the right tone, twisting his tongue, contorting his mouth. The result of all the inflections, the result of all the vocalizing and the diphthongizations . . . Baryton on his hobbyhorse, English, to the point that he even ends up mounting the pretty bicycle "all nice and chromed" he had promised his daughter, the day when she, too, would know how to say *the* properly, as she had been taught by Mr. Bardamu, "so patient, so kind."[107] The magical machine, with its "double cogwheel," too! A fairy-bike, just like Arlette's bicycle in *Faerie*, just like Céline's Imponder. No mere Peugeot . . . Plumes to the wind, a mere whisper . . .[108] Death is no sweeter, and no lighter. Death in the tales, in the beautiful legend. "And death very softly came over the Prince . . . He's no longer defending himself . . . His weight has flown . . . And then a beautiful dream fills his soul once more . . . The dream he often had when he was little, in his fur cradle, in the room of the Heirs, near his nurse Morave, in the castle of King René . . ."[109]

Sleep, child, sleep . . . It's the lullaby in honor of the little prince, the new prince born out of the slaughter, the atrocious melee. Out of the battle that was for him a second mother. Or, as it were, the same one, revisited. His own mother . . . The melody we were looking for, the forgotten song that Céline's text deposits on our lips, nice and soothing, even as he is trying to find a way out from under the mass of bodies now separating him from us.

⮌

But, come to think of it, neither more nor less than the other one; the joker who, in the meantime, is foundering in his English. Yet another effort, and he too will see it, the light at the end of the tunnel. The way he's gone off . . . Into music. Given that English, precisely, "is a kind of music."[110] Ferdinand's words. And a music, perhaps, akin to the music Robinson used to get drunk on in America, "their kind of music," as he says, anticipating the same expression. It is surprising that he uses it, because he's thinking not at all of the language, but of the music itself. Jazz music, "their kind of music in which they also try to leave their heavy habituation and the crushing misery of doing every day the same thing."[111]

To the point that, rather than wriggling to borrowed cadences, they would have been just as well inspired to try to exploit the virtualities of their language, so naturally dancing, so vivid and frisky: "it's playful," English; "it bounces too…rings…laughs at nothing…capers…quivers."[112] The professor's stroke of genius is that he realized it. Immediately. And, immediately, in unison. As true as his name is Baryton.

A name that predisposed.[113] Wherein the word *baryte* (from the Greek *barus,* meaning *heavy*) rises by its own momentum on the wings of song. Whereas Ferdinand, on the contrary, is sinking to his knees; whereas he is staggering under the load Céline has imposed on him in *Journey.* An awful burden, such a *barda,* such a gear! From the Greek, too, the word *barda,* even if the French owe it to the memory of the miserable life their African battalions had to endure. A word that has at least kept a vague resemblance (but kept after how much crossbreeding?) with the Greek *bastezein,* which weighs out with the Greek *baryte: bastezein,* indeed, means to carry a load. Nothing but a beast of burden (it's sung to you in every key, and in both languages at once, the vulgar and the learned), the *Barda*mu of *Journey*…It's Ferdinand alone, Ferdinand relieved of the cumbersome baggage of his patronymic, Punchinello without his hump, who will be allowed, across Channel, to join Cascade's troop, the *guignols* of the orchestra this latter conducts.

Who will not hesitate, for even a modest stand in this orchestra, to renounce the name of his fathers. Who will at least not have to be asked twice to give it up. Who will get rid of it without a fuss, like a man who knows that music demands sacrifices. What is necessary is necessary, in this as in everything. Necessity is law.

—Which law, exactly?

—The conjuring of Bardamu's name, this little bit of legerdemain first performed in *Death on the Installment Plan,* conceals from the reader something that may perhaps be discovered in the flash of the following revelation, preserved for us in the intimate notebooks of Lucienne Delforge. All the more moving, then, for having come down to us through someone who will have lent, for a time, to the demon Céline claimed he was possessed by, not only her talent as a pianist, but her beauty as a woman…He had heard her on April 4, 1935, during a recital she was giving. But it is only on May 3, a month later, Salle Gaveau, at a concert she was attending, that he takes advantage of the intermission to ask her to accept the homage of his admiration and to confide to her how the fire, the passion with which she had performed one of Chopin's Etudes (the so-called revolutionary one), "by shedding light for him on a certain meaning of cruelty," had allowed him, as if by miracle, to finally get the better of an episode of *Death on the Installment Plan* he had been struggling with for a long time, the chapter "in which the son kills the father."[114]

The confidence is worth its weight in gold, oh so rich with lessons. As long, obviously, as we are willing to understand, *à rebours,* that the murder of the father is the sacrificial gesture that, by breaking the enchantment, has freed music: beautiful prisoner calling in secret for her Saint George. To vanquish the dragon, the horrible monster, the massive beast: such is the task that has befallen the Célinian hero, the prowess we expect of him. The heroic act that, in Céline's thought, must lead to the establishing, over the world, of the definitive reign of the ideal, his great dream of harmony, a celestial music, concert of gambas and choir of angels, but from which he is torn, from which he is always more brutally awakened by the incessantly repeated spectacle of the paternal resurrections. For the fathers are reborn; book after book, more flourishing, more majestic, more enormous than ever. Veritable monuments of flesh, collapsing blubber balls under which music (listen to it moan) is dying, the poor little thing. Just look at Van Claben, with his hanging jowls, his rolls of flesh, fat Claben: he didn't take long; all the instruments confiscated, by the cartload, by the trainful; an entire continent reduced to silence. Or look at Normance, the other Horrible, Normance the mastodont; look at how, under the occupation, he makes it impossible for the narrator of *Faerie* to continue composing his "music for books,"[115] by jealously withholding all the available stocks of paper. Or look at the Jew finally, yes, the Jew of the pamphlets; look at him, the Plutus of Modern Times, refusing to invest a dime in Céline's ballets, and thus condemning them to remain what they are, not even pantomimes but a theater of shadows. *Without music, without anyone, without anything.*

— Drumont whispering its lesson to the Célinian Oedipus: we simply had to get back to that.

— Did we really? The question has been disputed, and will be disputed again. Alas! always in vain. What is done is done and brooks no excuses ... That being said, what is not done is not done. Is neither done nor to be done. It would be greatly unfair to forget this, and to put Baryton in the same boat as Bardamu. As a Bardamu who, what's more, feels like a prisoner of the gravity well of his evil star (call it the sun, in homage to the figure of the Father; yet science now calls it a yellow dwarf, this *outre* pouring forth without any restraint); as a Bardamu, consequently, all tangled up in malignant effluvium, whereas Baryton, on the contrary, and Baryton because he has no Oedipus, finds himself free as a bird.

—No Oedipus?

—We are in fairyland. The other scene, therefore. The names, even if they are still stage names, are no longer the same masks. No more fake noses, humps or protuberances, no more disgraceful warts; no more crosses to bear, but a call. And a call, let it be noted, of which the character, even before answering it, is already the living, the pathetic expression. Is it not written, after all, that though many are called, few will be chosen? Baryton is certainly one of the few.

—Well, with a name like that! The sublimation of heaviness through music: his work was cut out for him.

—Absolutely. Except for one detail, however (and not a negligible one): our man has never shown a hint of aptitude for this art. Yes, the truth now forces us to confess, "as a musician he wasn't worth a dime Baryton."[116] Not a musician, perhaps, yet, how to say it ... he speaks the musical French of Bordeaux.

And thus of Alcide's hometown; the town where the sergeant's niece, raised by the nuns, is presently undergoing therapy. For an infantile paralysis, treated with electricity. While waiting for the piano lessons. "What do you think you of the piano? ... It's nice, huh, the piano, for little girls?" And then the English lessons, because "it's useful English too?"[117] And thus useful to the lame; to all those who limp in their soul ...

But Bordeaux, but the electricity, but the music, but the English: can we still say that Céline isn't single-minded?

↝

Not a musician, Baryton? Strictly speaking, absolutely not. Yet *he had the accent.*

Has anyone ever wondered about the meaning of this phrase, *il avait l'accent*? A phrase that probably has no equivalent in any language other than French, where it is commonly taken in the absolute. Not so much the accent of such or such a region as the accent, period. Either you have it or you don't. And though it may be a charm to have it, though it may be yet another grace — no one, nonetheless, is beholden to the accent. Whereby French can be distinguished from English, in which the accent, on the contrary, "is everything."[118] One of Baryton's remarks, made in passing. Yet it's worth lingering on. The most profound truths always come in this way. Off the cuff, at the drop of a sentence, casually. Baryton's remark is no exception to the rule, and we will not be afraid, therefore, to take it for what it is: the statement of a general principle.

The accent, quite simply, is everything, is essential to our survival. At least what is called the accent, and defines in this case the faculty we have of accentuating, at any given point, the melodic movement of a language; a faculty, however, whose exercise is all too often thwarted by the use it is ordinarily enslaved to: the use of signifying, nearly the only use we recognize in language, when we refuse to conceive it other than as the simple vehicle of a message.

By constraining us to displace the question of language toward the accent, English forces us to operate a decisive subversion. As decisive, actually, as the subversion of argot can be in its own realm. But no less apt to second the efforts of a subject attempting to overcome his unfortunate inclusion in the social world. To such a point even that Céline's phrasing, compared to the shocking lapses he is such a noisy specialist of, could appear to us, reconsidered from the point of view of the qualities it acquired through its contact with English, as one of those revolutions that are euphemistically called gentle revolutions.

For, if argot is the manifestation of a sovereignty, it is but a sovereignty *à rebours*, a counterpower that can only maintain itself by force. Even if this is just the force, as Danièle Racelle-Latin has so clearly shown, of the challenge of the phrase, the swarm of rebellious metaphors with which one must, she says, ceaselessly harass the enemy.[119]

How gently, on the contrary, does Céline's text slip into us when it is speaking English! The term does not, of course, designate a specific language; and John Bull's language less than any. In this perspective, English wouldn't exist, the English I am thinking of, the English from which Céline's thought draws its strength; the beautiful thought he is secretly nursing, his writer's dream, his hope *to flee into language.*

To flee, I mean this time not by entrenching himself, imprisoning himself within the margins of the language, but on the contrary by following the lines of flight inscribed in it, first and foremost of which is the melodic line we were speaking of.

To flee down this line is to do exactly what Baryton did: to take English leave.

II

One will object that, under these conditions, it was hardly necessary, in order to take English leave, to go to England. Baryton's story is a fable. And to be read as such. The way you would read an apologue. A didactic narrative whose moral might be: no need to run, just make the language sing.

The reader will, however, grant me that England, in the work, does occupy the place legendarily assigned to the musical isle of antiquity. Doesn't Céline, from *Death on the Installment Plan* on, keep sending his Ferdinand precisely to this modern Delos? To go inquire, for him, about the lost treasure of the old music . . .

We know how Céline's conviction that the British Isles are indeed the guardian of this music — a conviction that he shares with Vallès, or believes he shares with him[120] — will have remained unshakable. A conviction often reaffirmed, from *Death on the Installment Plan* to *Guignol's band*, which is rather intriguing. The empire is certainly then at its peak. At the summit of its power, were it not, above all, at the limit of suffocation. Not so much immense as packed in on itself. England is massive, "nothing but bricks, warehouses."[121] For such is the truth *Guignol's band* will soon reveal, in its famous description of the docks of London, "monster stores!... fantasmagoric attics, citadels of merchandise [...] Himalayas of powdered sugar [...] Coffee for the entire planet."[122]

"London the stuffed," Céline also exclaims, in *The School of Corpses*.[123]

Death on the Installment Plan, granted, doesn't say it word for word, yet already says it in its own way. Ferdinand enters Chatham the way you enter a larder. Everywhere, victuals; everywhere, people devouring, and themselves devoured; people that look like fish, that smell of honey, of toast: food offered to God knows what gigantic appetite.

England is a belly.

But this belly has a soul... I don't mean an ordinary soul. I mean one of those souls such as give violins their heartrending accents. And there is no contradiction here. Simply the application of a very general law; an unwritten law, but whose effects can be felt throughout the work, and that I propose to consign, henceforth to refer to as *Céline's law.* It states, this law, that music is certainly a force that can raise mountains, but that this force is proportional to the masses in presence; that consequently the greater the masses, the more chances the music has of delighting our ears.

Put twenty bodies under a table. Make it thirty, just to be safe. Men, women, children intertwined, huddled, compressed "in a slimy pudding."[124] Press them more. Seal every breach. There must not be the least chink. The success of the experiment depends on it. Here, that little dog, to plug that hole... Alas! the dog was too much: the straw that breaks the camel's back, but that at the same time "discharges all the sounds."[125] For the fact is there. From under the table, rises a song. Yes, a song that sings: "What a world it is!"[126]

Treasures of harmony are lurking within the meat: "the streaming Aphrodites of musical inventions"[127] suddenly emerge from the ocean of mingled bodies. Music demands such holocausts. Because what we call music, in the end, is nothing but a qualitative leap — the product of a mutation that only occurs at the end of an exhausting race along the axis of volumes or the axis of quantities.

London, to return to it one last time, is all number: tons of this, tons of that and "kilometers in zigzag."[128] Airless passageways, "wells of fog";[129] pea soup in which the walker sinks, wandering, dawdling, and little by little disappearing — as if dissolved, absorbed. Returned to the common pot in which life, that ogre, is stirring its soup. But, like a sorghum beater, life is singing as it wields its pestle. *Policeman! Policeman! don't touch me! ... Dancing Dolly,*[130] or what else? Beyond a certain level (level, of course, of density), there is nothing as melodious, nothing as deliciously engaging, a veritable enchantment for the ear, as those long rows of bricks "that seem monotonous"; "greasy" bricks, "sticky with smoke," "sweats of fog, coal tars."[131]

〜

If Ferdinand's arrival in England is in fact, as we first suggested, an entrance into bodies, a return to the mass, it follows logically that Ferdinand's arrival must be trumpeted forth. And, in point of fact, as soon as he steps off the train, in Chatham, in the middle of all these rampant appetites and gluttonies, it's immediately nothing but songs, banjos, and mandolins; the drums of the minstrels, the trombones of the Salvation Army, the barrel organ of the merry-go-round, the farandole of the sailors on a binge, the racket of the mechanical piano, the waltz of love.

Yes, the waltz ... One, two, three ... One, two, three ... One, two, three ... Until he sets up shop. For there, too, to set up shop is to settle in music. To transport your lares, to take up residence in the college up there, on the hill. The college unfolding the pavilion of its great ear, quiet, listening.

> The noises from the city, the port, rose, filled the echo ... Especially those from the river down below ... It sounded as if the tugboat was pulling right into the garden ... You could even hear it puffing behind the house ... It would return again ... Head back into the valley ... All the whistlings of the train, they curled and snaked up through the mists of the sky ...[132]

Of a world that would no longer be anything but rumors. Certainly, the outside sounds still reach the inhabitants of the great ear. Yet only reach them relieved of that dimension of exteriority that is in itself so troubling. They are nothing, now, but light touches of being, whose charm, in part, is made of absence ...

All the charm, equally, of the English language, whose musicality must be paid, for Ferdinand, at the same price as the musicality of the world. Both of them, in all rigor, are only acquired by subtraction; language loses the dimension of meaning, just as the world, to become music, had to lose the dimension of exteriority.

And the loss, furthermore, if experienced in the same way, lived, in both cases, on the mode of withdrawal. You drew the great cloak of the fog over yourself; you now let yourself be drowned by the wave, the refreshing rain of unbelievable sounds, of syllables deprived of meaning that wash us, so it seems, of the sin of existence. "The *patronne* [...] I'd hear her like a song...Her voice, like everything else, was a spell of softness...What absorbed me in her English was the music, how it came dancing around, in the middle of the flames. I also lived wrapped up, me, a little bit like Jonkind, basically, in stupefaction."[133] Wrapped up in music, just as he is muffled up in the overcoat he never takes off ("I slept with it").[134] For to underline the comfortable side of the fabric is to insist here on the bubble of sound formed, for the child of man, and before his birth, by his mother's belly. A gently lapping paradise, full of sighs, of whispers. *No fear! No trouble...*

No fear! No trouble... As the poor creature goes about repeating, that Jonkind to whom Ferdinand was just comparing himself, the college idiot. Less of an idiot, actually, than it may seem. A happy fool, rather. And who actually knows his English better than Figaro; who knows enough, at least, to give its full meaning to the sort of return to the dark and musical sources of life that form Ferdinand's itinerary in England.

No fear! No trouble... The extraordinary sense of security one feels in this place. At the center of interference of all the sounds on earth, and, thereby, cut off from the rest. In the world, still, but as if one were already beyond the world...

Implying, as Clément Rosset would, that a little music more, when all is said and done, is a little reality less?[135] That's already something. A respite, a rest. And even the only way, probably, for the Célinian being temporarily to enjoy, on account as it were, the eternal repose. Like an advance drawn on death. The death he is owed, but that is taking so long to come; the death England (and England, precisely) has made him so impatient for, has given him a foretaste of. A sly desire that spread through his veins the minute he partook of the beverage handed to him over the counter of the pub. Something "thick foamy black."[136] And very bitter, at the same time. So evocative, in its bitterness, of the trial of the chalice, of the trial of the poison still in use among witch doctors.

So that Ferdinand, like Orpheus, has drunk the philter. It was enough, to tell the truth, for him to dip his lips in it to be worthy of joining the minstrels, of mingling with the street singers daubed with shoe polish, but who, when they wash up, appear all livid, "in the pale light of morning." Their complexion so sallow that you might think "that they were already dead";[137] that they have reached the dark shore and that, at this very moment, they must be in the *other world.*

How many times this expression appears, under Céline's pen, about England! "It was a whole other world [. . .] it made it seem that I'd never be caught again . . . that I'd become a memory, an unrecognizable."[138]

Gone in music, like another Baryton. Having entered alive into death. Only existing here below posthumously. "It was the lull, the great domain of the fogs . . . it became then all magical . . . it became like another world [. . .] It was a realm of phantoms."[139]

⌒

What can be said after such a stroke of the bow?

Phantom, *fantôme,* says it all, the most musical, one of the most beautiful words of the French language; the word, certainly, of all the words of this language, that sings the most harmoniously in Céline's ear.

But what does it mean, precisely, phantom? The ghost? The returning dead? But if they're returning, it means that they aren't happy where they are, and, no matter where they're returning from, that they haven't found a place anywhere . . .

To give the dead their place: one could demonstrate that this is the metaphysical goal of Céline's work. Demonstrate that Céline has taken on the cause of the ghosts; the cause of all these homeless dead. For homeless they are. We know perfectly well that coffins aren't little houses in which the dead lie comfortably, between four boards nailed tightly shut. It's not for nothing that these sorts of boxes have the shape of nacelles, the shape of boats . . . Prologue of *Death on the Installment Plan,* the fall of the curtain: "Then I clearly saw the thousands and thousands of little canoes over the left bank . . . They each had inside a little shriveled dead person under his sail . . . and his story . . . his little lies to catch the wind."[140]

Hasn't it been repeated often enough that death is the great journey? *E la nave va!* And the ship sails on! But sails where? Where it can. Comes and goes. Which explains why, under certain conditions, you'll see it go

by. Observe the movements of ports, plant yourself next to locks...
Who knows? With a little luck. Not to mention that life (life according
to Céline) is already nothing but a funereal odyssey, the interminable
story of the immense people of the dead, of all those unfortunates, those
wanderers seeking an impossible shelter.

— Could it be that they haven't paid the price of the journey?

— Eh! probably that's it. But, while we're on this subject, what, then,
is the price, and in what coin can it be paid? This is what Céline doesn't
have the slightest idea of, certain as he is that one must pay, but know-
ing neither how nor how much. And this ignorance eats at him. Which
is the reason he's always calculating, stirring numbers around in his
head. The reason the question of money is the great question of the
book. There's the rent to be paid, there's the boy's clothes. There are the
debts. All the worries of existence. But worries that are only so absorb-
ing, ultimately, because it is the apprehension of the day of reckoning
that is expressed through them. As he knows that he will never be able
to amass the sum (and, again, what sum? and in what currency?), the
Célinian being already feels in debt, ahead of time. He has come into
the world with the certainty of never, no matter what he does, being able
to afford his death. And to be convinced of this, believe me, is wearying.

So, then, to find some peace, to rest his mind a little, Céline sometimes finds himself dreaming that there exists somewhere, that there
must exist, for these vagabonds of time and space, a place to gather, to
pause. Even if it's just for a while. Not the Promised Land, of course, no
need to go so far; but, why not? England, so close, and yet so far it
seems it could be elsewhere. The elsewhere at our door. Within reach, it
would seem, of every wallet... Yes, it's England they need. And no need
to show them the way; they've found it all by themselves. In successive
waves, our dear departed, the deceased cross the Detroit, "a little British
halt, for a little laugh and oblivion."[141] Better than nothing, after all. If it
isn't paradise yet, at least it isn't hell anymore. Neither heaven nor earth,
but, between the two, an intermediary zone, a *no-man's-land.* The British
Isles are to the Célinian imagination what limbo is in Christian im-
agery. *Limbus,* the edge. He who has descended into limbo is halfway
between being and nothingness. A wasteland, with eternity as a view...

The result, meanwhile, is that between limbo and the world—whose edges, with Céline, are now abutting—there is a constant circulation. Jammed, the Passage, to a point you can't imagine. Of course, we knew it was congested on the surface. With all those ferries, those liners, those cargoes, superb ships mingling their wakes. We were perhaps unaware that it was just as bad down below.

We will learn it from Céline. In his *Journey to the End of the Night*... Ferdinand has a job at the Tarapout, a seedy little music hall where he's an extra. A nonspeaking part. The role of a policeman patrolling the Thames, while three English girls sing. "A little sorrow they were singing so-called! So they said!"

> Where I go... where I look...
> It's only for you... ou...
> Only for you... ou...

Like that they were singing [...]. It started in a nice little tone their song, it didn't sound like much, like every dancing tune, and then there it was making your heart lean from making you so sad as if hearing it you were going to lose the desire to live, because of how true it was that everything ends in nothing, youth and all, and you really leaned forward after the words, and after the song had already passed and their melody gone far away, to lie down in your own true bed, your very own, the real thing, the good hole to be done with it. Two returns of the refrain and it was as if you wanted it, that sweet land of death, that land forever tender and immediately forgetting like a fog. They had fog voices basically. We took it up in chorus, all of us, the lament of the reproach, against those who are still around, loitering alive, who are waiting along the quais, along all the quais of the world, to be done passing through life, while doing whatever, selling things and oranges to the other ghosts and pipes and fake money [...] talking about nothing, in this mist of patience that'll never be done with...[142]

The trio is spinning its romance. Like the Fates, their skein; the fatal sisters. Night after night, the stubborn ritornello. And then came the final night. One of the singers, taken ill, is replaced by a Polish girl; one Tania, "long girl powerful and pale."[143] Pale: all the more easy to believe that death is trailing behind her. Barely hired, she learns of the death of the man she loved. A small-time bank clerk living in Berlin.

Notice the sound of money to salute the entrance of Death; bills crackling between fingers, coins ringing. Crumpled paper, tinkling metal: the only language she understands. The very language in which Ferdinand, no sooner arrived in Chatham, will address her. "I had," says he, "a 'pound' in one pocket and then little coins in the other."[144] Not nearly enough, assuredly, to settle all his debts, but at least enough to hold off Madame Death. Let her wait till he's in the money... Note that she is patient, the lady. She extends credit. Even if, like everyone, to tell the truth, she prefers sure values, people that have plenty to fall back on. Bank clerks, not to name them. Gone for good, that one. Once again, they only lend to the rich.

Whereas for the others, for the penniless, for Tania and Ferdinand, Death forgets them. Impossible for them to go to the funeral. First, Berlin is far. And then there are no more trains... Out of reach, Death; beyond their means.

And this is what presently gives them that uncertain, somewhat suspicious look. People who have their feet firmly planted on the ground only owe their assurance to their certainty of being promised a grave one day. Such people walk on ballast. It's not like Tania, it's not like Ferdinand, who float, lost, who ramble in a nocturnal Paris with all the other losers. The great drifting. "Adieu, dead leaves, mischief and worries."[145]

They have landed in a little café, in Montmartre, the real tavern of nowhere. And there, while the same old song is still ringing in their ears

> It's only for you... ou...
> Only for you... ou...

a veil is torn and they have the revelation: they see the dead.

Well, those that, out of habit or laziness, we continue to call the dead. The whole ambiguity of the word, in Céline's language, comes from the fact that we cannot assimilate the dead to the defunct. *Defunctus*: who has paid. Céline's dead, in this sense, are dead in name only. To call them the "insolvent" might be more exact. But to say it, alas, doesn't do much good and still leaves us as far, still a hundred leagues away, from what causes the peculiarity of their condition. To grasp it to any extent, one should ideally be on the same side, on their side, basically. The impossible, in short! Barring truly exceptional circumstances; such as, for instance, the circumstances fate had in store for Tania and Ferdinand. Their vision on the Butte, the *axis mundi* through which run all the dividing lines of Céline's work. Midway between South and North, Today and Tomorrow, Today and Yesterday. Midway between the Living and the Dead.

They started at the Place du Tertre; nearby, the dead. We were in a good position to spot them. They were passing right over the Galeries Dufayel, to the east therefore.

[...] Especially from the cemetery next door they came, and more came and not very elegant ones. A small cemetery, though, Communards even, all bloody who had their mouths wide open as if to yell still and who couldn't anymore... They were waiting, the Communards, with the others, they were waiting for La Pérouse, the one from the Islands, who was commanding them all that night for the gathering... He was taking his time, La Pérouse, to prepare himself on account of his wooden leg that wouldn't fit on straight... and that first of all he'd always had a hard time putting it on, his wooden leg, and then also on account of his great spyglass that he had to find.

He didn't want to go out into the clouds without having it around his neck, the spyglass, an idea, his famous adventure telescope, a real laugh, the one that lets you see people and things from far away, from always farther away and always more desirable necessarily as and in spite of how you draw closer. Cossacks buried near the Moulin were having a hard time prying themselves from their graves. They made efforts like it was frightening, but they had tried many times already... They all fell back into the depths of their graves, they were still drunk since 1820.

But eventually a gust of rain made them surge forth too, finally refreshed high above the city. They dispersed then in their round and daubed the night with their turbulence, from one cloud to the next... The Opéra especially was attracting them, it seemed, its great blaze of advertisements in the middle, the ghosts were spurting from it, to go bounce off the other end of the sky and so agitated and so numerous that they made you dizzy. La Pérouse finally equipped wanted to be raised and steadied on the stroke of four [...]. Behind La Pérouse, it's the great rush of the sky. An abominable debacle, phantoms arrive whirling from all four corners, all the ghosts from all the epics... They chase each other, they challenge each other and charge each other century against century. The North remains weighed down for a long time by their abominable melee. The horizon clears up in bluishness and the day finally rises through a great hole they've punched through the night as they fled.

After that to go find them, it becomes absolutely difficult. You have to know how to go out of Time.

It's around England that you find them when you can, but the fog, in that area, is always so dense, so compact that it's like real sails that rise one in front of the other, from the earth to the highest reaches of the sky, and forever. With a little habit and some attentiveness you can manage to find them anyway, but never for long, on account of the wind that keeps bringing back new gusts and the mists of the open sea.[146]

Pure Céline. The Céline, it should have been clear, that I loved. What I love in Céline, and love above all, are passages like this one...That are *passages* in more ways than one. Part of a text or of a piece of music, and action of passing. As if the text itself and the music were only passing. Accompanying in their passage the passage of the dead.

Who are passing, it's obvious...Like a flight of ducks.

When the ducks head north, the wild geese or the cranes, it's a sure sign spring is near. The northern migrations of the souls, with Céline, are an equally good omen. We can feel Céline's pleasure at it. Céline jubilating...Nothing brings him as much joy as these great gatherings. Nothing shakes things up as much, nothing rattles as vigorously the oppositions on which things rest: oppositions of class, of periods, of moral categories. The good and the bad, the ancients, the moderns, the banished, the humiliated, the conquerors, see how they all dance in step. And what a round it is! How it whirls! Nothing wrong, not a hitch anymore. Meaning that the impetus, on the contrary, is contagious and sets the cadence for everyone, lameness itself having become the universal motor: the first motor. Not only does La Pérouse's peg leg not trip everything up, but it's his peg leg, it seems, that makes the machine run.

The opera machine directing the phantasmagoria, the fine machine, perfect assistant to the marvelous, blending its scenes one into the other; and we have the raising of the bodies, the funeral; we have the shades, larvae, or lemurs; we have their furtive disappearance: the dead all at once slipping away, with a deep bow. So that along with the dead, the dead who are also our roots, come loose our last ties to the real. Or at least the few that were left, because, after all, seriously, what was left? Long before the night on Bald Mountain, the "bamboula"[147] of the bombs — before *Faerie* sets Paris topsy-turvy, all the houses "like kites in Indian file,"[148] Lutry's building "at an altitude of four thousand meters,"[149] Lambrecaze's palace "in the zeniths"[150] — the whole Place du Tertre, already, the Butte itself is vanishing into thin air. While the story, on its side, opens up under our feet, gone out of time, too . . . For God's sake, let us not read amiss. Let us avoid, at least, the ridicule of wondering whether or not the page we have just read is an integral part or not of the narrative reality. What we are told Bardamu has seen, has he actually seen it with his own eyes? A pointless question. This is not the time to demand an explanation from a story that, manifestly, has abandoned us. That has freed itself of the obligation to have to narrate anything plausible anymore, ever since, at the Tarapout, it felt the call of the open sea, responded to the song of the Sirens who bore it far from here, along the wind of their fog voices. Implausibility, in the end, is its own way of going into weightlessness; to take English leave . . .

And this, in the final analysis, this going away, is what Céline's approval goes to. An approval lacking only music, perhaps, to be complete and whole. Unreticent. But the music that is lacking (although it isn't entirely lacking: it's from the cupola of the Palais Garnier that La Pérouse conducts the saraband), the long-awaited music can wait. Since it will be heard later. Will be heard elsewhere. In another book; but a book that connects with this one, and connects with it at this precise place.

The book is *Death on the Installment Plan*, which, as we could not fail to notice, anchored its reverie, the beautiful reverie its prologue ends on ("Across the Star my fine vessel tears into shadow"),[151] at that very place. Which is why, in *Death on the Installment Plan*, the lines in question begin with quotation marks. Because, really, they are a citation. But a citation that, on one point, improves upon the original. Music, which, as we had just pointed out, was cruelly lacking, has been put in, this time. And put in right. "He's understood the professor . . . he's playing downstairs the right tune . . . 'Black Joe.' "[152]

Yes, the professor, the downstairs neighbor, a pianist giving his lesson. Céline, no matter where he is, is never far from music.

But "Black Joe"? In what way is "Black Joe" the right tune? Because it's a minstrels' song, modest in tone, but serious, touching, "spirited, perky! whirlwinding!"[153] as Céline writes, growing exalted at the memory of his own song, the one he had promised Révol, his "dandy ritornello,"[154] a song whose lyrics (they are not in the book but have been found since) go like this:

> Gone are the days
> When my heart was young and gay.

Gone are the days. Passed, really... And nonetheless passing, always passing again. The magic of music. What, in music, is Céline grateful for, finally? Its power, even if it is just apparent, to bring back repetitively that which, on the contrary, only exists by going away. Or, to take dictation from Clément Rosset, who more than anyone else will have opened my ears to Céline's music: to confer duration upon the ephemeral.

And not a relative duration, a given duration. One must, to meet Céline, go to the end of Rosset's thought... Eternal duration!

Paradox of an essence of the fleeting.

⌒

It's in light of this paradox that appears, from a new angle, all the ambiguity of Céline's conception of death... When Céline proclaims that death is refused to us, when he complains about what is interminable about it, we must now read, conversely, that he is rejoicing in this as in the most precious good. The fact that the passage (since to die is to pass) can thus prolong itself indefinitely is, in Céline's opinion, the greatest luxury ever offered to mortals. What man will be eternally indebted to death for. What, in his whole life, he can never pay enough for.

We know, too, about Céline's claims to being the inhabitant, or rather the owner, of the Passage. But the time has come for us to realize that the Passage — the Passage Choiseul, where he did after all spend his whole childhood, and all those bridges he keeps crossing and recrossing — has the configuration, in the work, of what in logic is called an aporia. An aporia that consists in making last that which isn't destined to last. To make things last, as they say, and to make them last inasmuch as they are destined to perish...

Céline *writes*, for instance. But what is the meaning of this operation, where he is concerned? One usually writes against the clock; a "fetishist of seconds"[155] like no one else, the writer according to Céline. His dream, the mad hope he is nursing, which he one day confides the secret of to Albert Paraz: a chronograph. Patek Philipp, "*best brand in the world.*"[156]

— To ring the hours?

— As if that's what we're talking about! To Hell with it! The hours . . . No, but to put "the God of Time in his pocket." To have him on his side. Let him work for you . . . Bottom line, art is often no more than this illusion. Which is why, by tradition, marble interests him, and he would like to hijack its power; the power to challenge the effects of the years.

Except that, in fact, Céline doesn't share this illusion in the least. You can like watches, even platinum ones, without for all that sharing the fantasies of a stone lover. If friend Paraz were still doubting it, the following letter would fully reassure him: "The Patek Philipp is a dream. If I had it, it wouldn't be a dream anymore! [. . .] That's what it's like in fairy tales. It must be 'impossible.' "[157]

Perfect lucidity of the artist. For, after all, what writing is for him, Céline, on the other hand, has never made a secret of it. To dabble in the bobbin, and, as far as dexterity goes, to try to outdo lace. And there is nothing as fragile as lace. "You touch it, tear everything! . . . not repairable."[158] Not to mention that lace, anyhow, well, there isn't any left. No one, nowadays, knows what it is, real lace, "delicate inserts, netting, flighty trills, trills of nothing . . ."[159] Lace is gone like a flash in the pan.

All the more reason to stick to it. To thus defeat the enemy on his own ground. The music of Time may change, "it is never the same from one century to the next":[160] big deal! We'll sing its own music to it. Tit for tat, an exemplary answer; so typically Célinian in the turn it adopts, this way he has of always forcing the imagination of duration to invest itself in the ephemeral.

And in the ephemeral still, in the ephemeral always, with the argot. A word of argot, tomorrow, no one understands it. Brand-new, at first; as disheveled as you like, but frisky. Alive . . . Yet beware! There is life and there is life. And even death has its own sort of life, as Elie Faure said. Yet Elie Faure's expression wouldn't fall on deaf ears. Immediately taken up by Céline,[161] who would bake his bread from it. Concluding, in private, that, with argot, this was exactly the sort of life he intended to make language profit from. A life that the thinker in him has nothing to say about, other than to note that it keeps dying. An acknowledgment made over and over again, so decisive does it seem to him; so much does it seem to justify him in his choices, his conducts. And in his hatreds, too. His hatred of dead languages, of the French language, "dead since Voltaire." Céline, no matter what people claim, has no taste for death. He is far too convinced of what a waste a corpse is: "stiffs don't amuse me."[162] Dying, now, that's something else; something else also, a dying language, a language that is never done dying. A language, by this very fact, that survives itself in death. Such is, in any case, the movement that argot has been given the task of maintaining and constantly reactivating.

This movement, we would be justified in calling it music. For argot is music. Just as lace is music, just as all of Céline's things are music. Things that are only things, in truth, by virtue of no longer being things. But things nonetheless; and this is what is so strange. Our astonishment, in fact, will go to the capacity Céline's things have to endure in their decrepitude. To their capacity to endlessly end.

This is also because the end, in the Célinian regime, is a time of great complexity. Both very brief (a question of minutes, seconds perhaps, it only takes an instant) and very long (no matter how brief its duration, properly speaking, you never see the end of it). So that of the end, rigorously speaking, we only ever have, with Céline, the beginning. But a dilated beginning, opening up a space where things, one by one, array themselves under an oblique (occidental) light that extends the shadows, draws out their forms, sends their tip to the limits of the horizon; the fine tip that thus seems to be the goal these things aspire to reach, but on the path of which, immensely distended, they only continue diminishing...

↬

These things I am speaking so mysteriously of (but isn't the mystery constitutive of the thing itself? Thing, ghostling [*chose* ou *fantôme*], who can't hear it? It's more than an assonance: it's the same music...), these things are like the world. As long as one has the same point of view on the world as La Pérouse, atop the Opéra, directing his spyglass at it; the spyglass, as Céline wrote, "that lets you see people and things from far away, from always farther away"; the incomparable spyglass, his distancing spyglass.

Happy the farsighted, the Gustave Mandamours, cherished children of the gods for whom seeing is always different from seizing. The sight of the presbyopic, always going beyond, permanently creates an unbridgeable distance — the "perfect measure," the "infallible yardstick to evaluate desire . . ."[163] We've understood the lesson: that which gives distance is good. A natural disability (alas! you can't order it) or corrective glasses, to see from far away "and always farther away." And also high places, eagles' nests and belvederes, to see life through rose-tinted spectacles. How beautiful everything seems from up there! From the Val-de-Grâce, from the Bastion of Bicêtre or that Montretout, "Show-all," where Courtial has taken his quarters, and which shows nothing. Nothing but a backdrop, a panorama, a diorama with its effects of distance, of blurriness, of ghost; with its *dissolving views,* as English sings so prettily, once again the appropriate language; the music needed to accompany the world in its dissolution.

Were you to say in its departure, you wouldn't have said anything else. As much as possible, Céline's text strives to combine the advantages of the departure and the diorama. And we have Ferdinand, for instance, himself on the eve of his departure, Ferdinand, who, as he says, "glances one last time at the view":

> The weather was clear, ideal . . . It was nice and visible, all the ramps, the illuminated docks . . . the lights of the ships crossing . . . the great play of all the colors . . . like dots seeking each other in the depths of the dark . . . I had seen many of them leave, me, ships and passengers . . . sail . . . steam . . . they were at the devil now . . . on the other side . . . in Canada . . . and then others in Australia . . . full sail ahoy . . . They were picking up whales . . . I'd never, me, go see all that . . . I'd go to the Passage . . .[164]

To the *Passage.* To that place where you remain . . .

Could it be that the *Passage* brazenly puts the lie to its name? More subtly perhaps, that, as Jean-François Lyotard writes, "it's passing that we reside."[165] But that the residence, in turn, doesn't pass on. Neither a *mobile home* nor the shepherd's home.

Turning our backs on Alfred de Vigny, as Céline's text forces us to, let us now consider one last time what might be the meaning, under these conditions, of his feeling of never having left the *Passage*. Or, which comes down to the same, of being called to die two steps from the place where he was born; on the shore, these are his own words, "where close I was born."[166] Similar in that to the author of the *Mémoires d'outre-tombe*. From his little coffin to his cradle, how far is it, strictly measured? A hundred meters, "all the trouble he went to, René!...a hundred meters."[167] Something to think about.

Unless we imagine, conversely, that Céline, in turn, only dreams himself incarnating God knows what essence of the fleeting. And it must be recognized that the work, in its form, might have something to do with this ever so insane dream. That it often betrays Céline's effort — given the impossibility he finds himself in of arresting the course of things — to get a good head start on the ineluctable. To anticipate what he knows he can't avoid, and, instead of struggling to fix the fleeting spectacles life is so prodigal with, striving, on the contrary, to lose sight of them the minute they appear to him.

From a Célinian point of view, the world doesn't so much exist as persist: a pure effect of remanence. Persists for a moment, to the point of making us wonder, in certain pages, if it was ever anything more than a retinal afterimage. Thus, in *Death on the Installment Plan*, the page in which Céline tries out the power of his exorcisms on Ferdinand displays for him the full range of his evocative sorcery. Night falls, a veil of ash over the city. Ferdinand is sitting, Ferdinand at the end of his rope, frail silhouette surrounded by shades. Because this harassed pedestrian staring at the passersby, as the street around him screams dizzyingly, it's not Ferdinand anymore, it's Aeneas in Hell. Devouring the anonymous faces of his fellow men, of all these strangers rushing by — faces flashing to life in the glare of the shop windows, under the whiplash of the signs — washing them in the unreal light of his gaze, suffused with the certainty of their imminent extinction.[168]

"I am a lot more with people when I leave them": confidence of Céline to Lucienne Delforge.[169] A confidence that says a great deal about the lovingly desperate nature of his relation to the world. Waiting, to tie himself, for beings or things to be holding on only by a thread. Which he then lets run, out of fear that it might break. But lets run the way a fisherman does. Little by little, with a supple flick of the wrist; a movement all the more studied in that, finally freed of the worry of the catch, you can work at it, essentially, for the beauty of the gesture.

Thus Céline's sentence, a cord stretched and stretching out, unraveling as it goes, beautiful with a beauty of this order. And beautiful, for instance, for keeping all along the feeling of the necessary distance; for remaining to the end, having itself reached the limits of the breaking point, in an asymptotic relation to its object. Thereby ensured of never really losing it, never quite missing, though it may never reach it.

And what object, for that matter? What objects? . . . Fragile apparitions, they are still shivering with the memory of the nothingness they have emerged from, when already they are plunging back into it. Have they ever really even come out of it? A doubt takes hold of our mind, a Mallarméan doubt that once in place soon weakens the least, the most timid of our judgments of existence. Is Céline's gift actually the "gift of the retrospective," as he claims through a third party,[170] or, even rarer gift, wouldn't it rather be the nearly intuitive faculty to be in tune with the secretly dissipative dimension of the present?

Which, to be brought to light, does suppose this erosion of presence. Presence must be worn to the bone. Worn, worn more, as long as you still can't see the light of day through it. "Life is filigrees, what is clear isn't much, it's transparency that counts . . . the lace of Time, as they say . . . the 'blonde' basically, the blonde, you know? fine lace, so fine! with the bobbin, so sensitive!"[171]

And let no one, after this, come reproach life for its ephemeral nature. That is precisely what is so lovable about it . . . The great happinesses are always tragic. Why cry over Nora, once the last page of the British adventure has been turned? Yes, she is dead. But what does it matter? It was a foregone conclusion. And let us be honest. Let us admit that in Nora, and for some time, we had loved nothing so much as our premonition of her impending metamorphosis. Of the slow labor, the almost Baudelairean labor of decomposition Nora had become the object of, under the attentive, the passionately interested, gaze of Ferdinand, who was keeping track of the progress of the thing. Not wanting to miss any of it, not to lose a single crumb, ferociously determined not to leave the place till what was prescribed had been accomplished. "I can make it out clearly . . . it's a stain . . . it's vacillating through the shadows... White whirling... It's the kid, certainly, it's my mad girl! Flits from one lamppost to the next... It's like a butterfly, carrion."[172]

From the chrysalis to the butterfly. As if from one note to another, as if to the highest note: hat tossed over the score, the bars of the cage in which, its wings clipped, mopes the libretto of our all-too-human loves. Flown the coop, Nora! *Hallelujah!*... Let us rejoice. Just as we must learn to rejoice about time going by, and because it goes by; about time flying, and because it flies, falls into shreds. Goes up in smoke...

Fragile happiness, *a stippled happiness.* In the very image of a score.

Alas! in its image only.

Only music can testify for existence thus conceived, thus understood. Not literature. And that is its great disability. All the more afflicting inasmuch as taking the measure of it is not enough. There comes a moment when the writer, giving up, must hand over the job.

⤙

End of *Trifles*... Céline is back. Having returned empty-handed from Russia, where he had hoped to unearth the composer who would agree to toss a few notes at the feet of his ballets; little choreographies, trifles, a whim he'd had.

Quite inopportunely, it must be said. Russia, panicked, had stored away its pianos, its violins... A total failure.

The end of *Trifles* reads like a liquidation.

But we will see how, filing for bankruptcy, Céline, at the same time, gives us the conclusion that suited this essay. The ghosts will reappear; and, with the ghosts, many of the figures I will have briefly awakened, pulled from the shadows they were resting in. The whole round, the farandole starting up again; and going by in an absolutely tattered style, a real lace of style: fragile words, bits of sentences, *Nacht und Nebel.*

It's enough in the end, these three words we keep repeating: time goes by... it's enough for everything...

Nothing escapes time... but a few little echoes... more and more muted... more and more rare...

And then that's it...

Very gently, they'll become ghosts... and all of them... and all of them... and Yubelblat and Borokrom... and the grandmother... and Nathalie [...] all that will go as ghosts... *loûû... loûûû...* We'll see them on the moors... And good for them... They'll be happier, far happier, in the wind, in the folds of shadow... *volûûû*... *volûûû*... dancing in circles [...] And this ballet, then?... It was ready... I was pretty happy with it [...] I had intended it for Leningrad... And there it is!... the circumstances... a pity... so it goes!... I'm going to read you the beginning of this long entertainment... a trifle [...] A little twitch simply between death and existence... it distracts... carries you away [...] The Dream carries us away... But the Music?... Ah! that's my whole fear... I fall back down all tangled up!... Music!... wing of Dance! Outside of music everything collapses and crawls... Music the edifice of Dream!... Once again I'm toast... If you ever heard someone mention, by chance, among your re-lations... a rather fragile musician... who just wants to do the right thing... Please... a little sign... I'll give him terms... between death and existence... a light situation... We can surely reach an agreement...[173]

CITATION

Rigadoon. A place off to the wayside, somewhere in Copenhagen:

this alley is really quiet ... but wait! ... Lili sees better than I do ... it's nothing ... over there in the grass, a bird ... but not a usual bird ... a bird, I would say "prize," from a Jardin des Plantes ... a bird the size of a duck, but half pink, half black ... and disheveled! I would say feathers askew ... I look further ... another one! that one, I know it! ... I'm the one who saw it first! ... an ibis ... funny bird here ... and an "egret"! ... that one surely not from Denmark! ... a peacock now ... they're coming on purpose! ... and a "lyrebird" ... they want to eat ... the place isn't very nourishing, ruins, thorns, rocks ... another one! ... this time a toucan ... we have them nearly at three ... four meters ... they would be friendly if we had something to give them, but truly, truly, we've got nothing ... I say to Lili, "close the bag well, that he doesn't stick his head out!" ... I'm thinking of Bébert ... like that surrounded by birds if someone came he would wonder what we're doing to them, if by chance we wouldn't be charmers ... bird charmers ...

"Let's go!"

I think that for us everything is dangerous ... these birds, I'm sure are in "breach of aviary" ... they must have come like us from down there, from "zoos" in Germany, bombed ... in any case, my canes! ... and a great effort and up! ... and to the tramway! ... I told you, to the "terminus" ... where we came from ... we'll meet again ...[1]

161

Last recall (of the motif) of the birds. We are in June. The Saint John's fires of summer will soon be blazing. The work still has to bury the yellow peril. In the basements, real quick, in Champagne, between Reims and Épernay, "those sparkling depths where nothing exists anymore." And on July 1, silence. Céline dies of a stroke.

NOTES

FOREWORD

1. In the original, *faire la lumière.* — *Trans.*

2. "Absolument étranger," a conversation with Philippe Bonnefis collected by Fabrice Thumerel, *Les Cahiers de philosophie* 10: *Spécial Biographies* (spring 1990): p. 46.

3. Ibid., p. 47.

4. In English in the original text. — *Trans.*

5. "Absolument étranger," p. 45.

6. Ibid., p. 44.

7. Ibid., p. 38.

8. In English in the original text. — *Trans.*

9. In English in the original text. — *Trans.*

10. Letter to Jean Paulhan, January 7, 1949, in *Lettres à la N.R.F., 1931–1961,* ed. Pascal Fouché (Paris: Gallimard, N.R.F., 1991), p. 80.

11. Thumerel, *Cahiers de Philosophie* 10, p. 34.

12. Ibid.

13. Ibid.

14. Ibid.

15. The expression is Jean-Michel Reynaud's, cited in ibid., p. 40.

16. Ibid., p. 42.

17. Philippe Bonnefis, *Céline: Le Rappel des oiseaux* (Lille: Presses Universitaires de France, 1992), p. 195; here, p. 140.

18. Ibid., p. 122; here, pp. 85–86.

19. Ibid., p. 18; here, p. 5.

20. Dolorès Djidzek-Lyotard, "Lecture: *Céline: Le Rappel des oiseaux* de Philippe Bonnefis. Dans la chose, la musique de Céline," *Rue Descartes* 12–13 (May 1995), p. 210.

21. Bonnefis, *Céline*, p. 163.; here, p. 116.

22. Ibid., p. 169; here, p. 120.

23. Ibid., p. 135; here, p. 96.

24. Ibid., p. 21; here, p. 9.

25. Ibid., p. 135.; here, p. 95.

26. Ibid., p. 29; here, p. 16.

27. Ibid., p. 185; here, p. 132.

28. Ibid., p. 157; here, p. 112.

29. Ibid., pp. 155–56; here, p. 111.

30. Ibid., p. 167; here, p. 118.

31. The word *timbré* has many senses. It can mean a person with a lovely, resonant voice. It is also an idiomatic term for someone who is crazy. Lyotard is playing with the resonance between the two words. — *Trans.*

32. The author is playing on the double sense of the word *entendre,* to hear and to understand. *Entendre* is the root of *mésentendre,* to misunderstand. — *Trans.*

33. Another play on the homonymy of the French language. Grammatically, "his bad ear" should read *sa mauvaise oreille.* Lyotard replaces the adjective *mauvaise* with a deliberate misspelling of the adverb *mal,* making it at once refer to the action of doing something badly (*mal entendre,* for example) and to hearing in the masculine (*mâle oreille*). — *Trans.*

34. Bonnefis, *Céline,* p. 192; here, p. 137.

35. In English in the original text. — *Trans.*

A WARNING

This book draws on material that first appeared in the *Revue des Sciences Humaines* (nos. 198 and 200), in *Modern Languages Notes* (vol. 103, no. 4), and in the *Actes du Colloque de Toulouse* devoted to Céline (Éditions du Lerot, 1992).

1. *Guignol's band II,* t. III, p. 495; *Normance,* p. 40; *Rigodon,* t. II, p. 925; *Guignol's band II,* t. III, p. 537.

2. *Les Beaux draps,* p. 217.

3. Ibid., pp. 208–9.

4. *Maudits soupirs pour une autre fois,* p. 31.

5. Jean Giono, *Que ma joie demeure, in Œuvres romanesques complètes,* t. II (Paris: Gallimard, Bibliothèque de la Pléiade, 1971–83), p. 464; and "Promenade de la mort," in *L'Eau vive,* in ibid., t. III, p. 304.

1.   BRIDGES

1. Gustave Flaubert, *Bouvard et Pécuchet, in Œuvres Complètes,* t. V (Paris: Club de l'Honnête Homme), pp. 130–31.

2. *Guignol's band I,* t. III, p. 179.

3. Arthur Rimbaud, "Les ponts," *Illuminations.*

4. *Rigodon,* t. II, p. 883.

5. Céline, in *L'Herne,* no. 3, p. 182.

6. *Guignol's band I,* t. III, pp. 90–91.

7. *D'un château l'autre,* t. II, p. 243. ["Fifis" is short for the F.F.I. Resistance fighters. — *Trans.*]

8. Ibid., p. 242.

9. *Entretiens avec le Professeur Y,* pp. 97–99.

10. *Guignol's band II,* t. III, p. 709.

11. *Entretiens avec le Professeur Y,* pp. 102–5.

12. I wish to salute, in passing, Jean-Pierre Richard, who, more than anyone else, thanks to a chapter of his *Microlectures,* "Taking the metro" (Paris: Seuil, coll. "Poétique," 1979, pp. 205–19), helped me to see, in Céline's metropolitan scene, something akin to a primal scene.

13. *Guignol's band II,* t. III, p. 759.

14. *Rigodon,* t. II, p. 825.

15. Every French child knows this old eighteenth-century tune:

> Sur le Pont d'Avignon,
> On y danse, on y danse!
> Sur le Pont d'Avignon,
> On y danse tous en rond.

16. *Voyage au bout de la nuit,* t. I, p. 445.

17. *Maudits soupirs pour une autre fois,* p. 128.

18. *D'un château l'autre,* t. II, p. 41.

19. *Entretiens avec le Professeur Y,* p. 109.

20. *Maudits soupirs pour une autre fois,* p. 68.

21. I have taken the text of "London Bridge" from the *Oxford Dictionary of Nursery Rhymes,* ed Iona and Peter Ople (Oxford: Oxford University Press, 1951), pp. 270–71. My interpretation of it, in the following lines, was suggested to me by the editors themselves (pp. 272–75), as well as by Laurence Gomme's commentary in his *Dictionary of British Folklore,* vol. 1 (London, 1898), pp. 338–49.

22. *Guignol's band I,* t. III, p. 40.

23. Ibid., p. 106.

24. *Rigodon,* t. II, p. 884.

25. *Mort à crédit,* t. I, p. 539; *Rigodon,* t. II, p. 829.

26. *Les Beaux draps,* p. 221; *Féerie pour une autre fois,* p. 277; *Guignol's band I,* t. III, p. 187.

27. *La vie et l'œuvre de Philippe Ignace Semmelweis (1818–1865), Cahiers Céline,* no. 3, p. 25.

28. *Lettres à Albert Paraz, Cahiers Céline,* no. 6, p. 289.

29. *La vie et l'œuvre de Philippe Ignace Semmelweis,* p. 53.

30. *Lettres à Albert Paraz,* p. 289.

31. "Entretiens avec Jean Guénot et Jacques Darribehaude" (January 20, February 6 and 20, 1960), *Cahiers Céline,* no. 2, p. 148.

32. *La vie et l'œuvre de Philippe Ignace Semmelweis*, p. 45.

33. Ibid., p. 27.

34. Ibid., p. 63.

35. *Voyage au bout de la nuit*, t. I, p. 505.

36. *D'un château l'autre*, t. II, pp. 3–7 passim.

37. *Féerie pour une autre fois*, p. 137.

38. For the BBC, see *Féerie pour une autre fois*: "It's the beebeecee but slutier" (p. 44). Céline writes the word "bibici."

39. *Rigodon*, t. II, p. 883.

40. *D'un château l'autre*, t. II, p. 135.

41. Ibid., p. 71.

42. *Nord*, t. II, p. 359.

43. Frédéric Vitoux, *Céline* (Paris: Pierre Belfond, 1978), p. 163.

44. *Normance*, p. 346.

45. In, for example, his *Force majeure* (Paris: Éditions de Minuit, 1983).

46. *D'un château l'autre*, t. II, pp. 92–93.

47. "Louis-Ferdinand Céline vous parle," first side of the record devoted to Céline in the "Leur œuvre et leur voix" collection (Festival, F.L.D. 149). Henri Godard has transcribed it in vol. 2 of the Pléiade edition of Céline's works, pp. 931–36.

48. In vol. 2 of the Pléiade edition of Céline's works, p. 1223.

49. In Albert Paraz, *Le Gala des vaches* (Paris: Balland reprint, 1974), p. 165.

50. *Rigodon*, t. II, p. 870.

51. *D'un château l'autre*, t. II, p. 96.

52. *Féerie pour une autre fois*, p. 157.

53. *D'un château l'autre*, t. II, p. 159.

54. Ibid.

55. Ibid., pp. 282–83.

56. Ibid., p. 270.

57. *Ibid.*, pp. 290–91.

58. Claude Simon, *Histoire* (Paris: Éditions de Minuit, 1967), p. 213.

59. *Féerie pour une autre fois*, p. 157.

60. *Normance*, p. 70.

61. "Creux néant musicien" (Mallarmé, "Une dentelle s'abolit").

62. *Normance*, p. 70.

63. Ibid., p. 113.

64. Ibid., p. 230.

65. *Rigodon*, t. II, pp. 865–66.

66. *Lettres à Albert Paraz*, p. 136.

67. "I have to feel a resonance, work in the sinew, have the right contact. Then, I continue. I never worry about logic. I try to follow the right trail, to touch" — his hand feels the table — "to not let go, to reach the entrance of the cave, finally to enter into it, and then the least sound of my voice calls up a thousand echoes... 'Ho...Ho...' I go 'Ho' and it answers me." These words, that Robert de Saint-Jean, at the time editor-in-chief of the *Revue hebdomadaire*, attributes with a great deal of likelihood to L.-F. Céline, and that he transcribes in his diary on February 22,

1933 (*Journal d'un journaliste* [Paris: Grasset, 1974]), have been reprinted in the *Cahiers Céline*, no. 1, p. 51.

68. *Féerie pour une autre fois*, p. 158.

69. Ibid., p. 159.

70. Ibid., p. 158.

71. *Mort à crédit*, t. I, p. 537.

72. Michel Serres, *Les cinq sens* (Paris: Grasset, 1985), p. 116.

73. Gaston Bachelard, *La Terre et les rêveries du repos* (Paris: Corti, 1948), p. 194.

74. Blaise Cendrars, *Moravagine*, in *Œuvres complètes*, t. IV (Paris: Le Club Français du Livre), p. 69.

75. *Normance*, p. 182.

76. *Féerie pour une autre fois*, p. 162.

77. *Maudits soupirs pour une autre fois*, p. 45.

78. *La vie et l'œuvre de Philippe Ignace Semmelweis*, p. 31. The sentence applies to Skoda, Semmelweis's teacher at the new School of Medicine of Budapest. Skoda was then putting the final touches to an Auscultation Treatise, a continuation of Auenbrugger's work, about which more later.

79. Ibid., p. 22.

80. Ibid.

81. "Eblé's sappers!... White Dragoons of the Empress!... Withered Chasseurs, so rotten, cross-eyed..." (*Féerie pour une autre fois*, pp. 165–66).

82. "The Russian retreat was for him Poléon but the opportunity for a bad scare, to leave his fellows get good and chopped up by the cossacks and to skedaddle, in triple stages! troika! youp là!... to go screw his Polack!... the proof is you'll still find at the bottom of the Beresina plenty of shreds and bits of uniforms of the Great Army, and plenty of skeletons, and Legions of Honor, and drums too... all the skeletons, French flags, and uniforms you find... especially those of Eblé's pontoneers... this was actually the opportunity for nicely stimulating articles in the L.V.F. papers... Soldiers of the New Europe, you will follow in their footsteps, etc...." (*D'un château l'autre* [fragments of a primitive version], t. II, p. 1037).

83. As it appears in *Bagatelles pour un massacre*, p. 338.

84. In Godard's bibliographic note to *Guignol's band II*, t. III, p. 966.

85. Gordon Biddle, *The Railway Heritage of Britain* (London: Michael Joseph, 1983), p. 184.

86. *Lettres à Albert Paraz*, p. 47.

87. "Thus in this connection he told me that during the Russian retreat, Napoléon's generals had had a hell of a time stopping him from going to get sucked in Warsaw one last time supreme by the Polish woman of his heart. That's how he was, Napoléon, even in the midst of the greatest reversals and misfortunes. Basically not serious. Even him, the eagle of his Josephine! The behind on fire, you could say, and come what may. Nothing to be done anyway as long as you like pleasure and laughter and that's something we all like. That's the saddest. It's all we think of! In the cradle, at the café, on the throne, on the toilet. Everywhere! The dick! Napoléon or not! Cuckold or not! Pleasure first! Let them croak the four hundred thousand hallucinated emberesinated to the plume! said the great loser to himself,

as long as Poleon gets his rocks off one more time!" (*Voyage au bout de la nuit*, t. I, p. 353).

88. *Féerie pour une autre fois*, p. 171.

89. *Nord*, t. II, pp. 706–7.

90. Cf. Philippe Alméras (*Australian Journal of French Studies*, 1976, nos. 1–2, p. 58) and Henri Godard in his notes to the Pléiade edition of *Voyage au bout de la nuit*, t. I, p. 1291. Cf. especially Nicholas Hewitt and his lecture at the Colloque de La Haye, in July 1983, "*Voyage au bout de la nuit*: voyage imaginaire et histoire de fantômes" (*Actes du Colloque international de la Haye*, Bibliothèque L.-F. Céline, no. 8 [Paris: Bibliothèque de Littérature française contemporaine de l'Université de Paris VII, n.d.], pp. 9–19).

"It is now possible to specify," writes Nicholas Hewitt, "that this song exists since 1812 and wasn't invented, in spite of Henri Mahé's testimony, by Céline himself. It is indeed the Song of the Beresina, sung by the Swiss Regiment of the Great Army of Napoléon I, at dawn on the day of the crossing of the Beresina during the Russian retreat. In his book *Honneur et fidélité. Histoire des Suisses au service de l'étranger*, P. de Vallière narrates the meaning of this song: 'Long before daylight, Commandant Blattman and Lieutenant Legler, from the 1st, were walking up and down the road to shake off the mortal numbness of the night. Legler began to hum a tune he had sung as a child, in Glaris. Blattman encouraged him; the voice rose, warm, in the frozen air:

Notre vie est un voyage
Dans l'hiver et dans la nuit,
Nous cherchons notre passage
Sous un Ciel où rien ne luit.

"'Officers drew near, soldiers rose to listen to this song that awoke in them the magic of memory. Men arrived from all sides, drawn by this echo of the distant country. Hundreds of voices took up, in chorus, the following stanzas. The melody swelled; always fuller, it passed over the bivouacs, over the white plain:

La souffrance est le bagage
Qui meurtrit nos reins courbés;
Dans la plaine aux vents sauvages
Combien sont déjà tombés!

Demain, la fin du voyage,
Le repos après l'effort,
La patrie et le village,
Le printemps, l'espoir — la
mort!

"'It was the reveille of the Swiss, in the gray day, their farewell to life, their salute to the homeland.'"

91. *La vie et l'œuvre de Philippe Ignace Semmelweis*, pp. 22–23.

92. *Voyage au bout de la nuit*, t. I, p. 17.

93. *Mort à crédit*, t. I, p. 536.

94. *Nord*, t. II, p. 459.

95. *Féerie pour une autre fois*, pp. 156–57.

96. Interview of Céline by Louis le Cunff (*Le Monde et la vie*, no. 90, November 1960); *Cahiers Céline*, no. 2, p. 182.

97. Interview of Céline by Madeleine Chapsal (*L'Express*, no. 312); *Cahiers Céline*, no. 2, p. 24.

98. "Entretiens avec Jean Guénot et Jacques Darribehaude" (January 20, February 6 and 20, 1960), *Cahiers Céline*, no. 2, p. 147.

99. *Guignol's band II*, t. III, p. 469.

100. "With a nearly pathological obsession, he mused about his poor fractured head, responsible, he admitted, for 'certain lacks, absences, ramblings'" (Henri Mondor, foreword to the first Pléiade edition, p. xi).

101. "Due to a trepanation required in 1914 by a wound to the head, a trepanation he said had been badly performed, he had always suffered from violent migraines" (Marcel Aymé, "On a Legend," *L'Herne*, no. 3, p. 214).

102. Milton Hindus, *L.-F. Céline, tel que je l'ai vu* (Paris: Éditions de L'Herne, coll. "Essais et philosophie," 1969), p. 35.

103. Robert Poulet, *Mon ami Bardamu* (Paris: Plon, 1971), p. 120.

104. Franz Kafka, "The Bridge," trans. Willa Muir and Edwin Muir, in *The Complete Stories*, "Centennial Edition," ed. Nahum N. Glazer (New York: Shocken Books, 1983), p. 411.

105. *Féerie pour une autre fois*, p. 206.

106. Ibid., p. 252.

2. STEPS

1. Pierre Dumayet, "Lectures pour tous," Radio-Télévision française, first channel, July 17, 1957; *Cahiers Céline*, no. 2, p. 67.

2. *Mort à crédit*, t. I, p. 828.

3. *Voyage au bout de la nuit*, t. I, p. 373.

4. *Mort à crédit*, t. I, p. 1089.

5. Camille Flammarion, *Les Étoiles et les curiosités du ciel. Description complète du ciel visible à l'œil nu (Supplément de l'astronomie populaire)* (Paris: Ernest Flammarion, 1899), p. 452.

6. *Mort à crédit*, t. I, p. 544.

7. Ibid., p. 546.

8. "*Malaise d'irréalité*"; letter to Clément Camus, June 28, 1949, in Bibliothèque L.-F. Céline, *Textes et documents 3* (Paris: Bibliothèque de la Littérature française et contemporaine, Université de Paris VII, 1984), p. 153.

9. *Guignol's band II, Le pont de Londres* (Paris: Gallimard, "Folio," 1944 version), p. 154.

10. *Mort à crédit*, t. I, p. 545.

11. *Maudits soupirs pour une autre fois*, p. 114.

12. *Guignol's band I*, t. III, p. 308.

13. *Guignol's band II, Le pont de Londres,* 1944 version, p. 21. The word is lost, alas, in the copy revised by Céline in 1944–45, in favor of "men of shards," undoubtedly judged, and wrongly perhaps, more picturesque. It is a pleasure, in any case, to see Marie-Christine Bellosta salvaging it for the title of her book — an excellent book, let it be added, and from which this reading has profited — *Le capharnaüm célinien; ou la place des objets dans* Mort à crédit (Paris: Minard, "Archives des Lettres Modernes," 1976).

14. *Guignol's band I*, t. III, p. 191.

15. *Mort à crédit,* t. I, p. 933.

16. Ibid.

17. "*Voici la Céline,*" "Here's old Céline," sung Céline in the first version of *Règlement,* evincing a femininity that the definitive version, the 1937 one, will conceal, substituting "Clémentine" for "la Céline"; *Chansons. Nouvelle édition revue et augmentée* (Paris: La Flûte de Pan, 1985), p. 30. There would be a great deal to say on this hesitation.

18. *Mort à crédit,* t. I, p. 581.

19. In the first scene of this *comédie-ballet* in four scenes, written, apparently, ca. 1927. *Progrès,* let it be repeated, belongs to the prehistory of *Mort à crédit.* I will therefore often have occasion to return to it.

20. *Voyage au bout de la nuit,* t. I, pp. 366–69.

21. *Guignol's band II,* t. III, p. 351.

22. *Voyage au bout de la nuit,* t. I, p. 366.

23. "Across the Star my fine vessel tears into shadow... loaded with canvas to the mizzenmast..." (*Mort à crédit,* t. I, p. 542).

24. Ibid., p. 543.

25. "He'd return to sky level... He reappeared... He rubbed his weepers... He straightened out his frock coat... He found himself all dizzy in the shop.../ 'I'm dazed Ferdinand! It's pretty... It's pretty... It's magical!'" (*Mort à crédit,* t. I, p. 867).

26. Flammarion, *Les Étoiles et les curiosités du ciel,* p. 427.

27. To quote an expression that Céline himself used to characterize *Voyage au bout de la nuit* in a letter dated April 1932 "aux éditions de la N.R.F.," sent along with his manuscript. "It is," the letter stated, "a sort of literary symphony, emotive rather than a true novel [...] this story is close to what one obtains or should obtain with music. [...] Hence numerous diversions that little by little enter into the theme and eventually make it sing as in musical composition. [...] The intrigue is both complex and simplistic. It also belongs to the Opera genre" (L.-F. Céline, *Lettres à la N.R.F., 1931–1961,* ed. Pascal Fouché [Paris: Gallimard, N.R.F., 1991], p. 14).

28. Milton Hindus, *L.-F. Céline tel que je l'ai vu* (Paris: Éditions de L'Herne, coll. "Essais et philosophie," 1969), p. 152.

29. Ibid.

30. *Voyage au bout de la nuit,* t. I, pp. 349–50.

31. "I kept on circling for weeks and months around the Place Clichy, where I'd left from" (ibid., p. 237).

32. *Guignol's band II*, t. III, p. 448.

33. *Noé* was first published by the Éditions de la Table Ronde in 1947. The text has been reprinted in Giono's *Œuvres romanesques complètes*, t. III (Paris: Gallimard, Bibliothèque de la Pléiade, 1971–83).

34. *L'homme foudroyé* was first published by Denoël in 1945. It is quoted here from the *Œuvres complètes* of Blaise Cendrars, t. IX (Paris: Le Club Français du Livre, 1970), p. 116.

35. An obsessive reference in Céline's work, Noah, for instance, appears in *Voyage au bout de la nuit*, t. I, p. 175; in *Mort à crédit*, t. I, p. 725; and in *Normance*, pp. 69–70 and 129.

36. "Vous êtes en rab" (*D'un château l'autre*, t. II, p. 98).

37. *Voyage au bout de la nuit*, t. I, p. 74.

38. *D'un château l'autre*, t. II, p. 224.

39. On this question of the weight of things, cf. Bellosta's *Le capharnaüm célinien ou la place des objets dans* Mort à crédit.

40. *Mort à crédit*, t. I, p. 797.

41. Ibid., p. 1094.

42. Read: Fort Gonorrhea, *Admiral Crotch, Infanta Cunt-Dick. — Trans.*

43. *Progrès*, "Premier Tableau," *Cahiers Céline*, no. 8, pp. 38–40.

44. *Guignol's band II*, t. III, p. 399.

45. *Progrès*, "Quatrième Tableau," p. 67.

46. *Voyage au bout de la nuit*, t. I, p. 194.

47. *Guignol's band II*, t. III, p. 397.

48. *Bagatelles pour un massacre*, p. 12.

49. *Progrès*, "Troisième Tableau," p. 57.

50. Who has read, for instance, in Mallarmé, that "the dancer *is not a woman who is dancing,* for these juxtaposed reasons that she *is not a woman,* but a metaphor capturing one of the elementary aspects of our form, sword, cup, flower, etc., and that *she isn't dancing,* suggesting, thanks to the prodigy of shortcuts or leaps, with a corporal writing what it would take paragraphs of dialogued as well as descriptive prose to express in writing: poem freed from any scribe's trappings" (Mallarmé, "Ballets," in *Crayonné au théâtre, Œuvres complètes* (Paris: Gallimard, Bibliothèque de la Pléiade, n.d.), p. 304.

51. *Bagatelles pour un massacre*, p. 12.

52. "*Appareil*" (*Maudits soupirs pour une autre fois*, p. 256).

53. *Féerie pour une autre fois*, p. 138.

54. *Maudits soupirs pour une autre fois*, p. 144.

55. Letter to Karen Marie Jensen, March 2, 1937, *Cahiers Céline*, no. 5, p. 241.

56. Ibid.

57. Letter to Erika Irrgang, July 19, 1934, *Cahiers Céline*, no. 5, p. 56.

58. *D'un château l'autre*, t. II, p. 42.

59. Ibid.

60. *Mort à crédit*, t. I, p. 560.

61. Ibid., p. 565.

62. Jacques Chancel, "L.-F. Céline: 'La télévision achèvera l'esprit de l'homme comme la fusée lui simplifiera l'existence,'" *Télé magazine*, no. 177 (January 19–29, 1958), in *Cahiers Céline*, no. 2, p. 97.

63. "*Francs lourds*," "heavy francs"; revalued francs; *Cahiers Céline*, no. 2, p. 109.

64. *Guignol's band II*, t. III, p. 389.

65. Ibid.

66. *Maudits soupirs pour une autre fois*, p. 129.

67. Ibid., p. 170.

68. Ibid., p. 178.

69. "I don't like the sun," writes Céline to Elisabeth Porquerol, in a letter dated June 29, 1933. "I don't have what it takes. My skin is too thin, my eyes too unprotected" (*Cahiers Céline*, no. 5, p. 154).

70. Jules Laforgue, "Soleil couchant."

71. *La Valse brune*... Les Chevaliers de la Lune: "It's what they sang at Cascade's, but then from morning to night!..." (*Guignol's band II*, t. III, p. 617).

72. On the question of the phallic idealization of women, which I am only treating in passing, cf. Julia Kristeva, *Pouvoirs de l'horreur* (Paris: Seuil, coll. "Tel Quel," 1980), pp. 190–202.

73. Confidence of Céline to the journalist Max Descaves, from *Paris-Midi*, in a movie theater on the Place Blanche (*Cahiers Céline*, no. 1, pp. 68–69).

74. Ibid.

75. *L'Église*, p. 73.

76. *Voyou Paul, Brave Virginie*, ballet-mime, in *Bagatelles pour un massacre*, p. 38.

77. *La Naissance d'une fée*, ballet, in *Bagatelles pour un massacre*, p. 20.

78. *Foudres et flèches*, mythological ballet (1945–1947), *Cahiers Céline*, no. 8, p. 171.

79. *L'Église*, p. 253.

80. *Voyage au bout de la nuit*, t. I, p. 418.

81. Ibid., p. 160.

82. Ibid., p. 150.

83. Because she is an English girl and English girls all are. Cf. *Guignol's band I*, t. III, p. 106.

84. "Sosthène was toiling behind us... he was moaning because of his corns" (*Guignol's band II*, t. III, p. 747).

85. Ibid., p. 609.

86. *Bagatelles pour un massacre*, p. 18.

87. Ibid.

88. Ibid., p. 35.

89. Ibid., p. 374.

90. *Naissance d'une fée*, in ibid., p. 26.

91. *D'un château l'autre*, t. II, p. 113.

92. On this point, cf. François Gibault, *Céline (1894–1932). Le temps des espérances* (Paris: Mercure de France, 1977), pp. 32–33.

93. *D'un château l'autre*, t. II, p. 103.

94. *Progrès*, "Premier Tableau," pp. 29–30.

95. *Mort à crédit*, p. 659.

96. Expressions he himself uses to underline their unreal nature; *Maudits soupirs pour une autre fois*, pp. 134 and 163.

97. *Féerie pour une autre fois*, p. 208.

98. "A ring, enter a twenty-five-year-old woman, American, accent, luxurious muscles, luxurious dress, whole" (*Progrès*, "Troisième Tableau," p. 54).

99. *Normance*, p. 259.

100. Claude-Louis Combet, on Salome, another dancer; in *Marinus et Marina* (Paris: Flammarion, 1979), p. 268.

101. Mimi, indeed, is in *Normance* only Mimi Pinson, Mimi Chaffinch. She sings and doesn't dance. Sings naked, as we have said; yet, if she sings naked, it is only to make us regret the dancer she isn't; to resurrect, for an instant, this unforgettable figure.

102. In a letter to Albert Paraz dated July 13, 1949 ("I admire your ardor as miraculous as Mistingo's legs"); *Cahiers Céline*, no. 6, p. 167.

103. *Progrès*, "Premier Tableau," pp. 31–32.

104. *Mort à crédit*, t. I, p. 821.

105. "A fantastic coach...enormous hubs...A boiler like a distillery cooker... A tall, immense chimney...in front...terrifying brass pistons...all sorts of balance wheels...valves...unbelievable utensils...and then nonetheless some dainty touches...Canopy, garlands, credences, a mix of machinery and romantic trimmings...On a banderole, an inscription: 'THE FULMICOACH TRANSPORT, LTD.'" (*Voyou Paul, Brave Virginie*, ballet-mime, in *Bagatelles pour un massacre*, p. 34).

106. *Les Beaux draps*, p. 165.

107. "Poustouflantes marmites" (*Guignol's band II*, t. III, p. 652).

108. *Mort à crédit*, t. I, pp. 569–70.

109. As the French nursery rhyme goes:

> Maman les p'tits bateaux
> Qui vont sur l'eau
> Ont-ils des jambes?
> Mais oui, mon bon enfant,
> S'ils n'en avaient pas,
> Ils ne marcheraient pas.

110. *Guignol's band II*, t. III, p. 662.

111. Ibid., p. 747.

112. Ibid., p. 673.

113. Ibid., p. 662.

114. *Guignol's band I*, t. III, p. 179.

115. "Qu'on s'explique...," *Candide*, March 16, 1933; in *Cahiers Céline*, no. 1, p. 56.

116. "Keel," *quille* in French, is also an argot term for "pin," "leg." — *Trans.*

117. *D'un château l'autre*, t. II, p. 70.

118. *Féerie pour une autre fois*, p. 54.

119. Ibid., p. 45.

120. The Vault, the Tomb, or the Cellar. — *Trans.*

121. Patrick Wald Lasowski, *L'Ardeur et la galanterie* (Paris: Gallimard, coll. "Les Essais," 1986), p. 50.

122. "And the Gambetta in his nacelle? and Sarah Bernhardt one-legged? weren't those sublime leaps?" (*Féerie pour une autre fois*, p. 54).

123. Quoted in Pierre-Louis Clément, *Montgolfières* (Paris: Tardy, coll. "Art et Industrie," 1982), p. 83.

124. *Mort à crédit*, t. I, p. 885.

125. Michel Serres, *La Naissance de la physique dans le texte de Lucrèce. Fleuves et turbulences* (Paris: Éditions de Minuit, 1977), p. 32.

126. *Outre-là*: "beyond," still, also, more literally, "to the devil"; we will soon see what significations this substitution might hold. — *Trans.*

127. "But I know ill-famers, blokes in perversity, people who've got a grim mind, ambitious men all hermetic, unbelievable in their diabolical gleaming who are in veritable pacts with the powers of *outre-là!* . . . " (*Les Beaux draps*, p. 218).

128. Entrusted by Arletty to Pierre Monnier, in the early 1950s, the letter (several pages long) is now available from La Flûte de Pan, where it was published in 1983 under the title—title taken from the first lines of the manuscript—of *Arletty, jeune fille dauphinoise*.

129. "Projet de ballet sans titre," *Cahiers Céline*, no. 8, p. 231.

130. "After our first meeting, I saw him every day; he came to see me as a visitor. It took a year. One year looking at each other. I looked at him as an extraordinary being whom you see, who doesn't talk, but who is there. He was sad and absent. Sadly absent. [. . .] He was haunted by his work. We didn't live. Me, I was in my dancing. That's why it worked. Because we were both taken. Otherwise, we never could have gotten along, not even for an hour. We met, we separated, there's not much to say. We were both taken by our work, his great, mine tiny. [. . .] Me, I followed him. I think I would have accepted everything. But, in fact, I knew why he did things. I could feel it, I was the animal, I didn't ask for explanations. I agreed in general, otherwise life wouldn't have been possible for a day, not even for an hour. If he'd had to speak to me, to explain to me, it wouldn't have been possible. He had to be alone" (Lucette Destouches, "Mes années Céline," *Libération*, October 25, 1985).

131. "Oultre! Foultre!" (letter to Jean Paulhan, February 27, 1949, in *Lettres à la N.R.F.*, p. 85; or, also, in *Féerie pour une autre fois*, p. 39: "got to split even more *oultre!*"

132. Suzanne Allen, "Plus oultre," *Revue des Sciences Humaines*, no. 168.

133. *Mort à crédit*, t. I, p. 911.

134. Ibid., p. 975

135. Plato, *Symposium*, trans. W. H. D. Rowse (New York: Mentor Books, 1956), p. 109.

136. *Mort à crédit*, t. I, p. 1051.

137. In French: *Ballon, Phédon.* — *Trans.*

138. *Mort à crédit*, t. I, p. 887.

139. Letter to Lucienne Delforge, August 26, 1935, *Cahiers Céline*, no. 5, p. 263.

140. "What, then, does such a refusal to breathe signify, since it is really a question of atrophying the respiratory apparatus, of reducing to a minimum the gaseous

exchanges between his own body and the medium around him? One must remember that at birth, right after the cutting and the ligaturing of the umbilical cord, the first autonomous action of the newborn is his cry, the cry that proves the air has entered the lungs and the beginning of respiration. Before, it was the maternal blood that directly oxygenated the fetus: the mother's lungs were then breathing for two. Leaving the womb, the little batrachian expelled from the amniotic fluid truly becomes a human being as soon as he starts to breathe. In other words, the more I breathe, the further I draw from my mother since with each breath I am repeating the inaugural gesture that irremediably separated me from her. Each new lungful of air commemorates and aggravates the original section. And, on the contrary, the less I breathe, the less I will widen the gap separating me every moment from my mother. Panting as a permanent nursing; no weaning for the asthmatic" (Alain Buisine, *Proust et ses lettres* (Lille: P.U.L., coll. "Objet," 1983), p. 69.

141. *Guignol's band II,* t. III, p. 498.

142. *Guignol's band I,* t. III, p. 106.

143. *Mort à crédit,* t. I, pp. 880–82.

144. "I find *that none of those babblers* are 'IN THE THING.' They are frantically beating off OUTSIDE" (letter to Jean Paulhan, January 7, 1949, in *Lettres à la N.R.F.,* p. 80).

145. *Mort à crédit,* t. I, p. 881.

146. Ibid., p. 905.

147. *Guignol's band II,* t. III, p. 499.

148. Ibid., p. 500.

149. *Mort à crédit,* t. I, pp. 905–6.

150. *Guignol's band II,* t. III, p. 500.

151. Ibid., p. 499.

152. *Mort à crédit,* t. I, p. 983.

153. Ibid., p. 984.

154. Ibid., pp. 974–75.

155. Of all the virtues preached by Céline, enthusiasm is perhaps the cardinal one; if by enthusiasm we understand the transport of the soul, the exaltation that follows the little leap within us of "the God who dances" (*Les Beaux draps,* p. 88). Even more precise is the definition he gives in a letter to Milton Hindus: "Enthusiasm is lacking and I'm not teaching you anything new from the Greek *the God within*" (quoted in Hindus, *L.-F. Céline tel que je l'ai vu,* p. 159). But it is only one example out of many. The etymology of *enthusiasm* fills Céline with delight. And there isn't one of his listeners (Paraz or another) that isn't invited to share this delight.

156. *Mort à crédit,* t. I, pp. 977–80.

157. Ibid., p. 814.

158. *Voyage au bout de la nuit,* t. I, p. 11.

159. *Mort à crédit,* t. I, p. 923.

160. *L'Église,* p. 246.

161. *Mort à crédit,* t. I, p. 1044.

162. Ibid., pp. 1058–60.

163. Ibid., pp. 1087–88.

164. "Lieu natal où nous n'avons naissance," "lieu royal où nous n'avons séance" (Saint-John Perse, *Amers*, in *Œuvres complètes* [Paris: Gallimard, Bibliothèque de la Pléiade, 1972], p. 300.

165. *Bagatelles pour un massacre*, p. 374.

3. PASSAGES

1. *Guignol's band I*, t. III, pp. 191–92.

2. *Bagatelles pour un massacre*, p. 366. The Borokrom of *Guignol's band* is a reappearing character.

3. *Guignol's band I*, t. III, p. 192.

4. Ibid., p. 100.

5. *Guignol's band II*, t. III, p. 402.

6. *Guignol's band II*, quoted here from the copy left in 1944 to Marie Canavaggia and published as such by Robert Poulet under the title *Le Pont de Londres* (Paris: Gallimard, "Folio"), p. 117. Céline's corrections in Copenhagen in 1945–46 curiously erase the reference to music. The inventor of the *Ferocious* is now only a botanist who "professed in a lycée in Dorchester" (t. III, p. 407). A pity!...

7. *Progrès*, p. 26.

8. *Féerie pour une autre fois*, p. 205.

9. *Cahiers Céline*, no. 2, p. 62.

10. "Rodolphe and Mimi [...] you should see them, I got to tell you, they are in 'Bohème' costumes ... perfectly 'Bohème'!... where'd they come from?... 'That is the question...' I hadn't seen them come down. 'They were rehearsing' at home... yes! yes!... that I knew... they were rehearsing a scene... now, no mistake, it was them, they were there... above me!... and rigged up like!... him, in a frock, a period one, eh!... and a curly wig!... she as a young goldilocked 'Mimi'! impish..." (*Normance*, pp. 192–93).

11. *Maudits soupirs pour une autre fois*, p. 92.

12. Ibid., pp. 95–96.

13. "He excelled in three, four things... tank warfare, surgery... ah, and also the ditty!... I heard him on the piano... very amusing!... he was improvising... so I can judge..." (*D'un château l'autre*, t. II, p. 243).

14. "The witnesses are no longer alive [...] for all sorts of genocides, little intimate Hiroshimas... oh, not that I really give much of a fuck for Hiroshima!... look at Trumann [*sic*], if he isn't happy, all pleased with himself, playing the harpsichord!... the idol of millions of voters!... the dream widower of a million widows!... Cosmic Landru!... him at Amadeus's harpsichord!" (ibid., p. 104).

15. *Mort à crédit*, t. I, p. 536.

16. Paul Schilder, *L'image du corps* (Paris: Gallimard, "Bibliothèque des Idées," 1968), pp. 146–61.

17. *Normance*, p. 98.

18. *Guignol's band I*, t. III, p. 268.

19. *Guignol's band II*, t. III, p. 536.

20. Ibid., p. 634.

21. *Féerie pour une autre fois,* p. 55.

22. Cf. the *Dictionnaire étymologique de la langue française* by O. Bloch and W. von Wartburg and the *Dictionnaire étymologique de la langue latine* by A. Ernout and A. Meillet. One should also consult the article by Pierre Lembeye, "Esclops ou la parole dans sa patte, la patte dans la parole: le patois," in *Affranchissement du transfert et de la lettre* (Paris: Confrontation, coll. "Vert et noir," 1982), p. 84.

23. *Normance,* p. 125.

24. *Maudits soupirs pour une autre fois,* p. 45.

25. *Normance,* p. 54.

26. Ibid., p. 84.

27. An epilepsy (must it be restated?) that has its seat "in the left temporal-occipi-tal lobe" (diagnosis of the Doctor Galérand, based on Du Camp's observations). Affecting this point of the temporal zone, the fits are accompanied by related phe-nomena of the sort commonly referred to as sight disorders: abnormally perceived objects, perceptions without object, hyperesthesia of the sensation of color... But this is not the place to deal with a question that I have treated elsewhere, and from two different angles, in "Exposition d'un perroquet," in *Mesures de l'ombre* (Lille: P.U.L., coll. "Objet," 1987), pp. 75–110, and in "*Aura epileptica,*" *Magazine littéraire,* no. 250 (February 1988): 41–43.

28. A point I have also discussed in *Comme Maupassant* (Lille: P.U.L., coll. "Ob-jet," 1981), and in my edition of *Le Horla* (Paris: Livre de Poche, 1984).

29. *Nord,* t. II, p. 588

30. *Normance,* p. 17.

31. *Féerie pour une autre fois,* p. 251.

32. Ibid., p. 225.

33. Blaise Cendrars, *Bourlinguer,* in *Œuvres complètes,* t. XI (Paris: Le Club Fran-çais du Livre, 1969), p. 253.

34. *Normance,* p. 208.

35. Ibid., p. 53.

36. Ibid., p. 97.

37. *Guignol's band II,* t. III, p. 500.

38. *Féerie pour une autre fois,* p. 32.

39. "Le *Voyage* au cinéma" (1960), *Cahiers Céline,* no. 8, p. 235.

40. *Guignol's band I,* t. III, p. 102.

41. Ibid., p. 192.

42. Ibid.

43. Inasmuch as it is a question of reproducing sounds. This is actually the original meaning of the word.

44. A word Jean-François Lyotard uses to define "the general hypothesis" un-derlying the articles he has collected in *L'inhumain: causeries sur le temps* (Paris: Galilée, coll. "Débats," 1988).

45. *Normance,* p. 57.

46. "This second book has been entirely dictated on a DICTAPHONE. What a shame that printing cannot also *record* Dan Yack's voice, and what a shame that the

pages of a book aren't *sonorous* yet. But it will come. Poor poets, let us work" (Blaise Cendrars, *Les confessions de Dan Yack*).

47. *Normance*, pp. 11, 91, and 298, respectively.

48. One could usefully compare this series to the similar one obtained by the alteration of the sound *vroum*. Here it is, also theoretically reconstituted, but no less exemplary (paradigmatic) than the little suite in *broum*:

Vrrrrroum (p. 19) *Vrrrooou* (p. 217) *Vvvrouh* (p. 14)

Vrrrrounb (p. 31)

Vromb (p. 178) *Vvromb* (p. 113) *Vrromb* (p. 36) *Vrrromb* (p. 232)

Vrrrromb (p. 31) *Vroomb* (p. 297)

Vramb (p. 202) *Vrramb* (p. 83)

Vlamb (p. 86)

Vlang (p. 191)

Vrang (p. 199) *Vrrang* (p. 202) *Vrrrang* (p. 79) *Vrrrrang* (p. 186)

Vrrong (p. 88)

Vr (p. 128) *Vrr* (p. 128) *Vrrr* (p. 63) *Vrrrr* (p. 100)

Vsss (p. 267) *Vzing* (p. 224)

Vrooob (p. 81)

Vrac (p. 71) *Vvvrac* (p. 71) *Vrrac* (p. 91)

Vraaa (p. 269)

Vlam (p. 125)

Vlaouf (p. 121) *Vrraouf* (p. 78) *Vlooouf* (p. 97) *Viouf* (p. 104)

Vioûûû (p. 132)

Vlof (p. 271) *Vloaf* (p. 82) *Vlooaf* (p. 345) *Vouaf* (p. 18) *Vlaf* (p. 100)

Vlaac (p. 76)

49. Jean-François Lyotard, in "L'obédience," lecture read at the "De l'écriture musicale" colloquium held at the Sorbonne in June 1986 by the Collège International de Philosophie, and collected in *L'inhumain*, p. 183.

50. *Normance*, pp. 133–35, passim.

51. *Nord*, t. II, p. 664.

52. *D'un château l'autre*, t. II, p. 232.

53. *Nord*, t. II, p. 356.

54. *Saint Cecilia, surrounded by four saints, renouncing instrumental music.* On this question, cf. Albert P. de Mirmonde, *Sainte Cécile. Métamorphoses d'un thème musical* (Geneva: Éditions Minkoff, 1974).

55. *Les Beaux draps*, p. 208.

56. *Guignol's band I*, t. III, p. 193.

57. "Marlène! la! la! sol sharp! in three...four parts! passionately! and entwined!... falling back all over the chairs!... three at once on the pianist's knees!" (*D'un château l'autre*, t. II, p. 155).

58. "...I was looking for a tune...an accompaniment...I ask Lili...'Can't you hear anything?'...yes!...she hears the sirens...that's all!...me alone then this music?...Felipe?...he listens...He doesn't hear any music either, just the show-

ers of mines and plenty of sirens... *uuuh!* how come?... me, I'm not a musician, am I... at all... I get airs [...] I can hear it, in my head, the air... the air that would go, I think... but the notes?... the precise, right notes? [...] three, four notes... notes of sweetness, if I dare say [...] a keyboard now! [...] I plunk about... that's it!... nearly right, yes!... yes!... the *la* of a keyboard as it is... I'm there!... no prodigy! you beat your head for twenty years, the devil if you won't find it!... as pigheaded, as unmelodious as you may be!... I go back down, I have the four notes... *sol sharp! sol! la sharp!... si!...* remember it!... I should have had them back there" (*Rigodon,* t. II, pp. 825–29, passim).

59. "There're only two or three more planes still diving... pulling back up in chandelle, they look like they're reappearing from the center, toward the Opéra..." (*Maudits soupirs pour une autre fois,* p. 98).

60. *Nord,* t. II, p. 523.

61. *Féerie pour une autre fois,* p. 228.

62. Ibid, p. 225.

63. *Maudits soupirs pour une autre fois,* p. 139.

64. Ibid., p. 272.

65. *Normance,* p. 211.

66. *Maudits soupirs pour une autre fois,* p. 183.

67. *Nord,* t. II, p. 515.

68. *Maudits soupirs pour une autre fois,* p. 88.

69. *Les Beaux draps,* p. 128. We will note, at this occasion, Céline's attachment to Couperin, to Rameau. "I'm for Couperin, Rameau" (Milton Hindus, *L.-F. Céline tel que je l'ai vu* [Paris: Éditions de L'Herne, coll. "Essais et philosophie," 1969], p. 166). "What I look for in books? A little French music, some Couperin or some Rameau" (interview of Céline by Gérard Jarlot in *France-Dimanche,* no. 504 [April 19–25 1956]; *Cahiers Céline,* no. 1, p. 165).

70. *Guignol's band I,* t. III, p. 146.

71. Claude Simon, *Les Géorgiques* (Paris: Éditions de Minuit, 1981), p. 164.

72. Interview of Céline by Jacques Izoard, *L'Essai,* no. 2 (November 1959); *Cahiers Céline,* no. 2, p. 138.

73. *Maudits soupirs pour une autre fois,* p. 247.

74. Letter of Céline to Albert Paraz, November 23, 1948, in *Cahiers Céline,* no. 6, p. 101.

75. Letter of Céline to Albert Paraz, November 10, 1948, in ibid., p. 92.

76. "[...] we go lock ourselves up at the movies to forget we exist, we put ourselves in cellars of illusion, all dark, that're already death, with the screen full of ghosts, we're already nicely croaked, curled up in the seats, we buy our little permit before entering, our permit to renounce everything, at the door, sly corpses, to go collapse in communal graves, padded, magical, damp" (*Les Beaux draps,* p. 148).

77. *Féerie pour une autre fois,* p. 130.

78. *L'Église,* p. 162.

79. *Guignol's band I,* t. III, p. 191.

80. Ibid., p. 189.

81. *Féerie pour une autre fois*, p. 130.

82. The capital letter is indeed due to Céline, in *Entretiens avec le Professeur Y*, p. 103.

83. Ibid., p. 105.

84. Ibid., p. 117.

85. "All this paintering makes me dizzy, all this daubing [...]. It's awful, the inside of a painter, that's what I think..." (*Maudits soupirs pour une autre fois*, p. 248).

86. Ibid., p. 86.

87. "résille de crickets," "du semi piqueté" (*Guignol's band II*, t. III, p. 544).

88. *Maudits soupirs pour une autre fois*, p. 230.

89. Ibid., pp. 246–47.

90. *D'un château l'autre*, t. II, p. 117.

91. *Voyage au bout de la nuit*, t. I, p. 441.

92. *Mort à crédit*, t. I, p. 565.

93. *Voyage au bout de la nuit*, t. I, p. 436.

94. "Vadrouiller dans les Septentrions" (ibid., p. 442).

95. Ibid., p. 172.

96. Ibid., p. 444.

97. Ibid., p. 5.

98. *Entretiens avec le Professeur Y*, pp. 29–30.

99. *Voyage au bout de la nuit*, t. I, p. 234.

100. Ibid., p. 195.

101. Ibid., pp. 329–30.

102. *Mort à crédit*, t. I, p. 735.

103. "The siren woke everything up. We hung on to the 'waters.' We emerged from the portholes... The jetties down the end of the port formed a whole lace of piles... We looked at England like you land into the Beyond..." (ibid., p. 625).

104. *Lunette*: "telescope" and also "toilet bowl" or "rim." — *Trans.*

105. The same thing will be said about the losers, after the defeat of Gwendor, Prince of Christania, at the hands of King Krogold, in the famous episode of the pretty legend that gives its Middle Ages atmosphere to the prologue of *Mort à crédit* (t. I, p. 523). On the possible connections between this legend and Macaulay's relation, see later on in this chapter.

106. *Voyage au bout de la nuit*, t. I, p. 437.

107. Ibid., p. 443.

108. "The bike so light it will nearly go without me, from the hint of my decision to mount it!... An 'Imponder'... faster than Arlette sprinting! you should see me!... Arlette, who's a pedaling sylph... Trinité-la-Butte: seven strides! a breeze... that's her! a breath!... gone! uphill!" (*Féerie pour une autre fois*, p. 116). We can also read, in *Maudits soupirs*, where Arlette is called Lucette: "She's got three bikes in her garage... They're not busted, the three... and another one rue Caulaincourt, at the patisserie, well in the back of the shop... and another also at the bookseller's. I don't want her to ever be without a bike... it's her sort of wings, the bike... she musn't be a second without her wings. Oh! I've planned ahead... It's our luxury!" (*Maudits soupirs pour une autre fois*, p. 232).

109. *Mort à crédit*, t. I, p. 523.

110. Ibid., p. 738.

111. *Voyage au bout de la nuit*, t. I, p. 296.

112. *Guignol's band II*, t. III, p. 334.

113. *Baryton* is the French form of English "Baritone." — *Trans.*

114. *Lettres à des amies, Cahiers Céline*, no. 5, p. 257.

115. *Féerie pour une autre fois*, p. 143.

116. *Voyage au bout de la nuit*, t. I, p. 427.

117. Ibid., p. 159.

118. Ibid., p. 432.

119. "Voyage au bout de la nuit ou l'inauguration d'une poétique 'argotique,'" in *La Revue des Lettres Modernes, Série L.-F. Céline*, no. 2 (Minard, 1976), pp. 54–77.

120. "I lifted my trills from the British music hall certainly like Vallès" (*Lettres à Albert Paraz, Cahiers Céline*, no. 6, p. 178).

121. *Guignol's band II*, t. III, p. 684.

122. *Guignol's band I*, t. III, p. 109.

123. *L'École des cadavres*, pp. 35–36.

124. *Normance*, p. 144.

125. Arthur Rimbaud, "À une raison."

126. *Normance*, p. 130.

127. Michel Serres, *Le Tiers Instruit* (Éditions François Bourin, 1991), p. 225.

128. *Guignol's band II*, t. III, p. 684.

129. *Guignol's band I*, t. III, p. 106.

130. Ibid., p. 105.

131. Ibid.

132. *Mort à crédit*, t. I, p. 725.

133. Ibid., p. 729.

134. Ibid., p. 731.

135. Clément Rosset, *La Force majeure* (Paris: Éditions de Minuit, 1983), p. 54.

136. *Mort à crédit*, t. I, p. 707.

137. Ibid., p. 718.

138. Ibid., p. 709.

139. Ibid., p. 725.

140. Ibid., p. 544.

141. *Lettres à Joseph Garin* (Paris: Librairie Monnier, 1987), p. 27.

142. *Voyage au bout de la nuit*, t. I, pp. 364–65.

143. Ibid., p. 364.

144. *Mort à crédit*, t. I, p. 705.

145. *Féerie pour une autre fois*, p. 141.

146. *Voyage au bout de la nuit*, t. I, pp. 366–68.

147. *Normance*, p. 58.

148. *Maudits soupirs pour une autre fois*, p. 86.

149. *Normance*, p. 116.

150. *Maudits soupirs pour une autre fois*, p. 86.

151. *Mort à crédit*, t. I, p. 542.

152. Ibid.

153. *Féerie pour une autre fois*, p. 62.

154. *Maudits soupirs pour une autre fois*, p. 142.

155. *Lettres à Albert Paraz, Cahiers Céline*, no. 6, p. 309.

156. Ibid., p. 319.

157. Ibid, pp. 310–19.

158. *Féerie pour une autre fois*, p. 124.

159. *Maudits soupirs pour une autre fois*, p. 183.

160. *Lettres à Albert Paraz*, p. 362.

161. Cf. Céline's letter to André Rousseaux, dated May 24, 1936, published by Henri Godard in his edition of Céline's works, t. I (Paris: Gallimard, Bibliothèque de la Pléiade), pp. 1119–20.

162. *Féerie pour une autre fois*, p. 228.

163. André Hardellet, "Répertoire," in *Les Chasseurs* (Paris: J.-J. Pauvert, 1966); cited in Michel Collot, *La Poésie moderne et la structure d'horizon* (Paris: P.U.F., coll. "Écritures," 1989), p. 69.

164. *Mort à crédit*, t. I, p. 768.

165. "*C'est à passer que nous demeurons*" (Jean-François Lyotard, "*Domus* et la mégapole," in *L'inhumain*, p. 210.

166. *Maudits soupirs pour une autre fois*, p. 182.

167. *Féerie pour une autre fois*, p. 96.

168. "Ah! it really is terrible . . . no matter how young you are when you realize it for the first time . . . how you lose people along the way . . . pals you won't see again . . . never again . . . that they've vanished like dreams . . . how it's finished . . . faded . . . that you too will go lose yourself . . . one day very far still . . . but necessarily . . . in the atrocious torrent of things, of people . . . of days . . . of forms that pass . . . that never stop . . . All the assholes, the peg legs, all the bystanders, all the street-show sauntering under the arcades, with their pince-nezs, their brollies and the little pooches on the string . . . All that, you'll never see it again . . . They are already passing . . . They are in dreams with others, they have arrangements . . . they are going to finish . . . It's sad, really . . . It's loathsome! . . . the innocents passing by the storefronts . . . I was getting a ferocious urge . . . it was making me shake with panic to go finally jump on them . . . to plant myself there in front . . . so that they stop dead . . . That I grab them by the suit . . . a dumb idea . . . that they stop . . . that they not move at all! . . . Right there, that they fix themselves! . . . once and for all! . . . That you no longer have to see them go . . ." (*Mort à crédit*, t. I, p. 901).

169. *Lettres à des amies, Cahiers Céline*, no. 5, p. 262.

170. *Maudits soupirs pour une autre fois*, p. 118.

171. *Féerie pour une autre fois*, p. 124.

172. *Mort à crédit*, t. I, p. 771.

173. *Bagatelles pour un massacre*, pp. 373–74.

CITATION

1. *Rigodon*, t. II, pp. 922–23.

PHILIPPE BONNEFIS is Asa G. Candler Professor of French at Emory University. Among his more recent works are *Comme Maupassant* (1993) and *L'Innommable: essai sur l'œuvre d'Emile Zola* (1984).

JEAN-FRANÇOIS LYOTARD is professor of philosophy at the Collège International de Philosophie in Paris and Robert W. Woodruff professor of French and Humanities at Emory University. The University of Minnesota Press has published his *Political Writings* (1993), *The Postmodern Explained: Correspondence 1982–1985* (1993), and *Heidegger and "the jews"* (1990).

PAUL WEIDMAN is a freelance translator.